An Unexpected Adventure

bucket lists *and* walking sticks

7 Months - 19 Countries - 1 Big Bucket List

Emma Scattergood

What happens when you plan it... and just go.

www.darmatravels.com

Copyright © 2019, 2025 by Emma Scattergood

All rights reserved. No part of this publication may be reproduced, stored in a retrieval system, or transmitted in any form or by any means—electronic, mechanical, photocopying, recording, or otherwise—without prior written permission from the copyright holder.

The information in this book is true and complete to the best of the author's knowledge. It is intended for informational and entertainment purposes only. The author and publisher make no representations or warranties regarding the accuracy or applicability of the content and disclaim any liability for any loss or damage resulting from its use.

Cover design and interior formatting by 100Covers

First Published in 2019 by Olympia Publishers
Second Edition 2021 (Epub)
This Revised Edition with updated text 2025 by Emma Scattergood

Paperback ISBN 978-0-6453070-8-5
Ebook ISBN 978-0-6453070-3-0

Contents

Preface: The Unexpected Retirees xi
Chapter 1: Australia to Singapore 1
Chapter 2: Hanging Around in Asia 12
Chapter 3: Rediscovering Penang 20
Chapter 4: A Milestone Birthday 28
Chapter 5: Life Aboard a Boat to England 39
Chapter 6: The Indian Ocean 47
Chapter 7: Petra and the Suez 60
Chapter 8: It's All Just Greek to Me 71
Chapter 9: Across the Mediterranean 79
Chapter 10: At Home in England 89
Chapter 11: Exploring Paris 100
Chapter 12: South West France 113
Chapter 13: Finding Vincent in Provence 124
Chapter 14: Under the Tuscan Sun 136
Chapter 15: Towards the Sound of Music 149
Chapter 16: A Theme Park Called Prague 162
Chapter 17: Wars and Marijuana 174
Chapter 18: The Beauty of Brugge 186
Chapter 19: Living Life as a Pom 193
Chapter 20: Meeting Martin Clunes 204
Chapter 21: Living in London 217
Chapter 22: Circumnavigating Ireland 231
Chapter 23: Hong Kong and Home 242

Author's Note 253
Previous Books by Emma Scattergood 254
About the Author 257

In memory of my cousin Emma.

Books by Emma Scattergood

The Bucket List Adventure Series
Bucket Lists and Walking Sticks
Itchy Feet & Bucket Lists
Next Chapter Travel

Other
My Breast Cancer Adventure

Free Photo Book

Want to see it for yourself? Discover the photographs that accompany and enrich this book.

Browse or download the free photo book.

Visit: **https://darmatravels.com/photo-books/**

PREFACE

The Unexpected Retirees

Extract from Darma Travels Blog-
Each journey starts with an idea, moves into the research and costing phase, crystallises into an itinerary and finally, heart pumping, booking buttons are pushed, and a journey is born.

On the evening of 4 August 2011, I was watching television with my two children when the phone rang. On the line was Grant, a good friend of my husband, Darryl. Both Darryl and Grant, along with 15 others, were on their way back from Cape York. They had spent a week riding their motorbikes from Byron Bay, Australia's most easterly point, to Cape York, its most northerly.

'Emma, it's Grant—Red. I'm on the trip with Darryl,' he said. 'I need to tell you that Darryl has been involved in an accident.'

He went on to explain that Darryl had been in a terrible accident earlier that afternoon and was currently being airlifted by the Royal Flying Doctor Service to Cairns Base Hospital. He was not expected to live. A mutual friend, also a close work colleague of Darryl's, had been involved in the same accident and had not survived.

That phone call became the catalyst for a whole new life. After a three-week coma, Darryl spent another four and a half months in hospital. He emerged unemployable, with a fused spine, nerve damage, chronic pain, foot drop, memory issues, and other lasting complications. He could no longer sit, stand, or walk for long stretches—limitations that affected, and often ended, many parts of his former life, from work to leisure. The years that followed blurred into surgeries, physiotherapy, rehabilitation, and an endless circuit of doctors, appointments, and lawyers.

Four frustrating years later, as Darryl's body slowly began to strengthen, depression—long kept at bay—started to take hold. That was when I resigned from my role as operations manager at the Crystal Castle, a large tourism business near our home. I was overdue for time off, and stepping away meant we could spend more time together, easing Darryl's long, difficult days. Financially, we could just manage: an earlier property investment had worked in our favour, and, thankfully, Darryl had taken out an insurance policy in his early thirties.

Four years later also meant that Pierce, our son, had finished secondary school. After one year of studying for a Bachelor of Education at university, he decided it was not for him. Armed with his British passport, he promptly boarded a plane bound for London. His departure, and the stream of travel stories that followed, had a twofold effect on us. First, it left just us and our daughter Paige rattling around in our large house—a former Baptist church we had converted into a family home 16 years earlier. Second, it rekindled our own slumbering desire to travel.

'We always said we'd do more travelling once the kids were older. Maybe now's the time to start thinking about it,' I suggested to Darryl.

'We still have Paige for another year. And what about Jordie?' he replied.

'I'm not saying we go now. Maybe we can just start looking into it.'

'And how can we just leave the house?'

He had a point. Our two biggest stumbling blocks were clear: the house—located in Mullumbimby, large, with a swimming pool, a fishpond, and Turkle the turtle, all needing regular care—and Jordie, our ten-year-old Cavoodle, a happy 'I love everyone' sort of dog who rarely spent a night away from us.

Unexpectedly, in early 2016, just a few months after that conversation, our first hurdle cleared itself. A funky, modern townhouse came on the market in nearby Brunswick Heads. This small seaside town has it all: ocean beaches, a sparkling river, a lively collection of cafés and shops, and arguably the best pub in the world. Dolphins are often seen frolicking offshore, and depending on the season, migrating whales pass by as well. Properties here rarely come up for sale, and when they do, you need to be both quick and lucky. This time, we were both. We sold our converted church in record time and, thanks to Mullumbimby's booming property market, at a record price. A few weeks later, riding the adrenaline rush of a fiercely contested auction, we emerged as the successful bidders. Before long, we were rearranging furniture in our new, low-maintenance Brunswick Heads home.

Jordie, our second hurdle, was overcome when Patma, my stepmother and owner of a large garden full of native water dragons, offered to look after him if we decided to travel.

'Are you sure, Patma? We won't be going anywhere until next year, once Paige finishes high school, but if we do go, it could be for a while.'

'I'm very sure. He'll be good company—so long as he doesn't chase my water dragons.'

With Jordie's care settled and our living situation now blissfully low-maintenance, we finally made the decision: we would spend as much of 2017 as possible travelling. Our main destination would be England, and to help with costs, I planned to look into house swaps or staying with family. By then, Paige would have finished her exams and would either head to university or take a gap year.

I was born in England, a fact that has brought several fortunate consequences. The most important is that Pierce, Paige, and I are dual nationals, holding both Australian and British passports. This gives us the freedom to live, work, and travel not only in Australia but also throughout the European Union. Another advantage is having family who still live in England. These factors, combined with a long-held desire to finish a journey we first began in the 1990s, made England the natural choice for our travels.

Back in 1991, Darryl and I were living in London with rewarding, successful jobs. At the same time, we were still financing a mortgage in Australia, and when the first Gulf War broke out, work in both our industries quickly dried up. With few options, we packed up and returned home. We promised ourselves that we would one day return to England, and spent three months slowly making our way back through Southeast Asia. By the time we arrived in Australia, the war was already over. But life moved on—careers, children, and responsibilities took over—and the idea of returning to England quietly slipped away.

Perhaps it was inevitable. I grew up in a family of travellers. My English father met and married my Kiwi mother, Nancy, in New Zealand, and before eventually settling in Australia, they spent several years roaming across Europe and the United Kingdom in a motor caravan. My arrival did little to slow them down. I spent the first year of my life in the back of that van, journeying through Europe, Afghanistan, Türkiye, and India before we finally reached Australia.

That early experience, along with a childhood filled with more travel, firmly planted in me a desire to explore. Growing up, I dreamed constantly of far-off destinations and slowly compiled a series of bucket lists. When I met Darryl in my late teens, I introduced him to the idea of world travel, and over time our lists merged into one. At one stage,

BUCKET LISTS AND WALKING STICKS

I even laminated what I thought was the ultimate version and carried it in my wallet.

Now, with the prospect of extended travel ahead, we dug out the list to see what we might finally tick off. Aside from entries like 'have Christmas lunch with the (yet-to-be-born) grandkids,' and a few necessary updates, it looked much the same:

- Have a Singapore Sling at Raffles, Singapore.
- Spend a week in Provence and/or Tuscany.
- Visit the Wailing Wall, Jerusalem.
- Explore Petra, Jordan.
- See the Pyramids, Egypt.
- Travel the Trans-Mongolian Express, China to Russia.
- See the cherry blossoms in Japan.
- Gaze at the Mona Lisa, Paris.
- Traverse the Suez and Panama canals.
- Visit the Parthenon, Greece.
- Go to Istanbul.
- Stand beside the Leaning Tower of Pisa.
- Look at Michelangelo's David, Florence.
- Kiss the Blarney Stone and have a Guinness, Ireland.
- Visit the Red-Light District, Amsterdam.
- Visit Venice.
- See the Terracotta Warriors, China.
- View the Swiss Alps.
- Gaze at the Burj Khalifa, UAE.
- Find the Cornish village where *Doc Martin* was filmed.

It was clearly an ambitious list, spanning continents and cultures. The cost of ticking off all 20 would be significant, so we resolved to build an itinerary that balanced bucket list dreams with practicality. Anything not covered this time could always wait for the next adventure.

While attempts to arrange a house swap through various agencies came to nothing, reaching out to family proved more successful. A plea for help from their colonial relatives led to my Aunt Charlotte, based in Caversham, a small town near Reading, generously offering us a house to use as a base. Having recently completed the renovation of an old family home she had inherited, she was in the enviable position of owning two houses. Rather than leave one sitting empty, she offered it to us while she and her partner Derek decided on their next steps.

In the meantime, Darryl's doctors and insurance company were supportive. As long as he registered with a British doctor on arrival, he was given the all-clear to travel. Five years on from his accident, his physiotherapy sessions had lessened, but he was still living with a new hip, chronic pain, nerve damage, memory problems, foot drop, and a twisted spine. A walking stick was essential, and each afternoon had to be spent lying flat—the only position that eased his pain and restored his energy.

So, we now had a base in England, a medical clearance for Darryl to travel, and a timeframe of approximately seven to eight months. It was time to start planning the actual itinerary. With travel options limited due to Australia's isolated location, a well-timed comment from a friend and some extensive internet research led me to consider cruising to England as a viable option.

Cruising offered several advantages. Most importantly, it would accommodate Darryl's injuries. The 22-plus hours required to fly to Europe were not ideal for him. Secondly, the idea of slowly and calmly making our way to the other side of the world, stopping at exciting destinations along the way, was incredibly appealing. Frankly, with flying, you miss so much.

'There's a P&O world cruise departing Brisbane in early March that could take us to England via the Suez Canal,' I told Darryl one morning. 'The itinerary looks amazing, and it would let us tick off some bucket list items.'

'How much does it cost?' was his reply.

BUCKET LISTS AND WALKING STICKS

'It's doable—but I've also found a cheaper option,' I said.

'If we join this same cruise in Singapore instead of Brisbane, it's nearly half the price. Feels like a bargain too good to miss. We just need to figure out how to get to Singapore.'

As if it were meant to be, a way of reaching Singapore soon presented itself with the discovery of a repositioning cruise. These cruises occur when a cruise company moves one of its vessels from one home port to another—typically at the start or end of a season. They are worth knowing about as they are usually significantly cheaper than regular cruises, with the company eager to fill cabins.

'I've found a recently released, very cheap Royal Caribbean repositioning cruise leaving Brisbane on the 20th of February,' I told Darryl.

'How long does it take to reach Singapore?'

'Eleven days, then we'll have a three-week gap before the next cruise, which gives us time to travel around Asia if we want.'

With the discovery of these two affordable cruises, our itinerary began to take shape. Cruise with Royal Caribbean to Singapore, spend three weeks exploring Southeast Asia, then board the P&O cruise to England. As I have mentioned, years ago, we spent three months travelling throughout Asia, and I am fortunate that Patma, my stepmother, comes from Penang, giving us a family connection there. We decided that we would spend the three-week gap first exploring Singapore, followed by a train ride north through Malaysia to Penang. After spending time with family, we would retrace our journey back to Singapore to begin the next leg of our adventure.

With our journey from Australia to England organised, it would take nine weeks, visit ten countries, tick at least five bucket list items, and, with our base in England settled, we just had to decide what to do with the other five months available to us. Visiting Europe was the obvious option.

Back in our 20s, it was common for young Australians to buy a cheap campervan and travel the continent. Now in our 50s, with injuries to accommodate and a deeper appreciation for comfort, we considered and quickly rejected that option. Instead, we turned to more practical modes: bus, plane, or train—ultimately deciding that rail travel best suited our needs.

Touring Europe using a Eurail pass is a popular option for Australians. After some research, I also discovered it could be an expensive one. Fortunately, on finding a website called The Man in Seat 61 (now my go-to train travel guru) and following his advice, 'buy your tickets as far in advance as possible', meant we could skip the passes. Advance-purchase tickets were cheap, and we could save as much as 30% on each one.

It was fortunate that Paige was busy with her final-year exams, our internet was fast, and we had months to spare—because from mid-to-late 2016, we spent much of our time refining a route and booking accommodation to match. Guided by *The Man in Seat 61* and various travel forums, we gradually locked in each of the 17 train journeys needed to complete our European loop, along with five more to take us through Southeast Asia.

By Christmas 2016, the itinerary was nearly complete. Incredibly, we would be ticking off 13 bucket list items and visiting 17 countries—without taking a single flight.

'This trip's grown bigger than I expected,' Darryl commented wryly.

'It has somewhat,' I agreed. 'Although we've left about three months free just to live a normal life in England. I want to experience being a Pom.'

'I still want to get to Ireland,' Darryl added. 'And we have not worked out how we're getting home.'

We decided that part, our return to Australia, could wait until later.

By now, friends and family were becoming aware of our plans, and it was for them that we created darmatravels.com, our travel blog. We named it Darma Travels—firstly because it's a blend of our names, and secondly because Darma (although spelt differently) holds philosophical meaning in both Hinduism and Buddhism, two traditions we respect. The blog was intended to keep friends and family updated, help us stay mindful of the values we admired, and (hopefully) keep me occupied during the many sea, land, and rail miles ahead.

By February 2017, Paige, glad to be done with exams and even happier about taking a gap year, had left home and was job-hunting in the Whitsunday region of Northern Queensland. Pierce, looking forward to our arrival, was working in a pub in Twickenham, England. Jordie, happily settled in his temporary new home, was already causing trouble chasing water dragons. And we were preparing to leave Brunswick Heads. Phone and internet plans were cancelled. Mail was redirected. The fridge emptied. Steps were taken to cover rates, insurances, and car registrations.

Finally, on 20 February, after one last look around, we locked the doors, shut the gate, and took our first steps towards a new adventure. As I wheeled my overstuffed bag to the local bus stop, I tried to push aside a nagging thought:

Would Darryl be able to handle this journey?

CHAPTER 1

Australia to Singapore

Extract from Darma Travels Blog-
The past few days spent at sea have been incredible. We had no idea that we would be travelling so close to the Queensland coastline. At times, it has felt that we could just dive in and swim to shore.

20 February is a Monday, and as is typical in our region of Australia at this time of year, the day dawns blue, bright and beautiful. With our bags packed, passports and travel money cards safely tucked into various niches, we call out our farewells to the neighbours.

'See you when we get back—and could you please keep an eye on the house for us?'

'No problem. Have a great time, guys,' yell back Trish, Dave and Kay.

Our Royal Caribbean cruise, the Legend of the Seas, departs from Brisbane Cruise Terminal later that afternoon. To get there, we have booked seats on the local Byron Easy Bus. Unfortunately, Brunswick

Heads does not have much in the way of public transport—like most of the Byron Shire. The local train was decommissioned years ago, its tracks now rusting into ruin. Buses are infrequent.

What is fortunate is that the nearby town of Byron Bay, home to stars such as Chris Hemsworth, Simon Baker and Olivia Newton-John, has become an international tourism hotspot. Its status as a 'must-visit' destination has spawned several businesses catering to travellers. One of them is Byron Easy Bus: a fast, cheap and efficient way to access cities, airports and cruise terminals.

Boarding the Easy Bus, we find that seating is limited. It's packed with sleepy, slightly grungy backpackers who have spent the past few days ticking off their own bucket lists in Byron Bay.

'Excuse me, can you please move over?' I ask a guy stretched across two seats.

'Aah. Okay. Sure,' he grunts.

With our grey hair, Darryl's walking stick, and my hybrid backpack (the kind with wheels), we do stand out slightly among the younger backpackers. This becomes even more obvious some three hours later, when we're the only ones to alight at Brisbane Cruise Terminal.

In recent years, cruising in Australia has increased in popularity tenfold—although judging by the warehouse-type structure in front of me, you wouldn't think so. Situated in what feels like the middle of nowhere, with only a handful of cafés to support it, this bleak building is a far cry from the airport-style duty-free shopping plaza I had expected.

While the terminal itself and the lack of shopping options seem a little outdated, the service offered by the cruise staff certainly isn't. Stepping into the terminal, our bags are quickly whisked from us, and we are efficiently directed towards check-in. Here, the long queue we eye with some resignation quickly disappears when a staff member spots Darryl's walking stick and ushers us into a fast-track lane.

BUCKET LISTS AND WALKING STICKS

All goes well—until we realise Darryl's cruise ticket has gone missing.

'So, you still have your ticket, but you don't have mine?' Darryl asks.

'I did have it. I've no idea what's happened to it.'

What could have turned into an argument is thankfully avoided when the receptionist, sounding a little weary, steps in.

'If you fill out this declaration, I can print a new ticket for Darryl.'

It's here at check-in that we receive our onboard cruise cards—highly sensitive magnetic identity cards that not only open our cabin door but are also used for all onboard purchases. Because they function as ID, a photo must be assigned to each card, which leads to the following familiar exchange:

'Please stand still and smile directly at the camera.'

'No. Smile and stand still, Darryl. Let's try that again, shall we?'

With newly minted cruise cards in hand, it's onward to security and customs. Cruise terminal security is much like airport security: metal detectors, X-rays, and sniffer dogs. From a previous trip, we know that since his accident, Darryl—with his metal hip, femur rod, and fused spine—is now a guaranteed security alarm. Aware that he will set the alarms pealing, we quickly fall into a routine established on that previous journey. I go through security first and collect all of Darryl's belongings as they follow—his walking stick, belt, wallet and phone. Darryl, after receiving his customary pat-down, joins me a few minutes later. It's important we follow this routine, or else Darryl's possessions could be left unattended for quite some time.

With security and customs behind, all that's left is to step aboard—where a smartly dressed waiter promptly, and rather unexpectedly, greets us.

'Glass of champagne, sir, madame?'

'Champagne! Definitely. Thank you.'

'Oh yes. I'll have another. Thank you.'

Champagne clutched in one hand, phone for the photos in the other, I turn to Darryl and grin.

'Can you believe this? After nearly six crazy years, look where we are—on board a cruise ship with seven months of travel ahead of us.'

'It's pretty crazy,' Darryl replies.

'Cheers, Darryl.'

'Cheers, babe.'

As much as we'd love to savour champagne all afternoon, there's too much to see and explore. Our home for the next eleven days is a balcony cabin, located forward on Deck 10. Keen to inspect it, patience is required when seeking its location; we find ourselves continuously getting lost. More patience is needed when eventually arriving at our cabin door; we find that my highly sensitive magnetic cruise card does not work. Although I was warned, I have obviously put it too close to my mobile phone, thus rendering it useless. I make a mental note not to do this again, a mental note I take no heed of, as between the two cruises, I do this three more times.

Our cabin, on entering, we find is worn, but still, it exceeds our expectations. It is spacious, and the bed looks comfortable and inviting. A fresh gerbera, a flower Darryl closely associates with his late mother, Barbara, sits on the coffee table. Nearby is a dish of hard-boiled sweets and an impressive variety of teas and coffees. There are even packets of biscuits.

For some years now, I've made a habit of practising a 30-minute yoga routine each morning. Standing in the cabin on that first day, I mentally rearrange the furniture and decide there should be just enough space to continue my routine over the next eleven days. I even look forward to stretching and flowing through the poses while gazing out over the vast Pacific Ocean through our balcony doors. Time will soon reveal, however, that certain poses cannot be performed without bumping into either the television or the well-stocked bar fridge.

The rest of the afternoon is spent exploring and trying to make sense of the ship's layout. With eleven decks, six dining venues, eight bars, and more than 1,800 guests on board, there's a lot to take in. Before dinner that evening, we discover that the bathroom in our cabin is a good size, with excellent water pressure and plenty of hot water.

'The shower's great,' I say to Darryl. 'But watch out for the curtain—it has a habit of sticking to you.'

We've chosen 'My Time' or 'Freedom' dining at the Romeo and Juliet dining room, which means we're not locked into a set mealtime. Instead, we can eat when it suits us. This first evening sets the tone for most nights on board: a delicious three-course meal paired with a crisp French rosé, followed by a stroll around the promenade deck, a quick peek at that night's cabaret show, before collapsing into our queen-size bed.

The only nights we won't be dining in the main restaurant are the formal 'black-tie' evenings. Travelling with small suitcases meant something had to give—and in our case, it was formalwear. No suits, ties, or ball gowns for us. On those nights, our alternative is the more casual Windjammer Restaurant up on the top deck, where each evening, a decadent themed buffet is offered.

Following a restorative night's sleep, lulled by the ship's gentle rocking as she slowly starts to make her way up the Queensland coast, the following days take on a semblance of routine. I wake, do my yoga, then walk a few laps around the ship's exercise deck. Once Darryl is awake, we usually head to the Windjammer for the breakfast buffet, or, if we prefer, to the set breakfast in Romeo and Juliet.

After breakfast and following another stroll around the promenade, we find somewhere to sit and tackle the sudoku and crossword obtained each morning from the ship's library. This might be by the pool, in one of the plush lounges, or out on our private balcony. If the mood strikes, we join a talk, film, game, quiz, or other activity listed in the ship's daily newsletter.

Lunch brings another choice: buffet or three-course dining. It doesn't take long to realise we'll need to practise some restraint when it comes to food. For the past year, we've followed the 5:2 diet—or more recently, the 6:1 version, now that we're maintaining. That means six days of normal eating and one day of carefully watching our calories. It's worked well for us—and on board a cruise ship, it's more important than ever to stick with it.

In the early hours of Wednesday, 22 February, our cruise ship glides gently into Cairns Harbour. We wake to the sight of the long, low buildings of downtown Cairns, dotted with taller hotels and office blocks, visible from our balcony. Established in 1876 to serve miners heading to the nearby goldfields, Cairns today is best known as the gateway to the Great Barrier Reef.

It feels strangely significant that Cairns—a place where Darryl spent so many months in hospital—is our first port of call. While I lived here, shopped for groceries, paid bills, and drove around town, Darryl was either in a coma or slowly recovering. He has no memory of the layout or the place itself. Once well enough to leave Cairns Base Hospital, he was flown straight to John Flynn Hospital on the Gold Coast, where he spent another two months in rehabilitation.

This visit gives us a chance to experience Cairns together—to walk its streets and take in the sights, all while sweltering under its tropical heat. We browse the local shopping centre, pop our heads into the nearby casino, and stroll along the well-known esplanade, with its unique, topless-bathing-permitted swimming lagoon.

Unlike many of our fellow passengers, we have no interest in excursions to the Great Barrier Reef—we've done that—or the nearby Daintree Rainforest. This stop is not about sightseeing. It's about quietly closing a door on something that happened nearly six years ago, and finally moving on.

We spend two days in Cairns—enough time to seek a little closure. In truth, we're eager to move on, to begin the next leg of our journey: travelling further up the Queensland coast before turning west at the top of Australia and heading towards Darwin, our next port of call.

Although previously unknown to both of us, it turns out that Australia has a defined cyclone season. Covering the eastern and northern seaboards, it typically runs from November to the end of April—though cyclones have been known to occur outside these dates. We're lucky. Despite travelling smack in the middle of the season, we encounter no extreme weather. In fact, we're surprised and mesmerised by just how calm the ocean is. We hadn't realised we'd be travelling so close to the Australian mainland, and we certainly hadn't expected the sea to be, at times, as smooth as glass.

It takes two full days to travel up and over the tip of Cape York, heading west towards Darwin. Passing Cape York is a momentous occasion for us. As mentioned earlier, it was on the way back from here that Darryl had his accident. While he remembers reaching the top, there's very little he recalls after that. To mark the occasion, we manage to secure a bottle of Veuve Clicquot Ponsardin from the ship's cellars for fifty Australian dollars, along with a few chocolate-coated strawberries. While negotiating the purchase, we learn that the *Legend of the Seas* is actively trying to clear out its stock.

'How come you're selling all this alcohol? And why so cheap?' we ask.

'The ship's been sold to Thomson's. This is our last cruise. Once we reach Barcelona, she'll be overhauled,' replies one crew member—which explains the unusually low repositioning fare we paid.

'Do you still have jobs?' we ask.

'Yes, everyone's transferring to other ships. I'm going to the Caribbean,' answers one lovely Chinese stewardess.

As we were told, the ship has recently been sold, and this voyage is part of her final journey for Royal Caribbean. After a planned refit in

Barcelona, she'll begin a new life in the Mediterranean. We're happy to take advantage of the clearance sales and can't help but wonder—with so many items being sold off—what state the ship's cellars and gift shops will be in by the time she reaches her destination.

'Sorry, mate, there's no more alcohol left—it's all been sold,' we suspect will become a familiar refrain.

We drink our champagne and eat our strawberries out on our private balcony. The sea, a bathwater-warm 27 degrees, is millpond smooth and at times only twenty metres deep. The sun is hot, but the breeze created by the ship's momentum is cool. It feels as though we could almost reach out and touch the tip of Australia. Adding to the surrealness of it all are dolphins, countless jellyfish, and even the occasional sea snake.

Somewhere near the top of the country, we raise our glasses—not just to the day's travel, but also to Jeff, the mate Darryl lost up here.

The following day is spent sailing across the Gulf of Carpentaria and into the Timor Sea before arriving in Darwin in the early hours of Sunday morning. As we dock, the cooling breeze created by the ship's propulsion disappears, and it's immediately clear we've arrived in steamy, tropical Darwin—former frontier outpost and capital of Australia's Northern Territory. We're looking forward to this visit. Known to us as the city that was flattened twice—first by Japanese air raids during World War II, and again in 1974 by Cyclone Tracy—it will be interesting to see what a relatively newly-built city looks like.

With just eight hours in port, we've decided to skip the ship's organised excursions and explore on our own. The past few days have highlighted a few gaps in our packing—particularly in the toiletries department—and we're keen to make the most of familiar department stores and currency to restock.

'I thought we could share a hairbrush to save space, but I don't like that idea anymore,' I had said to Darryl just that morning.

'And I want my own toothpaste—I don't like yours,' was his quick reply.

First stop: the nearest supermarket.

Disembarking and walking along the harbour, Darwin's status as a recently rebuilt city is immediately apparent. The waterfront looks modern, and clearly a lot of money has been invested in its development. Cafés, bars, and restaurants line the foreshore, bordered by wide, open parklands. Residential apartments are plentiful, and a large communal wave pool enhances the resort-like feel. The walkways leading away from the harbour are impressively pedestrian-friendly, guiding us straight into the city via a skybridge and a state-of-the-art glass-walled lift. It's a pleasant surprise—and we find ourselves wondering what the rest of Darwin will look like.

As we walk along the pedestrian walkway from the harbour to the city centre, we come across a fellow cruiser in tears.

'What's happened?' we ask.

'She's dropped her phone into the harbour. It had all her credit cards and cruise card in it,' someone explains.

'We're going to try diving for it,' chimes another.

Moments later, a young man comes sprinting back from the ship carrying a pair of goggles. He hands them to a fit-looking teenager, who promptly slips them on and dives into the murky water. After a few duck-dives, he surfaces triumphantly, phone held high above his head.

The relief on the young woman's face is contagious, and we are both smiling broadly as we walk away.

After making our supermarket purchases, we spend the next few hours exploring Darwin's city centre. Compared to the modern harbour foreshore, the city itself feels underwhelming—smaller and more subdued than we expected. We visit the ruins of the old town hall, wander through Civic Park and Smith Street Mall, and pause to enjoy live music in the bustling outdoor market.

With 1,800 tourists suddenly in town, Darwin tourism has pulled out all stops, organising a Sunday market right in the heart of the pedestrian precinct. Local artists and craftspeople eagerly showcase their work, hoping to catch our eye—and our wallets.

It's a scorching and muggy day, and by mid-afternoon, we are exhausted and sweating profusely. Making our way back to the harbour, we spy a cafe with a large awning creating a deeply shaded, inviting area. There's even free Wi-Fi on offer. Internet on board the Legend of the Seas must be purchased—something we are keen to avoid. This means that each time the ship docks, we, along with most of the other passengers, immediately seek out a source of free Wi-Fi to maintain contact with the outside world. Over time, we become quite accomplished at finding it. Today, given the welcoming appearance of this cafe, we immediately settle ourselves down and order two cold beers.

Typical of this time of year, as late afternoon approaches and we take our first reviving mouthfuls, the sky starts to cloud over, eventually turning a forbidding, thunderstorm-imminent grey. Although hard to believe possible, the humidity becomes even more cloying and the day stickier. We make our way back on board minutes before a powerful Australian tropical thunderstorm crashes down over Darwin.

It takes three full days at sea to reach Singapore. We cross into the Flores Sea, hugging Indonesia's western coast, and celebrate crossing the equator. The heat and humidity persist. The ship's pools are full, the air conditioning is cranked down, and the free soft-serve ice cream machine works overtime.

An enticement many cruise companies offer when encouraging you to book is onboard spending money, a credit against your account that can be used to make onboard purchases. Our credit for the 11 days is 200 Australian dollars each. This is enough to fund any cocktail purchases, and so the afternoons often see us, celebratory drink in hand, saluting the setting sun. A movie is often shown poolside on the top deck, which we watch before making our way to dinner.

BUCKET LISTS AND WALKING STICKS

In the early hours of Friday, 3 March, we sit on our balcony, watching as the ship glides into Singapore Harbour. The activity is staggering—cranes, cargo ships and containers everywhere. We later learn this is the second busiest port in the world by shipping tonnage, with over a thousand vessels here at any given time. Even the skyline is striking—tall, futuristic buildings silhouetted in the early morning haze, a preview of the ultra-modern city we will soon step into. We breakfast on our final buffet as we watch the sun rise, the mist dissipate, and Singapore gently reveal herself in all her splendour.

As we discover at the end of each of our cruises, passengers are expected to disembark early and quickly to make way for the ship's new passengers. Eight am finds us stepping off the Legend of the Seas, making our way through customs and out into the bustle of Singapore.

It is with some relief that customs go without a hitch. Before leaving Australia, the Smartraveller website had warned us that certain medications required prior approval to enter Singapore. After weeks of back-and-forth with doctors and Singapore customs, we had finally received the necessary paperwork for Darryl's medications. Of course, after going through all this trouble, no one asks to see any documentation. No one bats an eyelid. We are simply waved through.

'Well, I'm glad we didn't need it,' I say, 'but I do feel slightly hard done by.'

'I just hope it's as easy when we return from Malaysia,' Darryl replies.

CHAPTER 2

Hanging Around in Asia

Extract from Darma Travels Blog-
What a truly amazing, futuristic, spotless, dynamic city. A city where east does meet west. A city showcasing an awe-inspiring juxtaposition of buildings, people and cultures.

Outside the Singapore Cruise Terminal, we are lucky to be among the first cruise passengers waiting at the taxi rank. One advantage of travelling with such small suitcases is that we can self-disembark, in other words, wheel our cases off the ship ourselves. Due to the various dress codes required on board, most passengers travel with one or more enormous suitcases. Too bulky to carry themselves, they must rely on the ship's staff, which means they have little control over when they can actually leave the terminal.

Singapore, with its strict littering and chewing gum laws, looks immaculate, as expected. A taxi arrives within minutes, and before we know it, we are being whisked through the reclaimed harbour area and into the city centre. At just 719 square kilometres and home to over 5.5 million people, Singapore has spent the past 200 years expanding through land reclamation. The land we cross to reach our hotel was only reclaimed in 1992, with supporting infrastructure completed in the early 2000s. The result is a cityscape that has changed dramatically since we were last here in 1990.

Dominating the skyline is the extraordinary Marina Bay Sands Hotel, a futuristic structure that looks like a ship balanced atop three soaring towers. Other architectural landmarks catch our eye: the flying saucer-shaped Supreme Court, the spiky Theatres on the Bay that resemble a pair of durians, and the concrete giant that is the OCBC Centre. It is awe-inspiring and as we will come to realise, one of the most striking city skylines we will see on this entire journey.

Before our departure, much thought had gone into choosing which district of Singapore we would stay in: Chinatown, Little India, Beach Road, City Hall—some of the most popular options. In the end, we settled on the CBD (Central Business District), due to its proximity to Raffles Hotel, one of our bucket list items, as well as its access to shopping complexes and nearby MRT stations. Through Booking.com, we had reserved a room at the Peninsula Excelsior Hotel, and by 10 am, we have dropped off our bags, been advised to return at 2 pm, caught up on the news via the free Wi-Fi in the hotel lobby, and set off to explore the surrounding area.

Exploring the CBD and nearby streets confirms that we have chosen well. Two food halls nearby offer easy access to cheap, local meals. City Hall MRT (short for Mass Rapid Transit and Singapore's equivalent of the Underground) is just around the corner. Raffles Hotel is only a block away, as is Raffles Shopping Centre. Although we do not discover it on this first day, we later come across a vast network of underground pedestrian tunnels linking many of the MRT stations and shopping centres. Stretching from Raffles to the Marina, it spans kilometres and means that, if we choose, we never have to walk above ground, contend with traffic, or burn under the fierce tropical sun.

Two o'clock that afternoon finds us back at reception, waiting for our room. Another couple is also waiting. Some casual chatting surprisingly reveals them to be the aunt and uncle of an acquaintance from Mullumbimby.

'Our niece is from Mullumbimby. Name's Vicky. Do you know her?'

It is an amazing and delightful coincidence—briefly. The moment is soured when the uncle begins to turn quite churlish.

'Is our room ready yet? We've been waiting since eleven this morning. You must have some clean rooms in this 600-room hotel!'

His constant badgering of the reception staff is embarrassing, and as we are sitting nearby—also Australian—we cannot help but feel we are being lumped in with his arrogance. The moment they are handed their key, we take care to distance ourselves. 'I'm not sure what his problem was, but please know we're not with them,' I say.

'We're actually pretty embarrassed by his behaviour,' Darryl adds.

That evening, after filling our bellies at a local noodle and dumpling place not far from the hotel, we notice the ground seems to sway slightly. It is the lingering after-effect of being at sea. Our bodies have not yet remembered how to stand still. Darryl adjusts quickly, but it takes me another day or two.

Our second day in Singapore dawns bright, humid, and hot. After a great buffet breakfast—included in our rate—we head back upstairs and decide to catch up on washing. With no self-service options aboard the cruise, our clean clothes are running low. We managed to hand-wash a fair amount during the voyage, but drying racks were limited. Now, back on land and with plenty of space, the room quickly begins to resemble a Chinese laundry, with damp clothes hanging everywhere.

The rest of the day is spent exploring. Little India is crowded and chaotic, while the Buddha Tooth Relic Temple in Chinatown (so named for the canine tooth of Buddha displayed inside) is stunning.

BUCKET LISTS AND WALKING STICKS

We arrive during puja, and it is easy to lose track of time watching the monks and worshippers in quiet devotion. The Botanic Gardens are beautiful, although our enthusiasm is somewhat dampened when we find ourselves soaked by an afternoon rain shower. Dinner is yet more noodles, eaten in one of the many restaurants that line Beach Road.

To explore Singapore more thoroughly, we begin our third day by conquering the MRT system. From purchasing tickets at the user-friendly vending machines to grasping the east–west and north–south layout, we find it fast, simple, and incredibly convenient. This small victory grants us access to hours of exploration—first along Orchard Road, home to more than 40 shopping malls, and later at Gardens by the Bay: 101 hectares of waterfront gardens built on reclaimed land in central Singapore.

Gardens by the Bay mesmerises us with its strikingly designed greenhouses, enormous tree-like light structures, serene waterways, and lush greenery. As night falls, a light show set to a pulsing soundtrack takes place among the 'supertrees'—but we miss it this evening, as we are dining two storeys underground at a popular Burmese/Myanmar restaurant, where we try, and unexpectedly enjoy, a salad made from tea leaves.

As mentioned earlier, one of the main reasons we chose to stay in the CBD was its proximity to Raffles Hotel. Sipping a Singapore Sling in the iconic Long Bar has been a bucket list item for over two decades. Unfortunately, our previous visit to Singapore—more than 20 years ago—coincided with the hotel being closed for renovations. This time, we are determined not to miss out.

Raffles Hotel, once situated on the waterfront but now some distance from the sea thanks to extensive land reclamation, has stood since around 1887. In 1915, a gin-based cocktail was invented here for ladies, who at the time were not permitted to drink alcohol in public. Disguised as fruit juice, the cocktail became wildly popular and a tradition developed—enjoy a Singapore Sling in the Long Bar and toss your peanut shells onto the floor.

It turns out that the experience more than lives up to our expectations. Knowing it can get busy, we arrive just after breakfast, around 10 am. Despite yet another round of renovations, the hotel has cleverly repurposed the historic Billiard Room to serve drinks in place of the Long Bar. It is here that we order our first Singapore Slings.

'Which one of these is the original Singapore Sling?' we ask our waiter, pointing to an array of choices on the menu. 'And are we really allowed to throw the peanut shells on the floor?' I say, because, as it was early, the floors appeared peanut-shell free.

'Yes, yes. Just throw them like this,' he replies cheerfully, flicking a handful of shells into the air and watching them scatter.

Each cocktail costs approximately 35 Australian dollars, so while the first drink is an ode to the bucket list, the second round requires a little more justification.

'Shall we have another?'

'Well, with both our birthdays coming up… why not?'

Credit card slightly bruised, lips sticky, and bellies full of peanuts, we spill back out onto the street an hour later—euphoric. We have managed to tick one of our many bucket list items.

One meal I absolutely adore is chicken satay—especially when cooked and served the authentic Asian way. Not the great big lumps of chicken on a stick, as we tend to prepare it in Australia, but delicate, tender, bite-sized pieces grilled over a smoky wood fire and (if I have my way) smothered in peanut sauce. In the heart of Gardens by the Bay lies Satay by the Bay, and it is here that we choose to have our final meal in Singapore. Ordering a serve of 40 satay skewers and a large coconut to drink, I am in my element. Even more so when I finish with ice-kachang: a dessert of shaved ice heaped with red beans, jelly and sweet syrup.

With suitcases now filled with clean clothes and much of Singapore still left unexplored, we awaken on our final morning and make our way to the hotel concierge to ask about options for crossing into

Malaysia. Catching a train directly from Singapore to Malaysia is out of the question. Some years earlier, the Singapore government had reclaimed control of the city's majestic central train station, once the departure point for trains across the causeway, and closed it. Now, southern Malaysian trains originate from Johor Bahru, across the border in Malaysia. To catch one, you must first leave Singapore.

Prior Googling had shown that the easiest way to cross into Malaysia was by taxi—specifically, a special cross-border cab from the Queen Street Bus Terminal. For about 80 Australian dollars, this taxi would drop us directly at Johor Bahru train station, handling the border formalities en route from the back seat.

Alternatively—and this is the method our hotel concierge insists is both efficient and far cheaper—we could do the following for just three Australian dollars:

'You take a taxi to Queen Street Bus Terminal. From there, catch a bus to the Singapore border. Disembark and go through customs. Then board another bus across the causeway to the Malaysian border. Disembark again. Go through Malaysian customs. The train station will be just beyond the checkpoint.'

Obviously, the significantly cheaper option has its appeal—but what finally sways us is the sheer fun of the challenge.

'Let's do it. It'll be much more fun and satisfying,' I manage to convince Darryl.

Everything unfolds just as the concierge described. Two hours later, slightly dishevelled but only six Australian dollars lighter, we arrive in Johor Bahru, Malaysia's second-largest city. We buy some water, find our train, locate our seats—then sit back as the next chapter of our journey begins.

Unlike Australia, Malaysia has invested heavily in its rail infrastructure over the past few years. A new electric train line now allows for a faster, more efficient service. Unfortunately, it does not yet span the entire country. What this means for us is that we must first catch an old diesel rattler from Johor Bahru to a town called Gemas—a journey of around four and a half hours. From Gemas, we cross the platform and transfer to a modern electric train heading north.

It is all fairly straightforward, apart from the ticketing. For some reason, it is not possible to buy a single through-ticket from Johor Bahru to Kuala Lumpur, our destination for the night. We must instead purchase one ticket to Gemas, and then a separate one from Gemas to KL. It seems crazy—especially as, until six months ago, the through-ticket option had existed. We wonder what logic the Malaysian rail authorities have for creating such an inconvenient system.

We also wonder what excuse they have for keeping their trains so cold. When researching the Johor Bahru to Kuala Lumpur route, a recurring complaint on travel forums stood out: the air conditioning is freezing.

'Wear jeans, pullovers, everything—you'll freeze,' was the common refrain.

It turns out the forums were right. Of all the train journeys we take over the coming months, the Malaysian trains will prove to be the coldest by far.

Two trains, two crosswords, many sudokus, and nearly seven hours later, we arrive—blue with cold—at Kuala Lumpur Sentral Station. To give Darryl a break from travelling, we have planned an overnight stay here. It proves a wise decision, as by now, he is feeling the effects of the long day. We have booked a hotel close to the station, and with the sun setting and humidity still sky-high, we pull up Google Maps on my phone and set off in search of it. This pattern—arrive, locate the hotel on Google Maps, and walk—will become second nature to us over the next seven months.

Kuala Lumpur is hot, crowded and chaotic. Traffic is relentless, and the area around Sentral Station is as gritty and inner-city Asian as they come: narrow footpaths, open drains, hawker stalls, budget Chinese hotels, jumbles of smells, and throngs of people. It is so unmistakably Asian, you cannot help but love it. You quickly learn that to enjoy Asia, you must embrace everything—smells, noise, mess, and all.

Our hotel, the Sentral KL, sits in the middle of this urban tangle. After initially exiting the station from the wrong direction, we eventually find it. Its colourful, neon-lit exterior belies the small, ageing room within.

We check in and do our best to arrange suitcases and toiletries in the limited space before heading out to find dinner. Wandering the local streets gives us a fuller picture of just how grimy the area really is, before we notice a welcoming little bar offering happy hour. A few beers later, thirst quenched, we find a supermarket and pick up some takeaway noodle dishes and a few curious-looking cakes.

Breakfast is included in our stay, and we are stunned the next morning when we are shown to a large, airy dining room upstairs, complete with a balcony and a generous buffet spread. It feels worlds away from the shabby room below. We do not question it. We simply fill our plates and prepare to move on.

Back at Sentral Station, waiting for our next train, the one that will take us four hours north to Butterworth, the transit point for Penang Island, we witness a sight that will stay with us forever. Five men, sprawled in various relaxed positions across a row of coin-operated massage chairs, are fast asleep. They look so at ease, so completely comfortable, it is impossible not to smile. I take a photo and sit watching them until our train arrives and we step aboard.

CHAPTER 3

Rediscovering Penang

Extract from Darma Travels Blog-
Once heralded as 'The Pearl of the Orient', an island state with glistening seas, white sandy beaches, swaying palms and a vibrant multicultural society living in harmony, these days I found it to be more of an island of noisy cars, tall condominiums, patches of public beaches and disillusioned people.

Our train departs KL Sentral Station at 9 am, and approximately four and a half freezing hours later, we alight at Butterworth Station. From there, it is only a short distance to the harbour, where one can catch the ferry across to Penang Island.

The obvious option of travelling from the train station to the harbour is by a quick, efficient shuttle bus. For the uninitiated (or those slow on the uptake), there is also the option of lugging one's suitcase up a large flight of stairs, navigating a walkway that spans the rail tracks, and then lugging one's bags back down before accessing the ferry terminal via a ramp.

As Darryl slowly makes his way down the final flight of stairs, a porter at the bottom suddenly spots him with his walking stick.

'Why haven't you taken the shuttle bus?' he calls out, clearly unimpressed.

'Shuttle bus? What shuttle bus?' we yell back.

In this instance, ignorance of the first option makes us the foolish ones—me especially, as I have also had to lug Darryl's case.

The ferry, when it arrives, is big, bright, colourful and belches toxic fumes. Operating since the 1920s, it is the oldest ferry service in Malaysia. Crossing the causeway to Penang Island takes us a little over half an hour; the toxic fumes are offset by the view of George Town, Penang's capital, rising from the sparkling blue of the harbour. Disembarking, we are once again thrown into the chaos of Asia: tooting taxis, persistent hawkers, and a hot, burning sun. We could take a local bus, which would take another 40 minutes to reach our hotel, but instead, we opt for the convenience of a taxi.

For our Penang Island stay, we have booked two places. The first is six nights at the Rainbow Paradise Resort in the neighbourhood of Tanjung Bungah, en route to the popular tourist area of Batu Ferringhi. We chose this location because it is within walking distance of my aunt and cousins' home. It has been years since we last saw them, and we are looking forward to catching up over some delicious Malaysian food.

The resort, when we arrive, is typical of those found in Penang: a tall, narrow high-rise fronting a sliver of beach. Our 16th-floor room is large, with oversized brown wooden furnishings and, oddly, a lone kitchen sink—bereft of any other kitchen facilities. The best part of the room, though, is the very large balcony, where each night we will sit with a tea, beer, or wine in hand, watching the sun set over the Strait of Malacca.

That first night, we dine at the hotel's beachside restaurant. As it is low season, the place is almost deserted. We eat our chicken satay, roti canai, and chendol in near darkness.

'Where is everyone?' we ask our shy waitress.

'Not many here now,' she replies. 'But wait until the weekend. It will be very busy then.'

The following morning, it's up and off to visit the relatives. They live in an apartment just a ten-minute walk from our hotel, and it is on the way there that we begin to notice some of the harsher realities of life in Penang today. High-rise buildings dominate the skyline—many appear empty, their shuttered windows and air of neglect making them seem abandoned. The footpaths are haphazard and broken, and in places, the odour from open drains suggests possible sewer contamination. Few others are walking these footpaths.

On arriving, we find that Prabha, my aunt, has cooked up a storm of delicious Malaysian dishes. We tuck into chicken rice, dhal, salads, and over-the-top sticky Indian sweets we have picked up along the way. With stomachs groaning, we spend the rest of the day relaxing and chatting in their first-floor lounge room, gazing down at the bustling fishing village below.

'How much is a unit here?' we ask at one point.

'Prices have been dropping,' comes the reply. 'You can get a really nice two-bedroom apartment in a high-rise for about 300,000 Australian dollars.'

'How come they're so cheap?'

'There's been massive overdevelopment. The government approved too many projects, and now there's an oversupply. A lot were bought by wealthy overseas investors who can't rent them out, so they sit empty. Maybe only 10% are occupied.'

'There doesn't seem to be much supporting infrastructure,' we point out.

'No. Developers have been allowed to do whatever they want. They build the high-rises but are not required to improve footpaths or public services. Little money goes into maintaining or upgrading anything.'

We also discuss the apparent disparity between Penang's main ethnic groups: Malays, Chinese, and Indians.

'Government policies heavily favour the Malay (Muslim) majority,' we are told. 'That includes housing, finance, education—even jobs and university places. All key government roles must be held by Malays, so there's little hope of change.'

We find that all they tell us is later corroborated by hotel staff and taxi drivers.

It's all extremely disappointing and sad. I first visited Penang at age 14, and again in my 20s, when it was known as the Pearl of the Orient. My memories of Penang are of an island paradise of beachside cafes, swaying palms, blue seas, great food and friendly people. Memories that this visit has now reshaped.

Over the next few days, a routine forms. Some mornings, I will do my morning yoga followed by a stomach-stretching buffet breakfast before we head out into the Asian humidity to do some local sightseeing. This may include a visit to a local beach or temple or a browse through a nearby market. Asian markets are always interesting and chaotic with their displays of meat, their overwhelming selection of fruit, their wet floors and noisy crowds.

Afternoons are generally spent visiting the family or relaxing on our balcony or by the pool. Dinner might be simple snacks and drinks or a lavish Malaysian buffet. One lunch is spent eating the amazing birthday feast Prabha has prepared for Darryl, complete with cake and candles. We follow lunch that day with the family taking us to Batu Ferringhi, Penang's best-known beachside tourist district. Here, tucked right at the very end of this precinct, they introduce us to a small restaurant nestled on the sandy beach. We sit with our feet in the sand, toasting family and watching a glorious sunset. It's nice to see that hidden amongst the concrete high-rises and general overdevelopment here, one can still find a gem such as this.

Another evening, we are taken to one of Penang's famous food courts—a place where numbered tables are surrounded by dozens of small, individual food stalls, each offering its own speciality.

'How do we order?' we ask.

'Just choose your food from any stall, tell them our table number, and they'll bring it to you when it's ready.'

'And payment?'

'Pay them when they deliver it.'

It's an easy, simple system and very user-friendly. For the remainder of our stay in Penang, we seek out these food courts and experiment with the foods they offer. Probably an example of a not-such-a-good experiment is when I see a delicious-looking fruit salad covered in a caramel-like sauce.

'What's that?' I ask, pointing to the picture of this delicious-looking dish.

'Rojak.'

'What's in it?'

'Crushed shrimp.'

It looks so appealing that, despite both Darryl and me loathing seafood, I decide to order it. I do not tell Darryl what it contains, and when it arrives, we both tuck in. The sauce has an odd, slightly salty flavour. It is not terrible—but the thought of eating crushed shrimp stops me after just a few mouthfuls. Darryl, meanwhile, keeps going happily until guilt gets the better of me.

'Crushed shrimp! You're kidding. Yuck. You could have told me sooner.'

On our final day in Tanjung Bungah, Darryl pulls up a photo on his phone that has piqued our interest. He had recently noticed something odd on the ceilings of both our current hotel and the one in Kuala Lumpur.

'What does this sign mean?' he asks. 'It's not the first time we've seen it. Emma thought it might be an emergency exit or fire hydrant indicator, but I'm not so sure.'

'That's the Qibla arrow,' they laugh.

'What's that?'

'It shows Muslims the direction of Mecca so they can face it when they pray.'

Over the coming weeks, we develop a game whereby each time we enter a new hotel room, we must guess which way the Qibla arrow will be facing. Much to Darryl's annoyance, I usually win.

George Town, the capital of Penang, is a UNESCO-listed site with a rich and colourful history. Established as a free-trade port in the late 1700s, it attracted a large influx of ethnicities and religions. The result today is a vibrant multicultural city with an eclectic mix of colonial and architectural styles. It is also a food lover's paradise, drawing visitors not only for its cuisine but, surprisingly, for its growing medical tourism industry.

Our hotel, The Royale Bintang, is a restored 19th-century British colonial trading house situated on the old harbourfront of Weld Quay. From our room, located next to a noisy, creaking lift at the back of the hotel, we can just see another one of those bustling food courts we intend to frequent.

The following three days are filled with exploring George Town. Braving the humidity and scorching sun, we track down pieces of its world-famous street art, admire its grand colonial buildings, and retreat to various museums when the heat becomes too much. The Wonderfood Museum, featuring oversized replicas of local dishes made from synthetic materials, is more of a quirky photo stop than a true museum. By contrast, the Penang State Museum and Art Gallery, which traces the island's layered history, is genuinely engaging, and we spend a few enjoyable hours there. A personal highlight is a visit to China House, a cafe-restaurant created by joining three traditional heritage buildings. It is especially renowned for its cakes—particularly its tiramisu, which more than lives up to the hype.

Our final evening in Penang is spent eating chicken satay and drinking Tiger beer at the nearby food court before making a dash back to the hotel in teeming monsoonal rain. As we will be departing early the following day, we organise a packed breakfast to be delivered to our room. Our train, which will take us back through Malaysia, departs from Butterworth Station at 7 am. To catch the ferry over the causeway would mean waking at 4:30 am and leaving by 5 am. The alternative is to book an Uber to drive us the long way around via the Penang Bridge, a 13.5-kilometre dual carriageway linking Penang Island to the mainland. Primarily because we enjoy trying new things, and partly because it lets us sleep an hour longer, we choose the bridge option.

With our breakfast packs perched on top of our suitcases, we arrive early at Butterworth Station and are surprised to find it packed with grey-haired, middle-aged, white pensioners. We had not thought this mode of travel popular enough to attract such a crowd, but we are slightly reassured when we realise it is just one large tour group, not a swarm of like-minded travellers.

Due to the train schedule, we are unable to repeat our stopover in Kuala Lumpur. Instead, we must make the journey in one stint, although, as our destination this time will be Johor Bahru, not Singapore, it will be a few hours shorter. Darryl ensures he has plenty of medication and routinely walks the carriages to ease his discomfort.

By the time we arrive in Johor Bahru, evening is falling. We hail a taxi, despite having read our hotel—the KSL Resort—is centrally located and within walking distance of the station. It is fortunate we did, because it turns out we were wrong. Fifteen minutes later, the taxi pulls up in what appears to be an outer suburb. Johor Bahru is Malaysia's second-largest city after Kuala Lumpur, with nearly two million residents. We had mistakenly equated it to a large town. It is not.

Stepping out of the cab, we are unsure what we are looking at.

'Is this a hotel or a shopping centre?' Darryl asks. 'And are those dinosaurs up on the roof—with water coming out of their mouths?'

Inside, the check-in queue is the largest we have seen at any hotel and while Darryl collapses into one of the nearby lounge chairs, I eventually secure a key card to one of the hotel's 900-plus rooms. We are on the 20th floor, and the lift ride—creaking, rattling and jerky—does little to inspire confidence. Worse, our bathroom floor is soaking wet. Bracing myself for another lift ride, I return to reception. This time, they assign us a room on the 24th floor. It seems I will be enduring 24 floors of this dubious lift for the next week.

That evening, sitting in the food court of the shopping mall attached to the hotel (explaining our earlier confusion), eating fried kway teow and pork lor bak, we exchange uncertain glances.

'What,' we ask each other, 'are we going to do here for the next eight days?'

CHAPTER 4

A Milestone Birthday

Extract from Darma Travels Blog-
   '...remember that whole week we spent in that city in Malaysia just waiting for the next boat to leave... couldn't swim cause the pool was full of little weeing kids... on top of a weird shopping mall... ate heaps... had a massage... had a haircut... stingy with the bathmats... kept flooding the bathroom...'

It does not take much exploration the following morning to realise that keeping ourselves occupied here will be quite a challenge. As in Penang, the area surrounding the hotel is not conducive to walking. The footpaths are virtually non-existent, and the traffic is both plentiful and toxic. From our 24th-floor window, there is little greenery to be seen—just a sea of residential and commercial buildings.

After showering, we quickly discover why the bathroom in our first room was so wet. Water streams out from the shower tray and pools across the floor. With no bath mats or hand towels supplied, we have nothing to mop it up with. This becomes a regular issue throughout the week, as does the non-appearance of replacement towels or mats—despite our repeated requests.

As breakfast is not included with our accommodation, one of the first tasks is to find a supermarket. Thankfully, there is a large Tesco in the basement of the multi-storey shopping centre attached to our hotel.

I love browsing foreign supermarkets. What's on offer can be so different from what one finds at home. Asian supermarkets are usually the most fascinating of all, overflowing with exotic and unidentifiable items. What catches our attention here, more than anything, is the sheer volume of rice and palm oil for sale. One entire aisle is dedicated to rice—huge 20-kilogram bags stacked five or six high. Nearby, another corridor is lined with bottles of palm oil. The amount of palm oil on display helps explain the mile upon mile of oil palms we saw planted along the railway tracks during our travels through Malaysia. It is clearly big business, which is disheartening. Our daughter Paige is a passionate advocate for orangutans and has often educated us on the devastating impact the palm oil industry has on their forest habitats.

We fill our basket with muesli, milk, yoghurt, fruit, nuts, noodle cups, Tiger beer and chocolate biscuits. We also pick up a set of plastic cutlery each, along with a plastic plate and bowl. If we are going to be self-catering breakfast, it makes sense to have something to eat it on—and with.

'If we buy the cutlery now, then we can also use it when we're travelling around Europe,' I suggest.

'As long as we can fit it into our bags,' Darryl replies.

'Look at the price of wine,' I say. 'I was thinking of getting a bottle, but not now. The cheapest is about 40 Australian dollars.'

'The wine's expensive, but the spirits aren't,' Darryl notes. 'They must want you drinking liquor instead.'

Following a breakfast prepared from our supermarket spoils, Darryl rests; yesterday's travel has taken its toll, while I head out to explore the nearby shopping mall. It is an older-style complex spread across four storeys. Shops are arranged in a square on each level, with elevators in the middle. Each floor is jam-packed with stores and people.

For the following week, with limited walking outside, this mall becomes my exercise arena. Each day I aim for 10,000 steps, a target I have set since gifting myself a Fitbit the previous Christmas. Circumnavigating each level twice and weaving through the crowds gets me to about 7,000 steps.

One floor is dedicated mainly to food outlets, and the combined smell of fish laksa and durian is overpowering—at times, nauseating. But if you can acclimatise to the ever-present odour, the Asian cake stalls and fruit stands make it worthwhile. The fruit in Asia really is the best you'll find anywhere in the world. Pre-peeled and sliced pawpaw, watermelon, pineapple, honeydew, and other exotic offerings fill the cold display units. Each day, I find myself buying copious amounts of pineapple and pawpaw.

'And I'll also have some slices of mango, please,' I say with increasing familiarity.

Another floor seems devoted almost entirely to hairdressing salons and nail bars. I have never seen so many hairdressers in one place—salon after salon. As it has been over six weeks since my last haircut, I seriously start scouting for one. Before the week is over, I vow to have my hair washed, cut, and blow-dried.

One of the upper levels houses a cinema complex. Interestingly, the screens display language options next to each film title. It makes sense. While the clientele here is mostly Asian, some foreigners would welcome the chance to watch a movie in their own language. Not that there seem to be many foreigners—we gradually realise that some days, we are the only white faces we see. This part of Johor Bahru appears to cater more to Chinese and Korean tourists than to Westerners.

BUCKET LISTS AND WALKING STICKS

The hotel's seventh floor features a large swimming pool complex, but it is filled with hundreds of small children. A dinosaur-themed water park is attached, which explains the prehistoric creatures we spotted on arrival and the many families in attendance. Seating is limited, and there is no grassy area. It is not very inviting, and we soon decide we will not be swimming during our stay here.

One wall of our hotel room is entirely glass, offering a sweeping 180-degree view across the city to the far horizon. That evening, we pull our chairs up to the window, sip green tea, and watch the sun go down. Dinner is two-minute noodles followed by chocolate biscuits for dessert.

The following days again begin to merge. We are only here, trying to live cheaply, while we wait for our P&O ship to arrive. Apart from Legoland, Johor Bahru does not have much to offer. It is a city where tertiary and service-based industries such as finance and commerce dominate the economy, and it serves as home to many Singaporeans who find it cheaper to live here while continuing to work across the border. All in all, it is not the most exciting place to be stuck for a week.

We cannot bring ourselves to visit the nearby Johor Zoo, wary of the conditions we might find. One day is spent escaping the heat by exploring the massive City Square Shopping Centre. Here we find most of the Westerners—and, unexpectedly, a replacement tip for Darryl's walking stick. His current one has deteriorated quickly with all the constant pounding on concrete footpaths.

'Look how cheap they are! With all the cobblestone streets coming up, why don't you buy a few packets?' I suggest, noting they cost about 70 cents each.

'I will, but I'm a bit sceptical about their quality.'

Another day sees us using my upcoming birthday as an excuse to indulge. I book us both into one of the nearby massage and spa parlours. I opt for the indulgence package: three hours of massage, body scrub, and steam room.

'Please come through. Please take off your clothes and put these on, then lie on the bed,' says our beautiful Malaysian masseuse, smiling as she hands us each a pair of paper underwear.

'What are these?' asks Darryl, inspecting the flimsy garment.

'Paper undies,' I reply.

'Paper undies?' he splutters. 'I'm not putting on paper undies.'

'You have to—or else go naked or wear your own.'

'I'll wear my own.'

'Then they'll get all wet and muddy from the scrub.'

Despite the underwear debate, the whole experience is fantastic. We are led into a large, dimly lit room where the air is heavy with incense. After choosing our massage oils, we lie on twin tables wearing our respective underwear choices. The ninety-minute massage is blissful, especially for Darryl's twisted spine, which clearly appreciates the attention.

We follow the massage with an hour's full-body scrub before entering a small, glass-enclosed steam chamber tucked into the corner of the room. Here, weeks of Asian grime, along with clumps of exfoliating scrub, pour from our skin in the heat.

'That was fantastic,' I say, glowing, as we sip lemon and ginger tea in the adjoining relaxation lounge.

'It was good—apart from the undies,' Darryl mutters.

After days spent inspecting every hair salon in the centre, I finally make my choice. As most women will agree, trusting your hair to a stranger is not a decision made lightly. Though slightly apprehensive, I commit—and step inside.

A young, very effeminate Asian male (most of the hairdressers here seem to be male) greets me. He continually checks his reflection in the mirror, running his fingers through his own styled locks. He seats me, drapes a cape around my shoulders, and—without warning—squirts copious amounts of shampoo directly onto my dry hair.

'Excuse me! You don't wet my hair first? And aren't you going to use a basin? It's dripping down my neck,' I protest, eyes wide.

'No,' he replies curtly.

Once the shock passes, I pull out my phone and take a picture—no one will believe this otherwise. As he begins to massage the shampoo into my scalp, the cold water continues to trickle down my back. He still seems more interested in admiring himself in the mirror than focusing on my head.

Eventually, I am led to a basin where the shampoo is rinsed out, then brought back to the chair. The haircut that follows feels amateur at best—a snip here, a snip there. None of the layering or texturing I usually get from Rachel, my trusted hairdresser back home.

'Excuse me,' I venture, 'I usually wear a side-part. You haven't given me any part at all.'

He barely responds. Still more focused on his own image than mine, he finishes up. I emerge 20 minutes later with hair that looks much the same as when I walked in. Thankfully, very little has been cut off—for which I am profoundly grateful. It is, without question, an experience I will not forget. And one I hope never to repeat.

Back in our room, I find Darryl deep in a FaceTime call with Paige. She has unexpectedly left the Whitsundays and is back in Brunswick Heads. She will be house-sitting while figuring out her next move.

'Can I Airbnb the house?' she asks.

'Absolutely no way,' we both say.

'But I thought it was a good idea,' she wheedles. 'I could live there and just Airbnb one room.'

'No way,' we say again—this time even firmer.

'Aww, okay. I won't advertise it then. If I can't do Airbnb, I might look into coming over to England and working in a pub like Pierce. I'll let you know.'

Day five, and we are well and truly over muesli for breakfast and noodles for dinner. With little else to occupy us, the laundry is completely up to date, and we have become intimately familiar with every shop in the adjoining mall. Even the view of the extensive horizon has begun to lose its appeal.

Our original plan was to stay the full week and return to Singapore early on 25 March, the day our ship is scheduled to sail. Since my birthday is 24 March, this plan had us celebrating my 50th birthday in Johor Bahru. By day five, realising that keeping to this schedule will make for a poor birthday, we decide to cut short our stay by one day. Travelling back to Singapore on the 24th means that I will memorably be spending my birthday not just in Malaysia, but also in Singapore—and somewhere in the limbo of no man's land between the two.

Friday, 24 March, dawns hot and humid. After completing my morning yoga and flooding the bathroom one last time, we book an Uber and make our way back to Johor Bahru train station and customs. With no time constraints, we opt once again for the more complicated but cheaper—and infinitely more fun—route back across the causeway into Singapore. This time, however, things are not so straightforward. It is a Malaysian public holiday, and the queues to enter Singapore are long. We pass the time chatting with a Malaysian father taking his two young, wide-eyed children to Disneyland Singapore.

What took two hours last time takes three today, but eventually we find ourselves back in Singapore—again without being asked to show Darryl's medical clearance. One taxi ride later and we are back at the Peninsula Excelsior Hotel. This time, though, we are return guests—and the difference is noticeable.

'Welcome back, sir, madam,' the concierge says as we alight from the taxi.

'Happy birthday, Mrs Emma. Please accept these chocolates and this card,' smiles the friendly receptionist at check-in. 'As returning guests, we're very pleased to offer you an upgraded room.'

BUCKET LISTS AND WALKING STICKS

So far, I feel it's been a pretty good start to my 50th birthday. It only gets better when we are shown to our room. Unlike the view of the fire station our previous stay here offered, this time we have the best outlook in Singapore. Our new room overlooks Marina Bay, with the spectacular Marina Bay Sands Hotel taking pride of place in the centre of the panorama. A long-cushioned seat runs along the floor-to-ceiling window, and we immediately claim it. It is, by far, the best hotel room view I have ever had—and I am blown away. It bodes well for the rest of the day.

With lunchtime creeping in and hunger setting in, we make our way to Raffles City Shopping Centre via the underground walkway and take our time choosing a restaurant. After weeks of eating rice and noodles, a French restaurant offering coq au vin proves irresistible—and soon we are tucking in. The meal is delicious, and with our bellies full, we contemplate how best to spend the rest of this special day. I am all for participating in a bit of retail therapy: it is a special occasion, after all. Darryl prefers to head back to our hotel, where he can rest a while.

I spend the remainder of the afternoon browsing the shops in Suntec and Raffles City Shopping Centres. My sister Michelle has given me some money as a present, as has my mum and Patma. I splurge and buy a MAC lipstick and a few T-shirts. On the way back to the hotel room, I spy a bottle of Veuve on sale, which more than completes my retail therapy.

Back in our room, the sun sets and Singapore's night lights begin to glitter across the harbour. The view is both spectacular and calming.

'What do you want to do for dinner?' Darryl asks eventually.

'I'd really prefer to order room service and just stay here,' I reply. 'We can drink the Veuve and watch the light show from the window. Besides, this way, we won't be dirtying any more clothes.'

And so, we spend the remainder of my unforgettable 50th birthday ensconced on our cushioned window seat, gazing out over Singapore.

We eat lamb cutlets and steamed vegetables, drink Veuve, and toast this wild, wonderful journey. At 7:45 pm and again at 8:45 pm, we turn our attention to Gardens by the Bay and watch the dazzling light show, a nightly marvel. It is going to be hard to top this birthday.

The following morning, we awaken full of anticipation. Today, we board our P&O cruise ship—the *Arcadia*—our home for the next five weeks. After a leisurely buffet breakfast, it's outside for a walk around the nearby park before farewelling our friendly hotel staff and hailing a taxi. At approximately 12:30 pm, we are back at the Singapore Cruise Terminal, but there's a different ship in front of us this time. Our bags are immediately taken from us, and check-in is straightforward, with Darryl propelled once more to the front of the queue.

We have booked another balcony cabin, this one on the port (left-hand) side of the ship on Deck 8—fittingly named *Australia Deck*. This time, my door key works immediately.

As on our previous cruise, we spend the remainder of this first afternoon exploring the ship—and getting lost. Although carrying roughly the same number of passengers as our last vessel, this one feels bigger. We have six dining venues to choose from, nine bars, a gym, a spa and beauty salon, a boutique cinema, a three-tier theatre and three swimming pools.

One difference is immediately clear: on our last cruise, the passenger mix was roughly one-third American, one-third Australian, and one-third other nationalities. Here, it seems to be 95% British, with the rest of the world squeezed into the remaining five per cent.

What appeals most, however, is the abundance of hiding spots. There are nooks and crannies everywhere, many with deep, comfortable chairs. There are window seats perfect for quiet reflection, small escape rooms for reading, and decks lined with loungers. Unlike the *Legend of the Seas*, on the *Arcadia* we will never struggle to find a poolside chair or a cosy corner—important when you are spending five weeks on board.

While wandering this first afternoon, and in one such quiet area, we come across a woman happily playing the piano. She tells us she often escapes to this room.

'I'm from England but I got on in Sydney a few weeks ago,' she says. 'A lot of Australians boarded then too, but most of them got off in Hong Kong. It was much quieter once they left.'

'Yes, Australians have been known to party,' we agree with a smile.

'Where are you going to?' she asks.

'We're on until the end—Southampton. We're really looking forward to Petra and the Suez Canal.'

'I suppose you know about adjusting your tipping?' she says suddenly.

'Sorry? Excuse me?' we reply.

'If you don't want to pay the full daily tipping charge that's added to your account, you can request at reception to have it adjusted,' she explains.

I had read about this somewhere but forgotten. As the daily charge adds up to quite a substantial amount over a five-week cruise, her reminder is timely. We do go on to adjust the fee, and we remain forever grateful to the lady who mentioned it. What is curious, though, is that we never saw her again. It was as if she had been placed in that room for the sole purpose of passing on that tip.

Late afternoon, we unpack our bags, making full use of the generous cupboard space. The layout of this cabin is different—slightly more spacious—and my morning yoga routine will be that much easier. One luxury of spending five weeks in the same room is that you can truly spread out.

I also notice that we have been well supplied with generous-sized toiletries. They are from The White Company, a well-known brand which I love. There is even a better choice of biscuits, although this time there is no supply of hard-boiled sweets.

We have once again chosen freedom dining, and that evening, with no tables for two available, we join a group of six in the Meridian Restaurant.

'We're all-rounders,' one couple tells us. 'We've been on since Southampton.'

'How many all-rounders are there?' I ask.

'About 500 of us.'

'Have you had much rough sea?' Darryl enquires.

'The roughest was just after leaving New York. A few days of very heavy seas—many of us stayed in bed.'

The evening's entertainment is a high-energy cabaret by the Headliners, P&O's dance troupe. We watch the show before returning to our cabin, where Robert, our steward, has dimmed the lights, turned down the bedcovers, and placed a small bar of chocolate on each pillow. Sinking into our extremely comfortable queen-size bed, it doesn't take long to fall asleep, lulled by the gentle rocking of the ship.

CHAPTER 5

Life Aboard a Boat to England

Extract from Darma Travels Blog-
Our clocks went back an hour this morning and will go back another hour tomorrow. This means that we are now four hours behind Australia. We know a cyclone is bearing down on Queensland but find it hard to get any actual facts about it.

The following morning, I work out that there is enough room for my yoga and find that the promenade deck, great for walking, is empty—a sharp contrast to the *Legend of the Seas*, where early-morning walkers were a regular sight. The passengers on this ship, it seems, are not the pre-breakfast exercise type.

After completing a few laps of the empty deck, I head back to our cabin, where I scan the day's entertainment programme, circling those activities that interest me. In the days to come, this becomes part of my morning routine. One highlight is discovering the daily presentations by guest speakers on a wide range of topics. Over the coming weeks, these speakers will include scientists, retired police officers and even former game show contestants. Another favourite is the port talks—informative sessions given by P&O guest services staff before each destination. These presentations cover everything from the port's history and local currency to transport options, possible excursions, and other practical tips.

Breakfast this first morning is taken in the glass-walled Belvedere Restaurant on the Lido Deck. From now on, this becomes our preferred breakfast spot instead of the more formal set dining in the Meridian. The buffet is excellent, the views are expansive, seating is plentiful, and the atmosphere is relaxed and informal.

Filling our trays, we share a table with a charming elderly British couple. She wears beautiful jewellery that catches the light as they tell us:

'This is our 13th around-the-world trip. There aren't many places left we haven't seen,' the gentleman says. 'But this will be our last.'

Why?' we ask.

'We're getting too old now. I'm 92 and my wife is 88. We may not be around for much longer.'

Ninety-two and eighty-eight!' I exclaim. 'You both look amazing.'

And they do. Sadly, we never see them again—a common occurrence on a ship of this size. It's a pity; I am sure they had many stories worth hearing.

Overnight, we have sailed north, hugging the Malaysian coastline through the Strait of Malacca. By the time we awaken, the *Arcadia* is already moored at Port Klang, the main cruise terminal for Kuala Lumpur. Having passed through Kuala Lumpur many times—and only a few weeks ago—we decide to take advantage of the ship being empty to do some more onboard exploring.

We are pleased to discover that this ship has washing machines and dryers available, although Darryl's dislike of dryers means we will probably avoid using them. The jewellery and shopping boutiques are closed while we are in port, but from what we can see, they look promising. We find a well-stocked library and help ourselves to the daily crossword and sudoku.

After a leisurely buffet lunch, the afternoon slips away as we lounge by the topside pool—reading, lazing and occasionally chatting with other passengers. That evening's entertainment in the Palladium, the *Arcadia*'s impressive three-tier theatre, is a lively comedy act that rounds off the day perfectly.

The following morning, with the *Arcadia* making her way further up the Malaysian coast, we find two letters slipped under our door.

The first is unexpected. It informs us that we will soon enter a High Piracy Zone (HPZ). Once inside the zone, passengers will be asked to keep curtains closed at night, avoid the decks from sunset to sunrise, and note that a Royal Navy officer will be coming aboard to support and advise the crew. It all sounds rather cloak-and-dagger, and we are both intrigued and eager to attend the upcoming mandatory piracy drill.

The second letter is an invitation from the ship's captain—Ashley Cook, or 'Captain Cook' (yes, really)—to attend a black-tie welcome-aboard drinks party that evening. Unfortunately, our lack of formal attire means we will have to miss out. A pity—we would have enjoyed the champagne and the chance to meet the captain.

This is our first full day at sea on this cruise, and it allows us the opportunity to attend our first guest lecture. The speaker is Gloria Barnett, a scientist and ocean expert, who spends the next 45 minutes captivating us with fascinating facts and stories about life beneath the waves. While it may be common knowledge to some, we both had no idea that about half of the Earth's oxygen is produced by the plankton in our oceans. Oceans that humans continue to treat as little more than dumping grounds! Following Gloria's excellent presentation, we just have time to make it to the theatre, where we proceed to spend the next hour listening to a talk on Phuket, Thailand, our next port of call.

Early in the afternoon, while Darryl rests, I go to investigate a 'Jewellery Making' session. I find two elegant instructors guiding a dozen or so chattering women in creating necklaces, bracelets, crystal suncatchers and other decorative pieces.

'Welcome,' one of them smiles. 'Today we're making necklaces using freshwater pearls. Just grab your supplies and take a seat.'

Jewellery-making classes will be offered several more times during this leg, and I'm already looking forward to each one.

That evening is a black-tie night—a detail that suddenly makes my afternoon pearls feel ironic. Without formal attire, Darryl and I are shut out of much of the ship's activity. We cannot attend the welcome drinks party, dine in the main Meridian Restaurant, visit the casino, enjoy the theatre or cinema, or even enter most of the bars. Our options narrow to the casual Belvedere or in-cabin dining via free room service. We choose the Belvedere and turn in early.

Before leaving Australia, we had often wondered how the time changes between Australia and England would be managed on board. The following morning, we find our answer: every few days, our entertainment guide instructs us to wind our clocks back an hour. This morning marks the first of seven such 'rewind' mornings to come.

Looking out from our cabin window, we see that the ship has moored in the Andaman Sea off the coast of Thailand. Ahead lies the long sandy sweep of Patong Beach—Phuket's most famous stretch of sand and our destination for the day. Phuket, located in Southern Thailand, is the country's largest island and boasts some of its most beautiful beaches. Once reliant on tin mining and rubber, its economy now thrives on tourism. Curious locals have jetted out to inspect the *Arcadia*, the constant buzz of their jet skis filling the air as they circle the ship again and again. Along Patong Beach, tourists parasail behind motorboats, dangling above the water like flies caught in a spider's web. After smothering ourselves in sunscreen, we make our way to the lower decks, where tenders stand ready to ferry passengers ashore. A quick 20-minute journey later and we take our first steps in over 22 years onto Patong Beach.

The last time we were here was 1994, when we had flown to Thailand to get married. Rather than a huge white wedding, which we both would have hated, we reasoned that for roughly the same price, we could spend a month travelling throughout Thailand and get married along the way. Telling only our workmates what we were doing, we locked up the house, placed a notice in the local paper saying we had eloped and would celebrate at the Brunswick Pub on our return, and caught a flight to Bangkok.

We had researched Thai marriages, and the Thai Consulate in Canberra had given us lengthy documents to complete and guidelines to follow. Only on our arrival in Thailand, armed with this paperwork, did we discover it was all completely useless. Attempts to tie the knot in Bangkok and then again in Phuket failed for the same reason. It was only after visiting the Australian Embassy back in Bangkok that we were given the correct information.

By the time we reached Chiang Mai in Northern Thailand, we were nearly ready to give up. Fortunately, we didn't—because after listening to a few words mumbled in Thai by a sleepy yet curious official at the local police station, we suddenly found ourselves married. The totally illegible documents he thrust into our hands—which we still have safely filed away—are apparently proof of this.

This time we have only one day here, rather than the full week of our last visit. That earlier trip left us with many great memories, and we are curious to see what has changed. We are also mindful that, in the intervening years, Phuket and Patong Beach were devastated by the horrendous 2004 tsunami, which claimed more than 5,000 lives here.

At the top of our list is a return to the Patong Merlin Hotel, where we stayed over 20 years ago, followed by a visit to the underground supermarket where we once bought Magnum ice creams or Singha beers. Each evening, we would sit on the beach and watch the sunset, ice cream or beer in hand—depending on our mood. While we feel fairly confident the hotel will still be there, we have doubts about the supermarket. Reports suggest it flooded during the tsunami, tragically drowning many.

To reach the Patong Merlin, we follow Patong's main beachside street, which is as chaotic as ever—bumper-to-bumper taxis, weaving scooters, and pedestrians darting between them. We pass fellow *Arcadia* passengers haggling with taxi drivers for private island tours. In the coming weeks, we will find this a common alternative to the organised excursions offered by P&O.

We stop briefly at the Patong Beach memorial, a poignant reminder of the lives lost in the tsunami, before continuing on to the hotel. Many changes have been made, but it is still recognisable, and the beachside bar remains. We sit for a while, sipping fresh juice, before exploring further. The supermarket is gone, replaced by a small mini-mart—a quiet confirmation of the loss we suspected.

We spend the next few hours idling through gift shops, chatting with locals, and wandering the streets in search of familiar landmarks. For some reason, Patong feels much smaller than we remember. It isn't, of course, but in our minds, it was somehow bigger, busier, grander. It remains very much a westerner's playground—particularly for backpackers. The beach is packed with them: some stretched out for beachside massages, others already working on their day's alcohol intake, and many simply lying in the sun, motionless.

That afternoon, in need of Wi-Fi to upload our Phuket blog, we find a beachside restaurant with shaded tables and an inviting breeze. Ignoring the lobsters staring at us with bulging eyes from the surrounding tanks, we tuck into plates of delicious pad thai.

It's with mixed feelings that we bid farewell to Patong Beach and head back to the *Arcadia*. The memories we carried here—of an island paradise where we eloped—are no longer reflected in what we see. It's less about Phuket having changed and more about us. The days of crowded beaches, long hours of sunbathing, and late nights of partying simply no longer appeal.

That evening, we leave the calm of the Andaman Sea and sail into the Bay of Bengal, north of the Indian Ocean. Our next destination is Colombo, Sri Lanka, a journey that will take two full days at sea. The first is spent attending a fascinating port talk on Colombo, followed by another engaging lecture from scientist Gloria Barnett. What makes the day most memorable, however, is sighting incredible numbers of dolphins swimming in front, alongside and behind our ship. If someone had told me we'd see that many dolphins, wake-surfing in every direction, I wouldn't have believed them.

The second day of our voyage, crossing the Bay of Bengal, and we awaken to some interesting news. First, and this is immediately apparent by the rate we are moving, is that something has gone wrong with our port-side engine. We are travelling considerably slower than previously, and if you peer over the ship's back—or stern—you can see that only the starboard side is producing a wake. Captain Cook, or 'Captaaain Cook' as he prefers to call himself, advises that engineers are busily working on the problem and, as we are still managing a steady speed, it will not affect our estimated arrival time at Colombo the following morning.

The second bit of news comes from a breakfast companion:

'The Royal Navy officer has now joined the ship,' she tells us. 'He's British, boarded in Phuket, and is here to advise the crew on what to expect—and what to do—when we cross the piracy zone.'

'We had no idea we'd be crossing a piracy zone,' we reply.

'Yes, interesting, isn't it?' she says. 'Have you seen the movie *Captain Phillips*? It's based on a true story—and that's the area we'll be travelling through. The film's showing in the cinema today, but you can also watch it in your cabin tomorrow.'

We are still digesting this when she adds, almost as an afterthought, 'Oh, and don't forget—the full emergency piracy drill is on this afternoon.'

That afternoon, during this drill, we meet our neighbours for the first time. Although we have occasionally heard them on the other side of our balcony partitions, we have never actually seen them. For passengers in balcony cabins, there is a risk that pirates could gain access through the balcony doors. In the event of a piracy situation, all balcony passengers must immediately vacate their cabins and, dressed warmly, wait in the corridors until the all-clear is given.

So, clutching our life jackets and wearing jumpers, we join others in the corridor, some perched on chairs dragged from cabins, others sitting cross-legged on the floor, for the next half hour. We compare cruising stories, share a few laughs, and, in true cruising fashion, never exchange names.

'Hope the pirates enter through your cabin rather than ours,' someone quips, and we all laugh, treating the whole exercise as one slightly absurd game.

In the early hours of Friday, 31 March, nearly a week after departing Singapore—and with the engine problem still unresolved—the *Arcadia* limps into Colombo, capital of Sri Lanka.

CHAPTER 6

The Indian Ocean

Extract from Darma Travels Blog-
Today I think that we have found the tuk-tuk capital of the world. We were warned before disembarking that the traffic would be crazy, and it was. Tuk-tuks, buses, cars, buffalo, bicycles, pedestrians, tractors and sometimes even elephants all jostle to navigate the narrow roads of Colombo.

As I do each time we arrive at a new port, I throw the curtains open on waking, step outside onto our balcony and gaze out over our new destination. What strikes me first about Colombo, Sri Lanka, is the sheer size of the dock—and then the convoy of coaches streaming in and lining up alongside our ship. There must be more than thirty of them, each one hurtling in at speed before slamming on the brakes to form a perfectly neat row. They are here to take the ship's passengers on their various booked shore excursions.

I sit watching all this activity for a little while, then start to laugh. The drivers, it seems, have parked in the wrong spot. Engines roar back to life, and the entire convoy surges forward another hundred metres before braking sharply again—this time in the correct place. Despite their bulk, the coaches are treated like racing cars, their drivers jockeying for pole position. From my vantage point high on deck eight, it is incredibly funny to watch.

This is not my first time in Colombo, though last time I got no further than the airport. Nearly 40 years ago, in transit from England to Australia, I spent six long hours there waiting for a connecting flight, my only distraction a large display of taxidermied animals. It is a memory that lasts to this day.

Sri Lanka, about the size of Tasmania, sits like a teardrop at the foot of India and is home to roughly 21 million people. Its history is chequered with Portugal, the Netherlands and Great Britain all ruling here at various times. More recently, in 2009, the country endured violent conflict in which around 70,000 people lost their lives in fighting between the Sinhalese majority and Tamil minority.

With a predominantly Buddhist population—about 70 per cent—world-renowned tea, and a celebrated cricket team, Sri Lanka has long been on our wish list.

For our stop in Colombo, we decided to join one of the ship's organised shore excursions. Our first choice was a journey into the countryside to visit one of Sri Lanka's (formerly Ceylon) famous tea plantations. Failing that, our second choice was Kandy, a UNESCO World Heritage city and home to many sacred Buddhist sites. Unfortunately, both were ruled out—not for lack of interest, but because of their distance and the mode of transport.

'Out of all the ports we visit,' our excursions officer warned, 'the coaches here in Colombo will be the worst. They are not up to the standard of other countries.'

She went on, 'If you have any injuries or back problems, you may want to reconsider.'

'How long is the coach trip, anyway?' we asked.

'About three and a half to four hours each way,' came her dampening reply.

With our inland options ruled out, we settle on a *Highlights of Colombo City* tour, promising a circuit of the capital's most notable sights. As we join the tide of passengers heading ashore, we cannot help but admire the choreography of the operation. Unloading and later reloading this many people—each destined for a different coach, taxi, or private tour—is no small feat, yet the crew manages it with practised precision.

Boarding our coach, we are warmly welcomed by Dudley, a fair-skinned, native-born Sri Lankan.

'Welcome. My name is Dudley, I am 80 years old, and I will be your tour guide for today. I was born in Sri Lanka but went to university in England, where I learned to speak English. I worked for many years as a geologist, but for the last ten years I have been a tour guide,' he tells us in his sing-song accent.

'Today we will be visiting, amongst other places, the Fort area of Colombo, Kelaniya Raja Maha Vihara, the National Museum, and the Independence Memorial Museum. We will also pass by Beira Lake and the beautiful Red Mosque.'

Finishing his recitation, Dudley surprises us by breaking into Shakespeare:

'And I am one who loved not wisely but too well.'

I adjust my air vent and settle back into my seat, already charmed by patriotic Dudley.

'This feels like it's going to be an interesting day,' mutters Darryl.

While Colombo Harbour, where our ship is moored, is large, spacious and relatively peaceful, leaving the safety of its patrolled gates is like stepping straight into a cauldron of humanity and noise. Within minutes, our coach is swallowed by streets heaving with tuk-tuks, buses, bicycles, cars, motorbikes and pedestrians. Navigating this chaos is undoubtedly a testament to the skill of our driver.

'Look, there's a buffalo!' I exclaim.

'And look, there's an elephant,' Darryl counters with a grin.

Our first stop is Kelaniya Raja Maha Vihara, a sacred historic temple said to have been visited by Buddha. Its interior walls are covered in breathtaking murals, each portraying a key event from his life. Beside the temple stands a stupa—a mound-like structure containing relics, usually the remains of Buddhist monks, and used as a place of meditation. Having once been closely involved in the construction of a stupa myself, I feel a particular pull towards it.

The calm of this beautiful, historic temple makes the city's chaos and noise feel a little less jarring. From here, we take in serene views over Beira Lake and admire the striking red-and-white Jami Ul-Alfar Mosque.

On the way to the Independence Memorial, we are fascinated by the sheer number of cricket fields we pass. In the middle of this crowded, bustling city, we count no fewer than five pitches.

'I knew Sri Lanka loved its cricket, but this is more than even I expected,' Darryl remarks.

'Imagine inner Sydney with five cricket fields right in the middle of it,' I reply.

The Independence Memorial itself is more of a leg-stretch stop than a sightseeing highlight, but it does come with its own entertainment. A tout with a huge python draped around his neck uses the snake to lure in tourists. The moment they get close, he tries to wrap it around them for a photo opportunity. The horrified expressions on their faces are priceless.

Guided all the while by the ever-quotable Dudley—'Some are born great, some achieve greatness, and some have greatness thrust upon them'—the day moves along quickly. We laugh when we discover that the promised 'refreshment' is a single bottle of water each, and 'lunch at a restaurant' translates to coffee and a bun, bought with our own money at the museum café.

The National Museum proves interesting, though our time is short. In truth, we spend more minutes admiring the sapphires (Sri Lanka is famous for them) and tea in the gift shop than studying the exhibits inside.

Throughout the tour, Dudley sprinkles in his own nuggets of information:

'Colombo has only two McDonald's—the first opened just a few years ago. There are no Starbucks.'

'How about public transport?' someone calls out.

'We still rely mostly on buses. That is why the traffic is so bad and the roads so congested.'

'And why are all the signs in English?' another passenger asks.

'Sri Lanka was ceded to the British in 1815 and only became independent in 1948. That is why there are many British buildings and English signs.'

Back at the port after what has been a lively and insightful day, I make one final observation.

'For a capital city, there don't seem to be many high-rise buildings.'

'No,' Dudley agrees. 'There are only about eight buildings above 30 floors—but that is changing quickly.'

Judging by the forest of cranes on the skyline and the many building sites we've passed, I am sure he is right.

While Darryl prefers to linger ashore a little longer, exploring the harbourfront, I head back on board for my first taste of what I later come to call *Laundry Wars*.

Deciding it is time to catch up on some washing, I gather our laundry and go in search of one of the three laundromats available to passengers. I find one on Deck Six, two levels below ours, and realise I will be competing with a good number of other cabins for just four machines.

On entering, my suspicions are confirmed. The small, steaming room is crammed with five other passengers—three queued in front of the washing machines, two in front of the dryers.

'This is the queue. You're fourth in line,' barks one elderly lady.

'Those three machines only take 40 minutes, but that one takes longer for some reason,' another queuer offers helpfully.

'You can't leave, or someone will take your spot. There's no holding places,' the first lady adds, even more firmly.

And so begins my first stint of standing in line, waiting for a machine to free up. I call it *Laundry Wars* because the atmosphere in these laundries can, at times, turn downright ugly. There is even a rumour circulating that a pair of passengers once came to blows over a machine and were promptly put off the cruise.

Later that evening, to the disappointment of myself and the rest of the jewellery-making group, I discover that our lovely instructors have disembarked in Colombo. Their classes have been replaced by lessons in Arabic.

'Who on earth would want to learn Arabic?' becomes the common refrain among the group.

Hoping that the entertainment crew will see sense and replace lessons in Arabic with something more appealing, I am nonetheless delighted with the five necklaces, three suncatchers and two bracelets I have managed to make.

That evening's sail-away party on the top deck brings better news. The ship's speed and the sight of two distinct wake lines suggest that the engine problems have been fixed—a fact soon confirmed by 'Captaaain Cook'. We are about to spend the next four days at sea, heading northwest across the Arabian Sea towards the United Arab Emirates. Doing so with a faulty engine would have been extremely disconcerting.

As mentioned earlier, we now have a Royal Navy officer on board, and it is with great interest that we attend his lecture the following morning. With a ship full of Brits—most well past retirement age—the talk is extremely well attended. Many have experienced war in one form or another, and most hold a deep pride in their Royal Navy.

Later that afternoon, he surpasses expectations by arranging for a British warship, currently patrolling the Indian Ocean, to rendezvous with us. With the Arcadia bedecked in Union Jacks and passengers belting out *Rule, Britannia!* at full volume, we wave enthusiastically to the crew aboard the warship. It is a stirring sight, and one we will not forget in a hurry.

On Tuesday, 4 April, with Oman to our port side, we enter the Gulf of Oman. We are now officially in the High Piracy Zone, and all precautions are put in place. At sunset, every exterior light is blacked out. No one is allowed on outside decks until sunrise. All topside entertainment is moved indoors.

With the weather glorious, we make our way further up the Gulf, arriving early Wednesday morning in Dubai—the most modern and progressive of the seven states that make up the United Arab Emirates.

Dubai, to me, has always been synonymous with oil, artificial islands, and the Burj Khalifa: the tallest building in the world. So, when I throw open the curtains that morning and see the Burj Khalifa framed perfectly in my cabin window, it is a genuine thrill. The fact that sighting it is one of our bucket list items makes it even more surreal. Stepping out onto the balcony, I'm met with a cloudless azure sky, criss-crossed with airplanes. The flat horizon stretches endlessly, and beneath that perfect sky lies a gleaming city of high-rise towers—a complete contrast to Colombo.

The Dubai we are about to explore today is barely 50 years old. For thousands of years, it was little more than a scattering of Bedouin settlements along a creek, sustained by fishing and pearl diving. Then, in 1966, oil was discovered, transforming the region beyond recognition. Just half a century ago, its people lived in tents, were desperately poor, and relied on animals for transport and farming. Today, the country is so wealthy that citizens pay no tax. They are eligible for free or subsidised housing, enjoy free healthcare, and receive free education up to secondary school. Generous grants help cover wedding expenses, while water and electricity are heavily subsidised.

Prior to our arrival, we had considered how best to see Dubai and, after speaking with fellow passengers, decided on the ubiquitous hop-on, hop-off buses found in most major cities. So, after a quick, light breakfast, we step ashore and board one of these double-decker buses conveniently stationed dockside.

Sitting on the upper deck with the wind blowing in our hair, earplugs in, we gaze in fascination as the bus makes its way from the harbour and into Dubai City. The landscape is utterly flat—no hills anywhere in sight. As expected, the buildings look relatively new, although many windows are coated in a fine layer of dust, likely the result of low rainfall and ever-present desert winds. The further we go into the heart of the city, the taller and more architecturally striking the buildings become, and the traffic grows steadily more chaotic.

Our first major stop is the Dubai Mall, the largest shopping centre in the world, located right next to the Burj Khalifa—at 828 metres, the tallest building on Earth. Since the bus will pass this stop several times, we decide to continue for now and return later.

As the tour continues, Dubai impresses us further. We glide along grand boulevards, pass stretches of gleaming waterfront, marvel at the Palm Islands—the world's largest man-made islands—and crane our necks for a glimpse of the Burj al-Arab Hotel, famed as the world's first seven-star hotel.

We finally disembark at the Bastakia Quarter, where time is spent browsing the Dubai Museum before exploring the historic Al Fahidi Fort.

Some of our fellow Arcadian passengers have shared colourful stories about Dubai's souks, and we are eager to see them for ourselves—especially the Gold and Spice Souks. Leaving Al Fahidi Fort, a short bus ride brings us to the Spice Souk, set along the Dubai Creek. Here, narrow aisles are lined with stalls overflowing with great sacks of saffron, cinnamon, cardamom, and other exotic spices. The air is rich with their mingled aromas, and it feels as though we have stepped straight into the pages of *Arabian Nights*.

Just across the creek lies the Gold Souk. While we could reach it by bus, the more appealing option is to take an *abra*—a traditional wooden boat. Boarding the crowded vessel, we squeeze onto a narrow bench, and with a roar of the engine and a plume of diesel fumes, we skim across the water.

On the far bank, we are greeted by more gold than we will likely ever see again in our lives. Streets are lined with shop after shop overflowing with it, their windows competing to showcase the most extravagant pieces—whether intricate jewellery or entire garments fashioned from gold. It is an incredible sight, and we spend our time snapping photos, watching locals haggle for bargains, and playfully pretending we are here to make a purchase.

With noon long gone, hunger sets in, and we begin searching for somewhere to eat—ideally with free Wi-Fi. Heading back towards our bus stop, we spot an interesting looking hotel with an on-site restaurant offering both traditional cuisine and the promised Wi-Fi.

'What do you recommend?' we ask our waiter. 'We're after something truly traditional.'

'If you'd like variety, I suggest one of the platters—they have a bit of everything,' he replies.

A short while later, a huge platter is placed before us.

'This is machboos—spiced lamb—this is chelo kebab, ghuzi or lamb skewers, rice, hummus, baba ghanoush, and bread,' he explains, pointing to only some of the dishes crowding the plate.

Happy with our choice, we tuck in. Afterwards, comfortably full, we sit back and catch up on the news from home.

Two updates stand out. The first is that Paige has booked a flight to England and will arrive shortly after we do. The second is that while we were floating somewhere in the Indian Ocean, my name was drawn in the members' raffle at the local RSL Club back in Mullumbimby. When your name comes up, you have four minutes to collect the day's cash prize. Apparently, if I had been four minutes away instead of 10,000 kilometres, I would have pocketed 2,500 Australian dollars.

Still, I argue I'd rather be here in Dubai than at the RSL in Mullumbimby. We pay our bill and step back onto the crowded streets. With the day slipping away and Darryl starting to feel fatigued, we decide to return to Dubai Mall.

Alighting from our bus in front of the mall, the first sight to greet us is the Dubai Fountain, shooting water 150 metres into the air. Earlier in the day, it would have been performing in time to music, but even now, with the Burj Khalifa towering beside it, it is captivating. The heat drives us indoors, and we are immediately drawn to a massive aquarium, three storeys high and teeming with sharks, fish, turtles—and scuba divers. Using this as our base (after all, this is the largest shopping mall in the world), we spend the next hour or so people-watching and window-shopping.

When it is time to return to the Arcadia, we board another hop-on bus, retracing our route through Dubai City before being set down in front of our ship. Tonight, we will sail further along the Gulf of Oman before entering the Persian Gulf. By early tomorrow morning, we will dock in Abu Dhabi, the largest and wealthiest of the seven emirates. Unlike Dubai, whose oil reserves are finite and which has turned to tourism and record-breaking attractions, Abu Dhabi still sits on vast, seemingly endless oil wealth.

We approach our visit to Abu Dhabi with mixed feelings. After the extravagance of Dubai, will this city feel like an anticlimax? Half an hour after boarding our organised coach excursion, any doubts vanish. Abu Dhabi, though more conservative, easily rivals its flashier neighbour.

From our coach windows, we watch the city unfold. In a desert nation with scant rainfall, the streets are thickly lined with flowerbeds. Golden-sand beaches are swept smooth, and a 13-kilometre promenade—the Corniche—hugs the city's northwest shore. If that is not enough of a display of wealth, the sight that truly makes our jaws drop is a drive along one of the main thoroughfares, where mile upon mile of palaces and opulent mansions sit behind security fences. Many belong to the ruling family or Abu Dhabi's elite—a remarkable showcase of affluence.

Our first stop is the Abu Dhabi Heritage Village, where we see just how much the city has transformed in half a century. Like Dubai, it was the discovery of oil in the late 1950s that catapulted it from poverty to extraordinary wealth. Inside the museum, we step into Bedouin tents made from goat or horsehair—the standard housing for most people just 50 years ago. We wander through recreated compounds, keeping a cautious distance from the smelly, cud-chewing camels. The Heritage Village sits on a spit of land, and when we look up from these life-size displays, the skyline of modern skyscrapers across the water provides a striking contrast.

Next, we visit Qasr Al Hosn, memorable for its lavish display of the ruling family's possessions—expensive cars, glittering trophies, and assorted treasures. A gallery illustrating Abu Dhabi's history in a visual timeline proves particularly informative. From here, our route takes us past the Emirates Palace, en route to the Sheikh Zayed Grand Mosque. The palace, one of the most opulent hotels in the world, cost more than four billion Australian dollars to build. We will likely never afford to stay there, but it is fascinating to glimpse where the mega-rich sleep.

Our final stop is the Sheikh Zayed Grand Mosque. Made of over 100,000 tonnes of pure white marble, adorned with semi-precious stones, and illuminated by chandeliers crafted from 24-karat gold and Swarovski crystals, it is a masterpiece not to be missed. Unfortunately, we must. While we can admire its 1,000 pillars and 80 domes from the outside, dress regulations prevent us from entering.

'To enter, women must be fully covered—no wrists or ankles visible—and white clothing is not permitted,' our guide explains.

As most of my wardrobe is white, I, along with several others, am left outside, trading stories of why we have been turned away.

The countries of the UAE are strictly Muslim, and as such, there are stringent rules on showing any signs of public affection. Kissing, hugging and holding hands in public are all forbidden. It is, therefore, not without some concern, that I mention it to an elderly couple from our tour group, happily walking along holding hands.

'Erm, did you know that you're not allowed to hold hands here?' I ask.

'Oh, my goodness. We had totally forgotten. We always hold hands,' is their sweet, albeit concerning reply.

Our third and final UAE stop is Khor Al Fakkan. Unlike Dubai and Abu Dhabi, the view from our cabin the next morning is one of bare hills, stripped of all vegetation. Low-rise, lime-washed houses sit at their base, fronting the sea. The scene is stark, almost bleak. Declining the organised tours, we opt instead for a free shuttle bus to explore the area, having no idea where it will take us.

Disembarking, the heat hits us immediately, intensifying the barren feel. We gratefully board the shuttle—until we realise the air conditioning is feeble at best.

'Any idea where we're going?' Darryl asks the gentleman, uncomfortably pressed against him in the heat.

'Not really. Maybe that town we can see from our cabin,' he guesses.

'That's what we thought,' Darryl nods.

We are all wrong. Rather than heading to the nearby cluster of white buildings and a central mosque, the bus turns toward the hills. For the next half-hour, we climb up and over them, emerging into a stark industrial landscape dominated by huge oil silos. Clearly, Khor Al Fakkan is a port whose main export is oil—judging by the endless ranks of storage tanks we pass. Eventually, we pull up outside a huge, white, windowless, box-like building, marooned in a sea of red dust with only a few scattered houses nearby.

Raising our eyebrows, we step inside—and burst out laughing. The cavernous space is a near-empty shopping mall, its walls plastered with posters of scantily clad lingerie models. In a nation as conservative as the UAE, the contrast is so jarring, so out of step with everything else we have seen in Khor Al Fakkan, that we can only chalk it up to the quirky contradictions of travel.

Leaving Khor Al Fakkan means six full sea days lie ahead before our next port of call, Aqaba, Jordan. Fortunately, we have 1,000 Australian dollars each in onboard credit. With six days at sea, we will have no shortage of opportunities to spend them.

CHAPTER 7

Petra and the Suez

Extract from Darma Travels Blog-
It takes two hours by bus to travel from Aqaba, our port city, to Petra. We pass through no towns, the entire journey occurring through rocky, barren terrain. Up mountains and through deserts such as the Wadi Rum Desert made famous by Lawrence of Arabia.

A day after leaving the UAE, the *Arcadia* re-enters the High Piracy Zone. As we push south towards Somalia, the risk rises—Somali pirates have long haunted these waters, hijacking ships for ransoms far more profitable than fishing. The ship's defences reflect the threat: night curfews, blackout lighting and armed guards now patrolling the decks around the clock. A water cannon stands ready on the promenade, alongside a long-range acoustic device capable of firing a pain-inducing sound beam. In one of his guest lectures, our Royal Navy officer mentions that we are now carrying extra guards and additional weapons.

It is, by any measure, serious—yet somehow, we find it more exciting than frightening. *Captain Phillips*, the Tom Hanks film about Somali pirates, happens to be showing again. We watch it from our cabin, fully aware we are sailing through the same waters.

The days pass quickly and easily. A new guest speaker, Margaret Gilmore—journalist and security and terrorism expert—delivers fascinating lectures on the aftermath of the 2005 London bombings and the poisoning of ex-KGB agent Alexander Litvinenko. Adding to the crime-and-security theme, former Detective Chief Inspector Terry Brown offers sessions on police interviewing. He helped write the British training manual and walks us through the PEACE method: Prepare and Plan, Engage and Explain, Account, Closure and Evaluate. We even try our hand at interrogating a 'suspect'—cruise ship style.

Hugging the Yemen coastline, we slip into the Gulf of Aden, pushing ahead at a brisk 20 knots—a good eight knots faster than the Chinese cargo ships we spot from our balcony, plodding along in protective convoys. On the third of our six sea days, we finally clear the High Piracy Zone. The armed guards and weaponry are quietly transferred to another vessel, and the mood on board shifts to one of relief.

With the tension gone, onboard activities and events are in full swing. At night, we wince through a Cilla Black impersonator but thoroughly enjoy the magician. The Headliners roll out fresh shows, and we watch them with genuine appreciation. Food is plentiful, and we have taken to afternoon tea in the main dining room—scones with clotted cream, finger sandwiches, tea cakes and gooey pastries, all accompanied by bottomless pots of tea. It is just as well I am keeping up my morning laps and yoga.

One evening, on our way to dinner, we share a lift with a couple who are clearly feeling the effects of a few drinks.

'We've probably had a bit too much,' they admit cheerfully. 'Been to the All-Rounder Party.'

'What's that?'

'A party for everyone doing the full world trip. Five hundred of us started from Southampton—there's 450 left.'

'What happened to the other 50?'

'Oh, some have died, some got ill, others had to leave for different reasons,' they say with unsettling chirpiness. 'Every cruise, at least a few die.'

As the lift doors close, I murmur to Darryl, 'Did they seem almost... gleeful about that?'

'A bit,' he agrees. 'But do you really believe them? That's a lot.'

The encounter stays with me for a while, but soon the days settle into a slow geography lesson. To port, Somalia, Eritrea and Egypt. To starboard, Yemen and Saudi Arabia. Leaving the Gulf of Aden, we slide into the Red Sea, passing Jeddah—gateway to Mecca, the destination of those Qibla arrows we saw in those Malaysian hotels.

In the early hours of Friday, 14 April, the Arcadia docks at Aqaba, Jordan, the main port for the ancient city of Petra and a good two-hour coach journey inland. Like most of the passengers, I have booked the ship's tour. It will be a 10-hour marathon, four of those spent on coaches. For this reason, plus the walking once we arrive, Darryl will not be coming.

'I'll hang around Aqaba and look for belly dancers,' he says, before adding, 'although after that passenger talent show last night, I'm not sure I want to see another one.'

Aqaba is Jordan's only coastal city. From our balcony, low-rise sandstone and limestone buildings sit pressed against steep red hills that stretch endlessly inland. Across the water to port, Egypt lies hazy in the distance.

Petra—the fabled Rose City—first entered my vocabulary thanks to my great-aunt Hilda. She was in her 80s at the time, yet her stories, especially her description of the 'Treasury' were so vivid that I could picture every detail. Until then, I had never heard of it. A little research later revealed an ancient city high in the desert hills of Jordan, lost to Western civilisation for hundreds of years and only rediscovered in 1812—and it went straight onto my bucket list.

Built by the Nabateans around 312 BC, their advanced building techniques, particularly their water conduit system, still survive today. Prosperity came from its strategic position on regional trade routes, and at its height, the city held over 20,000 people, living and trading in buildings carved almost entirely from stone. In the 7th century, destructive earthquakes and the growing power of the Roman Empire led to its abandonment. For more than a thousand years, it remained hidden, until 1812, when Swiss adventurer Johann Ludwig, disguised as a Bedouin and acting on local rumours, gained access to the city and opened it once again to the West.

It is Good Friday, a day I have a soft spot for, seeing as it was the day I was born, and I like the symmetry of visiting a place so meaningful to me today. Stepping off the *Arcadia*, we find 40 coaches lined up dockside. We have been warned of cooler weather, and I am grateful for it; at 12°C, it is a sharp contrast to the high 30s of the UAE.

The coach is warm and comfortable, and I manage to claim a double seat to myself. Departing the port, we quickly pass through Aqaba town centre and begin a two-hour journey I will never forget.

As we leave the city behind, I'm struck by the starkness of the landscape, and our guide begins to tell us more about the country we're travelling through.

'Jordan,' he begins, 'is a semi-arid, virtually landlocked nation. We are bordered by Syria to the north, Israel to the west, Iraq to the east, and Saudi Arabia to the south.'

He sweeps his arm towards the windows. 'This land has over 100,000 years of history, and more than 40,000 ancient archaeological sites. We call it the 'Land of the Rocks'—and as you can see, the name is well deserved.'

Travelling along a bitumen and, at times, concrete strip, we pass nothing but gravel plains and hills of stone. There are no towns, few cars, no grass or trees, and the only sign of water is a dry riverbed.

We pass through the Wadi Rum Desert, immortalised by *Lawrence of Arabia*, before climbing into the mountains. Here I see camels and sheep and later, Bedouins tending their flocks of goats beside their tents made from the hair of these goats. At the summit, we enter thick, nearly impenetrable fog, and we stop for a toilet and souvenir break.

Leaving the warmth of the coach, we find that outside, the temperature has dropped even further, and thus we scurry quickly towards and into the welcoming souvenir shop where small cups of thick coffee are thrust into our hands. We learn that here, temperatures can range from plus 50 degrees Celsius to minus five.

Fortified by the hot coffee and back in our warm coach, I continue to be mesmerised by the landscape. I could be travelling on the moon—mile after mile of rocky, barren earth. An hour later, buildings begin to appear, clinging to the slopes, signalling our arrival in Wadi Musa, the gateway town to Petra and the end of our bus journey.

It is a public holiday today—not our Christian Good Friday, but one of Jordan's own—and the queues are long, snaking under the PETRA sign and through airport-style security. Once through, I find myself standing at the entrance to the Siq: a mile-long chasm, at times only 90 feet wide but soaring to 130 feet high, winding its way into the heart of ancient Petra.

Making our way into this chasm, the pink, purple and cream sandstone walls that tower above us echo to the cries of touts, horses, donkeys, camels, carts and people. The carts and donkeys are there to ferry those who cannot or do not wish to walk: the cries are from people scrambling to avoid them. Our passage goes from dry, sandy and crumbly to wet, muddy and slippery the deeper we descend.

Advancing towards this long-held dream, I occasionally chat with others in my group, but mostly I walk in quiet anticipation. My shoes are wet and my hands are cold, yet all discomfort vanishes when, half an hour later, I catch my first glimpse—a sliver of ornate stone framed between the narrowing walls. The Treasury. Designed so that travellers would see it in this sudden, dramatic reveal, it takes my breath away.

Moments later, I round the final bend, and there it is in full—the rosy-hued facade carved from the sandstone cliff more than 2,000 years ago. Originally built as a mausoleum and crypt, its name comes from the legend that the carved urn crowning it once held great riches.

I stand for a moment, captivated by the history and beauty, yet fully aware of my surroundings. The square is alive with movement—donkeys, carts and camels pushing through the throng of hundreds of tourists. Underfoot, the ground shifts from dust and rock to a slick, unpleasant mix of mud, water, urine and dung. The smell, the press of bodies, and the constant jostling are impossible to ignore. It is my first real taste of what heavy tourism can do to a place—an experience I will meet again in Europe.

But still, the sight before me is utterly mesmerising. The skill, the time, and the sheer labour involved in carving this structure from solid rock must have been phenomenal. The Treasury, impressive as it is, is only one part of Petra—an ancient city that stretches across some ten square miles, of which archaeologists estimate only 15 per cent has been uncovered.

Eventually, tearing myself away from the Treasury, I continue to make my way further and deeper into the heart of Petra. I pass by the ruins of elevated tombs, streets, arched gates, temples, stairways, amphitheatres, cave houses and more. It really was, and still looks in part, like a city carved from rock.

'Bedouins still lived in these caves until 1985,' one of the guides tells me.

'They were forced to move into those buildings you saw back in Wadi Musa,' he adds, referring to the low-rise concrete blocks we passed earlier.

'That was the year Petra became a UNESCO World Heritage Site. In 2006, it was named one of the new Seven Wonders of the World.'

Three hours after passing through security, fully occupied and amazed the entire time, I have to concede defeat. I have not managed to see a tenth of what Petra holds. I would need a week to even try. As I retrace my steps up through the Siq and back towards the entrance, I do know that what I have seen has changed me forever.

Our tour also includes lunch at the nearby Movenpick Hotel, and here we feast on an absolute smorgasbord of Jordanian dishes. Lamb features heavily, alongside fragrant curries, rice and fresh bread.

Back on the coach, our guide uses the drive to tell us more about Jordan.

'Tourism is vital to our economy,' he begins, 'though our main export is actually phosphate. In recent years, we've also welcomed a large number of refugees from Syria—a humanitarian effort we are proud of, but one that has placed extra strain on our already limited resources.'

'One of our biggest challenges is water,' he adds.

No surprise there.

'To help address it, we are building more dams across the country.'

On reboarding the Arcadia at the end of a long and exhausting day, I find that Darryl has managed to keep himself occupied. He has browsed the nearby city of Aqaba.

'Although there's really not much to see and do.'

And has spent some interesting time hanging out on one of the nearby popular tourist beaches.

'I didn't see a belly dancer, though,' he adds. 'Which is, perhaps, fortunate.'

Our ship will not depart Aqaba until late evening, and so dinner is eaten in the casual Belvedere (it is black-tie night) while watching the lights of one country (Egypt) compete with the lights of another (Jordan).

BUCKET LISTS AND WALKING STICKS

At breakfast the following morning, the talk is all about our upcoming route. Overnight, we have retraced our way down through the Gulf of Aqaba and are now gliding slowly through the Gulf of Suez. Tonight, we will anchor alongside other ships, ready to take on the Suez Canal in the early hours.

'Yes, this will be our third time through the Suez,' one couple tells us. 'It's a bit different to the Panama Canal—shorter, and no locks.'

'What did you think of Petra?' I ask.

'Unforgettable. One of the best places we've ever visited.'

Early evening, our ship reaches the entrance to the Suez and drops anchor. Upwind, a factory sends a stream of acrid black smoke into the sky. Before long, it's in the air conditioning, and our cabin smells faintly toxic. Outside, though, the sea is calm, and dolphins arc and dive around us.

At dinner, we share a table with an elderly woman travelling alone.

'My husband died a few years ago,' she tells us. 'We used to cruise together, but now I go on my own.'

'Did you visit Petra yesterday?' Darryl asks.

'Oh no, I never leave the ship. My eyesight's very bad, and I'm scared I might fall.'

'You never leave the ship?' we echo in disbelief.

'Oh no. My daughter thinks it's better this way, and I agree. I'd hate to have a fall.'

While it is surprising that someone would take a world cruise and not actually leave the ship, her poor eyesight assertions are proven shortly afterwards.

'Look, there's a British warship,' Darryl says, pointing to one of the other ships anchored nearby.

'What is it?' she asks, squinting hard out the window.

'A whale?'

Nearly 150 years ago, the Suez Canal was created to link the Red Sea with the Mediterranean, saving ships the long voyage around the southern tip of Africa. It took 25,000 men ten years to complete and cost more than 100 million American dollars. Narrow and largely single-lane, it remains one of the world's most important shipping routes. At just over 200 metres wide, 25 metres deep and 193 kilometres long, the Suez Canal takes about ten hours to traverse. With an average of 76 ships passing through daily, traffic is organised into strict northbound and southbound convoys. Our northbound slot begins at 6 am this Easter Sunday, which means that, like many on board, we are up before dawn—jackets on, coffee in hand, ready for this long-anticipated passage.

In the darkness, the Arcadia eases into position behind a British warship—the one we spotted yesterday. Ahead of it, apparently, is an American warship. With two warships leading the way, our passage should be relatively uneventful.

From the top decks, passengers gather to watch in the cool morning air. With the sun just peeking over the horizon, we slip into the mouth of the canal. By breakfast, the light is full, and from our table we can see, on either side and seemingly within touching distance, armed guards posted every 400 metres, standing to attention in a landscape of empty sandy desert.

The conversation over coffee is as revealing as the view.

'It will cost P&O nearly £250,000 for the Arcadia to use the Suez today,' someone remarks.

'With about 75 ships using it each day, imagine the revenue,' another adds.

'Who gets it?' we ask.

'The Egyptian government.'

By late morning, the centre of the canal is reached. Here, a bypass has been created, allowing northbound and southbound convoys to pass. Unable to see the water level of the bypass, it appears as if the ships using this route are motoring through the sand.

As the hours start to slip by, so the scenery changes. To port, on the Egyptian mainland, patches of industry appear. The desert gives

BUCKET LISTS AND WALKING STICKS

way to cultivated fields, rows of crops, electricity pylons, and a train clattering along a track. To starboard, the Sinai Peninsula remains empty—just an expanse of pale sand stretching into the distance.

By lunchtime, we head inside after a morning spent roaming the decks for the best vantage points. From our window table, a car with a film crew keeps pace alongside the canal, barely 20 metres away, cameras fixed on the Arcadia. At one point, a train slides between them and us, and for a brief moment it feels like we are in a slow-motion race.

The hours that follow are quieter. The scenery changes little, and the earlier excitement fades into an easy rhythm—until, at 3:30 pm, the shipwide speakers crackle to life. It is Captaaain Cook announcing a medical emergency: the Arcadia will be making an unscheduled stop at Port Said, the canal's northernmost port. As we slow and peel away from our convoy, the two warships continue on without us.

We are lucky—as has happened at several ports—that our cabin faces the mainland. From our balcony, we have a front-row view of life in this bustling Egyptian city. Eye level, apartment blocks stand in various states of disrepair, their balconies crowded with satellite dishes, air conditioning units and drying laundry. At street level, helmetless motorbike riders weave through horse-drawn carriages, touts call out to passers-by, and cars ignore any semblance of traffic rules.

We watch as an ambulance pulls up beside the ship. Nearly an hour later, a stretcher makes its way down the gangway and into the ambulance, accompanied by an elderly woman and a pile of suitcases.

'A gentleman has had a stroke,' we learn later over dinner.

'It's fortunate we could stop so quickly at a port,' someone observes.

The general feeling, however, is one of unease. This is Egypt, after all—a place where nothing moves without forms, stamps and, often, a little haggling.

'Why are we still here?' a fellow passenger asks.

'Egyptian bureaucracy,' comes the dry reply. 'We won't move until the paperwork is done—and a price agreed.'

As darkness falls, we eventually pull away from Port Said and enter the Mediterranean Sea. Our 12-hour transit through the Suez is complete, and thus, another of our bucket list items has been ticked.

CHAPTER 8

It's All Just Greek to Me

Extract from Darma Travels Blog-
Although Crete does have its archaeological marvels—most notably the Minoan City of Knossos, whose discovery proved that Minoans were the earliest civilisation in Europe, existing around 1900 BC—what we were more in the mood for was some mixing with the locals: maybe a local taverna!

Having had the most incredible experience travelling the length of the Suez Canal, our adrenaline levels remain high, and with good reason—our next two ports of call will be in the Greek Islands. When we first booked this cruise, the stop after the Suez was to be Istanbul in Turkey, a country I have always wanted to visit. Sadly, in the months leading up to our departure, Turkey has faced both political turmoil and an escalation in extremist activities, and P&O had no choice but to cancel that leg in the interest of passenger safety. As a compromise, and to avoid widespread disappointment, our itinerary now takes us to Heraklion on the Greek island of Crete, followed by Piraeus, the port city of Athens.

We awaken in Heraklion to find the Arcadia already docked, and from our balcony we see a low-rise city sprawling across scrubby hills that, further inland, give way to large white-capped mountains.

'Is that snow on those mountains?' I ask. 'This is Greece—it can't be snow.'

'It does look like snow, but maybe it's sand,' Darryl replies.

We set aside our curiosity until breakfast, where our table companions settle the matter.

'Yes, it's snow. Crete sees it in the higher mountains each year, but every ten years or so it also falls in the lower ranges. That's what you're seeing today.'

According to the Heraklion port lecture, the best and cheapest way to see the city is by hop-on hop-off bus. At 15 euros each, it is apparently one of the cheapest such services anywhere. Hearing the word 'euro', we are grateful that before leaving Australia we had bought some notes 'just in case'. It means we can step straight off the ship, purchase our tickets, and board the bus—conveniently parked harbourside.

Heraklion, with a population of around 140,000, is the capital and largest city of Crete, as well as the fourth largest city in Greece. What Heraklion is most noted for, however, is the ancient, ruined city of Knossos, a place we are keen to visit. Dating back to 2600 BC, Knossos has the reputation of being the oldest city in Europe, but what makes it especially interesting are the legends that have evolved over the centuries featuring the Minotaur—a mythical, half-man, half-bull creature created when an ancient queen lay with a bull, and kept in a labyrinth here. As with most legends, there is death and sacrifice and a love story, this one with a successful outcome.

Apart from Knossos, Heraklion is also noteworthy for its 'Old Town', the oldest part of the city, located on the harbour and protected by massive defensive walls. We alight here and spend some hours just wandering the pedestrian-only streets, happily browsing interesting little boutiques. What captures our attention are shops full of huge rounds of cheese and tavernas full of ouzo-drinking locals.

'How about we explore more, then have a late lunch in one of these tavernas?' I suggest.

'Sounds like a plan,' Darryl enthusiastically replies.

Back on the hop-on bus, we exit the city and start weaving our way along the coastline, eschewing alighting at one of the numerous beaches—more than content just to watch the passing scenery. We note many more tavernas, all doing a great trade, and beaches that, while pleasant, are not nearly as good as ours back home.

At some stage, our bus pauses beside a large leafy square with numerous busy cafes and a gushing fountain. It is clearly a popular stop, as most of the passengers alight, and accordingly, we do likewise. Although we are unsure what has attracted them, what does attract us is the most tempting cake shop. Its window display is full of custard fruit tarts, chocolate eclairs, Danishes, strudels, and other pastries, and we just stand and gaze.

'Look how cheap everything is!' I eventually exclaim. 'And what a selection. We definitely have to buy something.'

With everything so inexpensive, it is hard to contain ourselves and we leave clutching large paper bags filled with bakery goods, all purchased for less than four Australian dollars. A marble-paved street cluttered with market stalls is nearby, and here we find a bench to enjoy our purchases before slowly browsing the unique little stalls.

It is sometime later that we reboard a bus and only realise when we find ourselves back in the Old Town that it is the wrong one.

'Either we get off and look for a bus heading towards Knossos, or we find a taverna, eat now and do Knossos later,' Darryl suggests.

'There are some really good-looking tavernas here,' I reply. 'How about we eat now and explore Knossos later?'

The taverna, when we enter, is exactly as we had imagined a little Greek restaurant to be—catchy Greek music strumming in the background, friendly waiters laying on the charm, and a menu in picture form, filled with our favourites: dolmades, Greek salads, feta dishes, baba ghanoush, souvlaki, and more.

'Can we have this, this, and this?' I say, pointing at the dolmades, cheese balls, crispy zucchini and baba ghanoush.

'That's way too much,' argues Darryl.

'You never get as much as what the pictures show,' I counter.

I am wrong. Before long, our table is groaning under the weight of the food placed before us.

'See,' says Darryl. 'We are never going to finish all this.'

With delicious food to enjoy, great music to listen to, and an incredible view of the harbour from our window table, we relax and let Greece weave her magic. After a while, our thoughts are interrupted by a couple of ladies seated nearby.

'We can't believe this! We must share with someone. Britain's going to the polls. We're going to have an early election!' one exclaims.

'We're not due for an election until next year at least! Why has Theresa May called one now?'

We have little to add to this conversation, so we just nod and murmur in agreement. They leave shortly after, still voicing their surprise.

Our musings are interrupted again—this time by our lovely, ever-smiling waiter. After clearing our numerous, half-finished plates, he places between us a huge dish of little sugary doughnuts piled high on a mound of ice cream.

'But we didn't order this!' we protest.

'All good. It is for you,' he replies, setting down a carafe of clear alcohol and two small shot glasses.

'Raki,' he says, nodding towards the carafe.

Assuming it's a generous thank-you for our enthusiastic ordering, we tuck into the doughnuts and take cautious sips of the Raki. It certainly catches the back of the throat, but it is not unpleasant. Time slips by easily as we finish the carafe, enjoy the sweet, and let our meal settle. So easily, in fact, that we realise we have left it too late to get to Knossos. We are due back on board the Arcadia, and Knossos will have to wait for another trip.

While disappointing, it hardly matters. The day has been fantastic—it did not go to plan; we must weigh a good few kilos heavier, but it is a day we will not forget.

It does not take long to reach Piraeus, Greece's busiest port and the gateway to Athens. A short cruise northward across the Mediterranean, and early on the morning of Wednesday, 19 April, we arrive at the second of our Greek stops. Pulling the curtains aside, as is my habit on waking, I get one huge surprise—we are docked so close to residential apartment blocks that I am virtually eyeballing the people inside. It is crazy, and it is incredible. On one side of the street: fully occupied apartments with washing flapping from balconies. On the other: us—a huge cruise ship.

Piraeus is only five kilometres from Athens. Once two distinct places, today they have merged into one sprawling city. It is incredibly exciting to be here. Athens, for which no introduction is needed, has been a dream destination all my life. To have the unexpected chance to visit is thrilling—and it means another bucket list item ticked.

Today, we have opted for separate tours. I will walk the stony, steep pathway up the Acropolis—the 'highest point of the city'—and stand in front of the Parthenon. I will also visit the site of the first-ever modern Olympic Stadium. Due to the walking involved, Darryl will not be accompanying me. Instead, he will view these along with other city highlights, from the comfort of a coach.

It turns out to be a wise decision. Darryl wakes feeling unwell, as he has on and off for the past few days. He has been on antidepressant medication for some time, but with our change in lifestyle, he recently decided this was the perfect opportunity to stop.

'Travelling and keeping busy like this seems the ideal time to wean myself off them,' he told me not long ago.

'Although I had no idea how hard it would be—or how sick I would feel. I would never have started them if I'd known how difficult it would be to get off.'

'What sort of symptoms?' I ask.

'Nausea and dizziness,' he says. 'The nausea I can cope with, but the dizziness is the worst.'

My tour has an early morning departure, so it is still relatively early when I find myself standing at the foot of the path that leads up onto the Acropolis. To get here, our coach has wound its way through the streets of Athens, giving me my first real glimpse of a city I had, until now, only seen on the news.

In the months before we left home, international channels had been full of reports on debt-ridden Greece—how severely it had been impacted by the global financial crisis, the intense debate over whether it should leave the European Union, and the unpopular austerity measures imposed to curb its mounting debt.

Sitting on the bus, I hear these headlines come alive through our tour guide's stories. Out of a population of 11 million, around two million are unemployed. More than 160,000 shops have closed in the past six years. There is a €200 weekly limit on cash withdrawals. Crime is rising. The police force is underfunded and overstretched.

Yet, what strikes me even more than these grim statistics is something I can see with my own eyes—the graffiti. It is everywhere. Some of it is old, untouched for years, because there is no money to remove it. Even beautiful, ancient buildings and monuments have not escaped this blight.

What makes this all so sad is that I am about to embark on a climb that will deposit me where, basically, 'life as we know it', originated. Around 2,500 years ago, in one miraculous century, the people of Greece created the foundations upon which our civilisation has since rested. Philosophy, politics, mathematics, the natural sciences, art were all invented or defined here. It is very hard to reconcile the Athens I have just driven through with the Athens I learned about in high school history.

My tour group numbers about 40, and when our coach pulls in, the parking area is already packed tight with other buses. This means the path up to the Acropolis is busy—jam-packed, actually. To make herself heard, our guide hands each of us a small receiver with an earpiece. It feels odd to be moving in near silence, her tinny voice murmuring in my ear as we shuffle up the rocky incline past ancient amphitheatres and onwards to the summit.

From here, the view over Athens is breathtaking—a sea of low-rise, lime-washed stone buildings, their rooftops punctuated by temples and monuments, with the Acropolis rising like a great white monolith in the centre. But it is the Parthenon that truly holds my gaze. Built around 447 BC to honour the Goddess Athena, its sheer size and elegance still inspire awe. Even the scaffolding and restoration work cannot diminish the beauty of this white marble temple. It is phenomenal to stand so close to where the ancients worked, played, and worshipped—to walk on the very stones worn smooth by their sandals. Perhaps it is because I come from so young a nation as Australia that this feels so extraordinary.

I spend two hours wandering, taking it all in, pausing often to gaze out across Athens, before making my way back to the coach.

'Before we visit the Olympic Stadium, we will stop at a little gift shop,' our guide announces once everyone is back on board.

'That's not in the itinerary,' someone behind me murmurs.
'It's probably her brother's or cousin's shop,' comes another whispered reply.

And on being deposited at a little gift shop, it appears that this statement could be true. Staffed by what appears to be grandma and various family members, all dressed in black, the shop is great fun. I leave ten euros lighter with a small owl necklace.

'Athena's owl, for wisdom,' grandma croons, pressing it into my hand.

Our next stop is the Panathenaic Stadium. I have always loved athletics, and the Olympics have been a much-anticipated event every four years, so I am keen to see it. Built entirely of marble in 144 AD, its greatest claim to fame is as the venue for the first modern Olympic Games in 1896. Standing here, I find it remarkable that such a pristine symbol of ancient and modern sporting history still sits in the middle of a city grappling with so many challenges.

With our heads full of images of beautiful ancient sites, the coach winds its way back to Piraeus. As we pass what looks like an entire alley piled high with clothes, shoes and household goods, our guide gestures towards it.

'Those are for the refugees,' she explains.

'Are there many?' someone asks.

She nods.

'Yes—many have come into Greece in recent years. A lot from Syria, but most from Africa.'

Back on board the Arcadia, I find that Darryl has already left for his own tour. Being almost entirely by coach, his excursion takes him further afield than mine, so it is interesting when comparing notes later that evening, that his experiences and views on Athens match mine. The sights in Athens are immeasurable, unforgettable, and stunning—yet it is impossible to ignore the sadness that comes with knowing the country and its people are enduring such financial hardship.

CHAPTER 9

Across the Mediterranean

Extract from Darma Travels Blog-
We had stepped into a limestone land of arresting, centuries-old shops, monuments and attractions accommodating a modern, English-speaking society.

Up early to walk my customary laps around the promenade, the chill in the air reminds me just how far north we have travelled. Only two weeks ago, our average daily temperature sat in the mid to high 30s; now, here in the Mediterranean, it has dropped to a brisk 15 to 20 degrees. On one side of Arcadia, the deep blue Mediterranean is dotted with sailing craft of every kind; on the other, a vision of limestone. We have docked at Valletta, the capital of Malta—a tiny nation in the heart of the Mediterranean.

Minuscule Malta, with a population of just 360,000, has a long and chequered history. Home to ancient archaeological remains such as the Megalithic Temples of Malta, reputedly the oldest freestanding structures on Earth, and boasting three UNESCO World Heritage sites, she may be small, but she packs a punch. With her deep, sheltered harbours and strategic Mediterranean location, it is little wonder she has been taken by Phoenicians, Greeks, Romans, Arabs, French, British and almost by the Turks.

From the promenade, all I can see for kilometres along the coast are towering fortified limestone walls and buildings. They rise so high from the water that I find myself wondering how we will reach the top, where the main city of Valletta appears to lie.

'The walls are 80 metres high,' we are told at breakfast.

'Most of us take the lift but you could climb the stairs. Or alternatively you could simply walk up, following one of the cobbled roads.'

Prior to our arrival, all I really associated with Malta was the Maltese Cross—that symbol so familiar on our ambulances, used for emergency medical services worldwide, that originated here. Now, seeing Valletta for the first time from our ship, I am fascinated.

After a quick game of Laundry Wars, we disembark and step out onto Valletta Harbour. We find ourselves at the base of the huge limestone wall, surrounded by countless little limestone buildings masquerading as cafés, bars, and gift shops. Deciding to save the lingering for our return, we head for the nearby lift and, before long, are 80 metres above sea level, gazing out over what appears to be limestone heaven. From our viewpoint, all we can see is limestone: limestone churches, monuments, buildings, shops, a palace, and of course, that amazing, never-ending limestone wall. It all looks exactly like one finds on the box of a jigsaw puzzle and is our first real indication that we have arrived in Europe.

Further indications come soon after, when we leave the harbour's edge and wander along cobbled streets into the heart of Valletta.

'There's an English pub… and another,' Darryl points out.

'And there's an English red phone box,' I counter.

With Britain's presence still strong here until as recently as 1979 (and Malta only becoming a republic in 1974), reminders are everywhere.

'Everyone speaks English. And this is the first place that offers free Wi-Fi everywhere,' I note.

With beautiful buildings to view or visit and photo opportunities everywhere, it's easy to spend the following hours walking and absorbing it all. The city is compact, its pedestrian malls plentiful, and around every corner there's another photo opportunity. At the end of almost every street, 'that wall' frames a view out over the glittering Mediterranean. At noon, we pause to watch the daily Saluting Battery tradition, a ritual dating back to 1565 when Malta, against all odds, repelled an Ottoman invasion. The boom of the guns echoes off the limestone, and for a moment it's easy to imagine the siege unfolding.

Outside the Casa Rocca Piccola, Valletta's 16th-century palace, men dressed in bright red military uniforms perform an intricate rifle drill. We had planned to see the famous frescoes of the St Francis of Assisi Church, but the snaking queue, already 40 minutes for those halfway along, changes our minds.

While an attractive little British pub has a certain appeal, it is the cafe boasting 'slightly thick or very, very thick hot chocolate' that wins our favour. The day is still cool enough to justify the indulgence, and we take our time over mugs of the very, very thick kind—rich, warming, and just right for a European spring day.

Back at the harbour, we spend a while simply watching the comings and goings, ferries, fishing boats and cruise tenders sliding in and out, before wandering into the cluster of little souvenir shops. Malta is famous for its hand-blown glass, and the pieces on display are stunning: swirling blues, fiery reds and intricate patterns captured in bowls, vases, and ornaments. We watch as fellow Arcadia passengers hand over their credit cards, emerging with carefully wrapped treasures.

Tempting as it is, the thought of lugging a fragile glass bowl through the rest of Europe, and then all the way home to Australia, is enough to keep my wallet firmly shut. Over

dinner that evening, I turn to Darryl.

'I think I could come back to Malta,' I say.

'It's certainly incredible,' he agrees.

'It's unlike anywhere I've ever seen. Next time, I'd love to visit Gozo and Comino too.'

Darryl laughs. 'Let's get Europe over with first.'

With our departure from Malta, the reality of just how close we are to England begins to set in. Only one port remains before our final destination—Lisbon, capital of Portugal—and we will be there in two days.

With our onboard credit still looking healthy, we decide to make the most of it. I book myself into the ship's beauty salon and emerge later, body scrubbed and massaged, nails neatly manicured. We swap the main dining room for one of Arcadia's speciality restaurants, indulging in a beautifully crafted Indian tasting menu that leaves us happily full and slightly smug about our good use of credit.

The ship's current guest speaker is Shaun Wallace—barrister, TV personality, Chelsea football devotee and one of the formidable Chasers from the hit quiz show *The Chase*. His talks are highly entertaining: part biography, part behind-the-scenes gossip. He tells stories from his childhood, his passion for Chelsea, how he won *Britain's Mastermind*, and the unexpected path that led him to become a Chaser.

'I was an average student,' he tells us with a grin, 'but I worked hard.'

On the eve of our arrival in Lisbon, Arcadia glides past the dramatic limestone bulk of the Rock of Gibraltar, a British Overseas Territory standing guard at the entrance to the Mediterranean. With so many patriotic Brits on board, the upper decks are busy with passengers keen to catch sight of this famously strategic, and often contested, outpost.

BUCKET LISTS AND WALKING STICKS

On Monday, 24 April, I am bundled into my thickest jumper with a jacket over the top, ready for the morning chill as we sail up the Tagus River. From the deck, Lisbon's skyline unfolds in striking fashion. First comes the 25th of April Bridge—its bold red span so reminiscent of San Francisco's Golden Gate that the likeness is uncanny. Officially, the longest suspension bridge in Europe, it feels as though Arcadia slides beneath it with barely centimetres to spare.

Not long after, another unexpected spectacle appears: the Cristo Rei (Christ the King) statue. Perched on an 82-metre plinth, the 30-metre figure stands with arms outstretched, echoing Rio de Janeiro's famous Christ the Redeemer. Towering above the river, it's a commanding and impressive welcome to Portugal's capital—and a sight I had not anticipated.

Our son Pierce was here only a few months earlier and raved about Lisbon, insisting we try the city's famous Portuguese egg tarts. With his glowing review in mind, we are keen to explore, but knowing the size of the city—home to around 1.5 million people—we decide to spend part of the day on an organised tour. This will take us out of Lisbon along the Portuguese coastline before leaving us for a few hours in Cascais, a seaside town renowned for its surfing.

Finding ourselves by far the youngest on our tour, time passes quickly and enjoyably as we navigate the at-times busy roads, pass scrubby vegetation, traverse sleepy little seaside towns, and eventually arrive in Cascais.

'Please be back here in three hours,' our guide instructs. 'Anyone not here by then will need to make their own way back to the ship.'

Considering it has taken nearly an hour to get here, the warning feels a little ominous.

'But first, follow me. I will show you where the main part of the town is,' she continues, before setting off at a brisk pace.

'Where are we?' I stage-whisper to a flagging Darryl about ten minutes later.

'I've no idea where the bus is now.'

83

'And at this rate, I think we've lost half the group,' he whispers back.

'I'm sure we're going to have to find our own way back to the ship,' sighs one elderly couple.

'I wish I'd taken a photo of the bus stop,' mutters another.

Deciding there's no point in worrying, we let the guide vanish into the distance and turn our attention to enjoying Cascais on our own. Our wanderings soon lead us onto a wide, cobbled pedestrian pathway laid in a striking black-and-white zigzag pattern. Everyone seems sensibly dressed in flats—high heels would be impossible on this uneven surface. The walkway winds through the town before spilling out onto a series of small sandy bays, flanked by low cliffs. Despite the cool day, sunbathers are scattered along the beaches, soaking up what few rays they can. The cliffs themselves are crowned with limestone buildings, seemingly added wherever there was space, one merging into the next in an appealing mishmash that appears to tumble toward the sand. For all its surfing fame, the sea today is calm; with no swell, there are no surfers in sight.

Eventually, we make our way back toward the main pedestrian precinct, where quaint little shops offer all the things Portugal is famous for: Mateus wine, port, fine embroidery, ceramic tiles, pottery, and cork souvenirs—all of impressive quality. The wine-tasting stalls along the footpaths look especially tempting, with generous samplings on offer for just a few euros.

'It's going to be hard enough finding our bus again, let alone after a few glasses of wine,' Darryl reasons.

'Another time,' I sigh regretfully.

Back shipside, we have the choice of reboarding the Arcadia or continuing our explorations. Like most seaside ports, this one brims with inviting bars, shops, and cafes, and it looks like an easy stroll into Lisbon's main commercial district. The decision to keep going is an easy one. Dodging colourful little trams, tooting scooters, and cars driving on the wrong side of the road, we meander along cobblestone streets until we find ourselves facing a maze of fascinating, narrow alleyways. These winding passages are dark and close, their tall buildings sheathed in patterned ceramic tiles.

Portugal is renowned for its azulejos or glazed ceramic tiles. Dating back to the 13th century, they are everywhere, and when used to cover every building in an entire apartment block, the effect is striking. Drawn in, we plunge into the nearest alley and wander for ages, eventually emerging onto a broad, pedestrian-only street near the city centre. It is lined with stylish shops and enticing cafes, and it is here that we spot the much-anticipated Portuguese custard tarts Pierce had raved about.

'The tarts are okay, but I prefer this chocolate éclair,' I decide after a few bites.

'Too eggy and sweet for me,' says Darryl.

Lisbon is the last of our port visits; in three days, we arrive in Southampton. Before then, a few things still lie ahead. First is the crossing of the notorious Bay of Biscay—a stretch that brings back some unpleasant childhood memories for me. We will also take part in an Anzac Day ceremony topside on the *Arcadia*. And on day thirty-three of our thirty-four-day cruise, we tackle customs—thankfully downstairs in the dining room. Rather than have thousands of passengers inundate Southampton Border Control when our cruise docks, customs agents have boarded in Portugal and will process everyone, neatly and calmly, the day before we reach the UK.

Nearly 40 years ago, my father decided it would be a great idea, after travelling through France and Spain in a motor-caravan, to take a shortcut back to England. After a few months caretaking a block of flats on the Mediterranean, we boarded a ferry in Santander, Spain, bound for Plymouth, nearly 20 hours away. We were told there would be dinner on board and a cosy little cabin for the night, so my sister and I, after negotiating who would get the top bunk, were looking forward to the adventure.

A few hours later, the story had changed completely. Not long after leaving Santander, the ferry sailed into rough weather. I can still picture myself on deck, staring at mountainous waves bearing down on us. That was where I truly learned the meaning of the word 'seasick'—and discovered, to my annoyance, that not everyone is affected. My father and I were confined to our bunks for most of the crossing, sick as dogs, while Michelle and Patma barely felt a twinge.

This crossing, however, is an entirely different experience. With her modern stabilisers, the *Arcadia* handles the Bay of Biscay as effortlessly as a chainsaw through a rose bush. We glide across this notoriously rough stretch almost without noticing.

Anzac Day in Mullumbimby is usually marked by a dawn service at the Cenotaph in front of the local RSL Club. Years ago, before children, the day might have continued with a few games of two-up in the RSL or a barbecue with friends. This Anzac Day is different. Mid-morning finds us standing in the icy wind on Arcadia's top deck, surrounded by a small cluster of fellow Australians and a lone Kiwi couple. One Australian pair nearby has draped the flag across their shoulders, a sight that stirs a quiet pride. Before us stands Captain Cook, who, after a few words, calls for the Australian flag to be raised.

'Please could everyone join me in saying the Ode,' he continues.

They shall grow not old, as we that are left grow old.
Age shall not weary them, nor the years condemn.
At the going down of the sun and in the morning
We will remember them. Amen.

Finishing with a minute's silence, it goes through my mind that while there have been many occasions where we have had to say the Ode, this cold, blustery day on board the Arcadia will be one I will never forget.

It is our final day on board the Arcadia. Cruising sedately alongside the French coastline, we are about to enter the English Channel. Our passports, taken from us when we boarded all those weeks ago, have now been returned, and we are standing in line with the other Australian and non-British passengers. It is around 3 pm, and the customs officers have been interviewing passengers since 8 am—a sign of just how long the process takes.

'Passports, please,' says an officious-looking customs officer.
'I have two. I'm also British,' I reply, handing both over.
'There have been a few of you,' he remarks, jotting down both passport numbers.
'And you, sir?' he says to Darryl.
'Just Australian,' Darryl answers, handing over his passport.
'What is your purpose of visit?'
'Holidaying and visiting family.'
'How long do you intend to stay in England?'
'Until October.'
'Will you be working?'
'Umm… no.'
'Have you a return ticket booked?'
'Umm… no.'
'How will you be returning to Australia?'
'We're not sure yet,' I volunteer.

After years of watching Customs and Border Security, we cannot help but feel a flicker of worry. But after a few more questions, Darryl's passport is stamped with a six-month tourist visa, and we are waved on.

'Phew!' we both exhale. 'Let's hope it's easier when we come back from Europe.'

That evening, we weave our way past the myriad suitcases lined up in the passageways, ready for collection and offloading by the ship's crew. We linger over one last gourmet three-course meal and take in a final show before heading back to our cabin. Our own bags are nearly packed; we have decided to offload them ourselves in the morning.

Excitement bubbles at the thought of arriving in England, but there is also a pang of sadness at leaving the Arcadia—our home for the past five weeks, a ship that has given us an incredible adventure and memories to last a lifetime.

'Southampton,' I sing the next morning, flinging the curtains open one last time.

'It's too early. It's still dark,' grumbles Darryl.

'We can self-disembark as long as it's before seven,' I counter.

'Let's get breakfast, then go. Otherwise, we could be waiting for hours.'

At exactly 7 am, suitcases happily rolling beside us, we step from the Arcadia onto British soil. Only a handful of other passengers are self-disembarking, and apart from them—nothing. No crew members, no customs officers, no terminal staff. The place feels eerily silent, the cavernous space broken only by rows of luggage awaiting collection. Picking our way past the mountains of bags, we head for the exit and find ourselves first in line at the taxi rank.

'The train station, please,' we call to the driver as he pulls up alongside.

CHAPTER 10

At Home in England

Extract from Darma Travels Blog-
We are now living about ten miles from George Clooney. Yes, George and Amal are now neighbours. And while I'm at it, Theresa May also owns a house nearby, although as she is currently residing at Number 10, it's probably empty at the moment.

Southampton Train Station is only a short drive from the cruise terminal, and we spend it explaining to the Pommy cab driver why two Australians have just disembarked a British ship. At the same time, we gaze eagerly out the windows, taking in the quintessentially British grey sky and equally British streetscapes. At the station, memories of costly train travel resurface when we learn it will be about 80 Australian dollars for the 50-minute trip to Reading. Still, we are happy to pay it—in the whole of England, our destination is less than an hour away, and the train is direct.

Aboard our train, we give ourselves away as freshly arrived tourists when we promptly settle into reserved seats. A brightly dressed African man with a broad English accent nods towards the tiny scrolling screens above the luggage racks.

'See that screen? If there's something on it, the seat's taken.'

The train soon fills with early-morning commuters, and before we know it, we are rolling into Reading Station.

That evening, as I unpacked my bag and settled into our room, I reflected on the day. Our journey from Reading Station had taken us along and over the River Thames, its banks edged with parklands and walkways where families of swans and ducks basked in what little sunlight England offers at this time of year. Leaving the Thames, we passed through Caversham, with its ancient ruins and manicured gardens, before arriving in our new neighbourhood—a place that looked lovely and felt worlds apart from Brunswick Heads.

At our new home, we were warmly greeted by my aunt Charlotte, her partner Derek and Fudge—their very noisy, very fluffy cat. After a brief walk in the drizzling rain through the nearby park, the afternoon slipped away over cups of tea, slices of Charlotte's delicious sponge cake—and the first stirrings of plans.

'Pierce will be coming to stay for a few nights this weekend,' I mentioned.

'He's also booked us into the hotel attached to the pub where he works, so we'll spend three nights in Twickenham after our ten days here. We're on the Eurostar for Paris on the 10th of May. Paige has booked her flight and will be arriving at Heathrow this time next week.'

'What's Paige going to do?' Charlotte asked.

'She'll be working as a waitress in an old pub in Beaconsfield and living on-site. She'll only have a few days with us before she starts.'

'What date do you return from Europe?' Derek asked.

BUCKET LISTS AND WALKING STICKS

'At this stage, the 26th of June—that gives us about eight weeks in Europe,' we replied.

As the conversation continued, our plans took shape. We would spend the next ten days with Charlotte and Derek, exploring Caversham, Reading and the surrounding area, with Pierce and Paige joining us at different times. After that, we would head closer to London for three nights with Pierce in Twickenham—at least Darryl and I would. Paige, soon to start work, would join us for only two nights. When we returned from the Continent, Charlotte and Derek would have moved into their new house, leaving this one for us to use as we wished.

A few days after our arrival, we return from a walk along the nearby Thames to find Pierce waiting for us. It is the first time in nearly two and a half years that we have seen him, and in that time, he has worked and travelled extensively across Europe. He has also grown—both upwards and outwards—and now towers at an impressive 195 centimetres.

It is wonderful to catch up and hear about his travels and his life in Britain. We celebrate with lunch at a nearby pub where, over the background of a football match, he shares a few of his adventures, including the story of how he broke his humerus, the large bone in his upper arm.

'I was arm wrestling one of the customers on Christmas Eve,' he explains.

'The customer was showing off, saying he could beat anyone. He was really annoying, so I said I'd take him on. I didn't hear the bone snap, but everyone else did. I just felt the pain. Christmas Day was awful, and on Boxing Day they operated at the University Hospital.'

As always, the days start to slip by. We say farewell to Pierce, knowing we will see him again in just a few days. A gentle routine soon forms—long, leisurely breakfasts with Charlotte, Derek and noisy Fudge, during which we map out the day. Sometimes the plan involves an outing; other times it is a trip into nearby Caversham or Reading to browse the shops and tackle practicalities like food shopping at the local Waitrose.

One matter needing urgent attention is Darryl's medication. He has managed to travel this far with what he brought from home, but it is now running low. To replenish it, he will need to see a doctor—our first experience of the NHS (National Health Service) on this trip. We had some dealings with it years ago when living in Britain, but that was a long time ago. More recently, we have heard plenty of talk: that it is sending England bankrupt, that foreign nationals are misusing it and that its condition was a key reason many older Brits voted for Brexit.

In Reading, a walk-in clinic offers our best chance. After some quick paperwork, Darryl is seen by a nurse who, after a brief interview, decides he should see a doctor. Twenty minutes later, he emerges from the doctor's office with the necessary prescriptions. Back at reception, we are told there is no charge. We are floored. An Australian, seen by both a nurse and a doctor, taking up a good 20 minutes of their time—all free of charge. We leave, agreeing that while it is nice to get something for nothing, it is easy to see why the locals complain.

Dealing with the mundane, it is time I had another haircut. It is starting to look bedraggled, and the attempt in Malaysia certainly did not help. A quick Google search shows plenty of hairdressers in Reading, many with glowing reviews, so I visit one that catches my eye to make an appointment.

'Would you like the manager? That would be £105 for a cut,' I am told. 'Or the senior stylist—£65.'

'Are there other options?' I ask.

'You could have a stylist for £40, or the senior apprentice for £30.'

'Okay. As long as they know what they are doing, could I book the stylist?'

Two days later, I return to the salon.

'Oh, we have been trying to contact you,' they say. 'The stylist is sick, but we have arranged for the senior stylist to cut your hair at the stylist's price.'

Still a little confused by the pricing hierarchy, I nonetheless feel I am getting a bargain somewhere along the line and happily take a seat.

'Would you like tea or coffee?'

'Coffee, please.'

A few minutes later, a tray appears with a cafetière of coffee, a jug of milk, an elegant mug and a plate of biscuits. I suspect this level of service partly explains why haircuts are so expensive here.

The senior stylist is clearly an expert. Nearly two hours later, I leave absolutely loving the cut—shorter than I have worn it in a long time, but stylish, flattering and easy to manage while travelling around Europe.

On one of our daily jaunts through the nearby countryside, Charlotte and Derek point to a stretch of riverbank almost hidden by drooping willow trees.

'That's where George Clooney and Amal live,' they say.

Another time, as we pass through the village of Sonning—just ten minutes from Caversham—they nod toward a quiet lane.

'Theresa May lives here. Or at least she does when she's not at Number 10.'

Pretty chuffed to have such illustrious neighbours, I mentally file this away for my next blog post.

A few mornings later, Charlotte asks, 'How about a visit to a National Trust property? We're members, and there are some great ones nearby.'

The National Trust, founded in 1895, is dedicated to preserving and protecting historic places and landscapes across Britain. Many grand old houses, too costly for their owners to maintain, have been saved from ruin thanks to the Trust. For a small fee, visitors can explore these properties, making for a leisurely and fascinating day out.

After some discussion, we settle on Nuffield Place, the former home of Lord Nuffield—better known as William Morris, the man behind the Morris Minor. We wander his gardens before joining a guided tour of the house. One of the most striking exhibits is an iron lung, a life-saving machine used for polio patients who could no longer breathe on their own. Seeing it stirs memories of my father's stories: how, in his childhood before the polio vaccine, classmates would be laughing and playing one day, only to fall ill and never return the next.

William Morris's house remains exactly as he left it over 80 years ago—a perfect snapshot of early 20th-century life. Childless, William and his wife were thrifty yet remarkably generous, donating many iron lungs to polio sufferers. Though they amassed an enormous fortune from manufacturing Morris cars, they gave most of it away—the equivalent of £700 million in today's money.

We finish our visit with what the Brits call a cream tea: warm scones piled with jam and cream, washed down with a hearty English Breakfast Tea from the on-site tearoom. Leaving the property, we feel both content and inspired. Not only have we been transported back in time and treated to an extraordinary history lesson, but we have also been reminded how deeply some people can impact the lives of others. The Nuffields' generosity changed many lives, and today's outing has reinforced just how valuable—and enjoyable—these National Trust properties are.

We have been in England for a week now, and today we are off to Heathrow to collect Paige. With the airport only a short drive from Reading, Derek offers to take us. In fact, everything seems close to Reading. Over the past few days, we have realised just how fortunate we are to be based here—excellent public transport, quick access to London and easy routes both north and south.

It is a quick whizz down the busy M4 to Heathrow, and somewhere along the way, Darryl and I discover something about England we do not love: the roads.

In our first week here, we have noticed that England's roads fall broadly into four categories:

Motorways ('M' roads): Huge, three or four lanes wide, extremely busy but with good visibility. They carry a constant stream of cars and trucks, allowing you to cover long distances quickly.

'A' roads: Smaller than motorways, often just as busy. The speed limits can feel far too high for the conditions, and in many places, they are lined on both sides by tall hedges.

'B' roads: Narrower again, frequently hemmed in by thick hedgerows, sometimes with no verge at all. Corners can be blind, visibility poor, yet traffic still barrels along at full speed.

All other roads: Smaller still—in some cases so tight and hedgebound that one vehicle has to reverse to let another pass.

'The state of your 'A' and 'B' roads is on par with our quietest back roads in Australia,' we tell them. 'They're far too narrow, with poor visibility, for the speed and number of cars using them.'

As Heathrow Terminal 4 has no short-term parking, it is fortunate that Paige has already made her way out of the airport. We spot her almost immediately. She has had a good flight but, like us, is a little dismayed by the weather.

'I thought England in May was meant to be nice,' she says. 'Not freezing and raining.'

'It has been like this since we arrived,' we reply. 'Welcome to England.'

The following morning dawns sunny—almost as if mocking our complaints—but still cold. To celebrate Paige's arrival, and to thank Charlotte and Derek, we decide on lunch at a Thames-side restaurant a few miles away.

Although the air bites, it is spring, and England is awash with bluebells. On the way, Derek pulls over at a spot he knows, and a short stroll along one of England's public walkways soon finds us knee-deep in a sea of blue. These 'rights of way' hold great memories for us. Legally open to the public, they meander through both public and private land, criss-crossing the countryside. On our last visit to Britain, we spent many a Sunday afternoon walking them off the back of a hearty roast.

Today, the wind quickly chases us back to the car, and before long, we arrive at our lunch venue, perched right on the riverbank. The menu is tempting, and as we eat, longboats drift past, broken here and there by a cruiser or canoe. Their slow, unhurried progress stirs an old dream of ours—spending time navigating England's canal-ways. I once spent two weeks on a longboat motoring through the Norfolk Broads as a child, and the memory still lingers. For now, the dream has been shelved in favour of other adventures, but perhaps one day it will surface again.

To help our lunch settle, we follow a nearby sign pointing to a local lock. The path curves gently along the river, a wide and easy 15-minute walk. Swans glide alongside us, many trailed by fluffy, grey-feathered cygnets.

'Did you know the Queen owns all the swans on the River Thames?' Derek remarks.

'Back in the 1500s, too many were being killed for eating. To save them, the monarchy claimed ownership, and it's now illegal to harm one.'

Paige is in England to work, so the next few days are taken up with getting her settled. The three of us travel to Slough, where she has an interview to obtain a National Insurance Number—the UK's equivalent of our Medicare card. There is no waiting area in the building, so Darryl and I perch on a fence outside, passing the time by watching the wonderfully multicultural life of Slough unfold before us.

Another day is devoted to opening a bank account for her, a surprisingly drawn-out process. On the way to one of these appointments, we are standing on a station platform when a train comes hurtling through without stopping—a blur of steel just centimetres from us, easily topping 100 kilometres an hour. The roar and draught it creates is staggering.

'Oh my god!' I gasp. 'That was terrifying!'

'Remind me to try and video it next time!' Darryl exclaims, after which we both convulse with laughter.

Before we know it, it is time to bid farewell to Charlotte, Derek and Fudge and make our way closer to London. With a key to their house safely stowed in our luggage, Darryl, Paige and I trundle our bags onto the first available train and, half an hour later, step off at Twickenham—home of Rugby Union. Pulling out my phone, I fire up Google Maps to locate Pierce's pub. It is a 15-minute walk, and, apart from a quick detour into a conveniently placed charity shop, we head straight there, soon arriving at a handsome old building fronting the River Thames.

While Darryl and I have booked and paid for a large, airy and extremely comfortable room overlooking the river, Pierce has arranged free accommodation for Paige in the room of a staff member currently on holiday. Unfortunately, it turns out to be dark, cramped and cluttered—a far cry from inviting. We reassure her that she can spend most of her time in our room instead.

'Besides,' I add, trying to put a positive spin on it, 'this will give you a chance to get used to living in staff quarters.'

It is the first time in over 30 months that the four of us have been together as a family, and it's surprising how quickly we fall back into familiar patterns. That night's conversation is fast-paced, with many sentences beginning, 'Remember when…?'

The next morning, Pierce—working the breakfast shift—sets down plates of full English breakfast and asks what our plans are for the day.

'I've downloaded an app called 'Find Near Me,"' I reply. 'It says Hampton Court Palace is a five-minute Uber ride away.'

'Never heard of it,' Pierce says.

'Me neither,' Paige chimes in.

Hampton Court Palace is one of only two surviving palaces once owned by King Henry VIII. Built in the mid-16th century, it draws crowds keen to stand where England's most notorious king once lived. Henry VIII—famed for his six wives, his extravagance, his charisma and his break with the Pope that led to the creation of the Church of England—is etched in my memory through the story of Anne Boleyn. I first learned about her during my impressionable teenage years and never forgot the story: Anne, failing to provide Henry with a legitimate male heir, was beheaded on his command.

'It's a huge palace once owned by a really famous English king,' I summarise. 'And there's a great maze in the grounds.'

While the palace and king fail to impress Paige, the promise of a maze challenge does, and so, rugged up warmly, we hail an Uber a short time later.

The day is wet, cold and grey, but that works in our favour, with short queues at the Hampton Court entrance. To get here, despite being in the middle of a major city, the Uber has passed through huge green parklands, and we are still excited from spotting herds of deer through the windows. That thrill only grows as we pass under the grand gatehouse into an enormous cobblestone courtyard, surrounded on all sides by the austere stone walls of the palace.

Inside, we collect wireless headsets that let us explore at our own pace, a steady stream of history and gossip flowing into our ears. At one point, a staff member announces that a play about Henry and Anne will shortly begin in the Great Hall. Watching it in that sumptuously decorated space, I have my first experience of underfloor heating.

'The floor's warm,' I whisper to Darryl, amazed.

Stone underfoot, yet enough heat rising to warm the entire vast room. Stepping back out into the palace's bitterly cold corridors feels like leaving a cosy winter lodge for the icy outdoors.

Deciding we have absorbed enough history for one day, we seek out the tea rooms and indulge in another enormous cream tea. The scones are fresh, the jam sweet and the tea strong enough to revive us for the next challenge—the Hampton Court Maze.

Built around 1700, it is England's oldest surviving maze, covering a third of an acre. World-famous, it has been on my must-do list since childhood. Supposedly, the average visitor reaches the centre in 20 minutes.

'Beat you there!' Paige yells, dashing into the entrance.

'You go next,' says Darryl.

Ten minutes later, Paige calls out that she has made it. Moments after, Darryl does the same. Another ten minutes on, I am still hopelessly lost. Frustration mounting, I abandon the hunt for the centre and focus on simply finding my way out. By the time I emerge—long after both of them—I am thoroughly over the whole experience and vow never to bother with a maze again.

That evening, our last together as a family for a while, we feast on pizza and pasta in a cosy upstairs room of a little Italian restaurant in Twickenham. From our table, we watch in awe as the waitress navigates the steep, winding staircase with arms full of food and drinks.

Early the next morning, Paige, Darryl and I head underground on the famous London 'Tube'. Paige's train to Beaconsfield departs from Marylebone Station, and along the way, we catch a glimpse of Wembley Stadium's distinctive arch.

Beaconsfield proves to be a quiet town of old houses, ancient pubs and just a handful of shops. Paige's pub appears to be the oldest of them all. We wave as she crosses the road and disappears through its oak-beamed entrance—she has prohibited us from coming any closer.

On Wednesday, 10 May, after a quick breakfast and the usual check of money, passports and bags, we say goodbye to Pierce and trundle back to Twickenham Station. Our destination: London St Pancras, where the Eurostar will carry us beneath the English Channel and into Europe.

CHAPTER 11

Exploring Paris

Extract from Darma Travels Blog-
It's a strange time to be visiting Paris, given its recent brush with terrorism. Smart Traveller advocates one uses a high degree of caution, and despite the city being full of tourists, I feel we are all slightly on edge.

It is fortunate that I bought our Eurostar tickets electronically and they are easily accessible in the Apple Wallet on my phone, because for some reason, time has become tight. With two customs queues to navigate—first British, to expedite our departure, then French—the minutes slip away faster than expected. While slightly anxious and wishing we had given ourselves an extra half an hour, the system does work and before we know it, we have found our seats aboard our high-speed train for Paris.

I must admit I am feeling slightly apprehensive about the upcoming train journey. Completed in 1994, this route boasts the longest undersea tunnel in the world. In just over two hours and fifteen minutes, the train will carry us from London to Paris at speeds exceeding 300 kilometres per hour—with 38 kilometres of the trip underwater, as deep as 115 metres below the surface at its lowest point. No surprise, then, that a small knot of unease sits in my stomach. Still, knowing that around 400 trains make this trip daily, I tell myself to set the fear aside and focus on enjoying the ride.

The seats are comfortable, there's ample luggage space and the buffet offers a passable chocolate muffin and coffee. We sit munching our muffins, watching the English countryside whip past. At one point, I pull out my book, only looking up when I feel the temperature drop. A glance out the window confirms we're in a tunnel—and it dawns on me: this is it, we're under the sea. I'm grateful there's been no grand announcement and I can only hope we've been down here for a while already.

The underwater stretch lasts about 30 minutes and not long after I register where we are, the train bursts back into daylight. Straining for proof we've made it to France, I breathe a sigh of relief when I spot French road signs, followed by cars driving on the right-hand side.

'We're in France,' I tell Darryl, grinning. 'That wasn't so bad after all.'

'Good,' he replies, deadpan. 'Because we'll be doing it again in eight weeks.'

Now that we are in France, the train seems to travel even faster and I find myself glued to the speeds flashing up on the overhead screens.

'We're at 295 kilometres an hour. Now 301.'

We peak at about 310 kilometres an hour—a speed unheard of in Australia. It is maddening to think that our vast, flat continent, perfectly suited for high-speed rail, has never had a government prepared to commit to such a project. The wasted potential is frustrating.

Exactly two hours and fifteen minutes after leaving London, our train glides into Paris Gare du Nord. Choosing where to stay in Paris was not easy. The city's 20 arrondissements each offer their own attractions, but fate intervened when, while reading a novel set in Paris,

I came across a reference to a hotel in the Latin Quarter—the 5th arrondissement. Drawn to the idea of an area described as 'narrow pedestrian streets full of cafés and restaurants,' I looked up the Hotel du Levant and found it not only real, but affordable, with rooms available. The final push came when I discovered it was within a five-minute walk of the Cathedral of Notre-Dame, the River Seine, the Sorbonne and the Pantheon.

'It's too far to walk to our hotel from the station,' I tell Darryl as we exit the station.

'Should we get an Uber or a taxi?'

'With an Uber, we won't have to use our euros. It'll come straight from the bank account,' he reminds me.

Finding our French-speaking Uber driver outside the chaotic Gare du Nord proves tricky. The crowds are thick and he calls to ask where we are. I dredge up enough high school French to direct him.

'You did well,' Darryl says as we sink into the back seat.

'Actually surprised me a bit.'

'I surprised myself,' I admit.

It is a short ride through noisy, bustling Paris before we turn into the cobbled, winding lanes of the Latin Quarter. As promised, cafés and restaurants line the streets, their menu du jour boards angled towards passing trade. Our driver stops outside a narrow, five-storey building with flower baskets spilling from its windows. Across the street, a violinist plays to the café tables—perhaps our personal soundtrack for the days ahead.

Inside the lobby, I spot a small, box-like contraption in the corner and raise an eyebrow. Is that the lift? Booking accommodation with a lift for Darryl's sake had been a challenge across Europe, but it was imperative. Now, looking at our first European example, we can only laugh.

'You're kidding. It's tiny,' Darryl grins.

'You take the bags up and I'll meet you there,' I say.

'Hopefully they'll fit in with you.'

Our room is on the fourth floor of the building's five floors, with a direct view of the busker across the road. Each day, his music will drift in through our partially open window, a gentle serenade for our stay in Paris. The room itself is tiny, dressed in gold and red velvet. In one corner sits what appears to be a wardrobe, but on opening the door, we discover it's actually a toilet. The bathroom—only marginally larger—occupies the opposite corner. Framed photographs of old movies and movie stars, some with signatures, line the walls. Quirky, compact and full of character, it feels just right. We are looking forward to spending the next six days here.

Although not quite as cold as England, there's still a nip in the Paris air, so we rug up in jumpers and jackets before heading out into the streets. The River Seine is only a short walk away, and we weave through the narrow lanes that define this quarter to reach it. Along the way, we pass the first of many small tourist gift shops and I am pleasantly surprised by the quality of what's on offer. Back home, our souvenir shops tend to be filled with clip-on koalas and sheep wool slippers, but here I find elegant scarves, neat little berets, and toiletry bags decorated with the artwork of renowned painters such as Picasso and Monet.

We also pass the first of what will become a familiar sight throughout our time in Europe—something we later dub 'Being a Pigeon.' These are cafes or bars where people sit in neat rows, drinking, smoking and watching the world go by. Most have small tables for resting drinks, but in many cases, there are none—just chairs lined up in horizontal rows, sometimes three or four deep, all facing a busy square or walkway.

'Look at all those people just sitting there facing the road!' Darryl says, surprised.

'Don't they remind you of the men on the bar stools at the RSL back home?' I laugh. 'They look like pigeons roosting on their perches! Shall we join them?'

'Definitely later.'

Used to Australia's strict no-smoking rules, Paris is a bit of a shock with its far more relaxed attitude towards smokers. Restaurants, cafes and bars are full of them and the streets are no different. We resolve that when we do decide to 'Be a Pigeon,' we'll aim for a spot with, hopefully, a little less smoke drifting our way.

Ahead lies the River Seine and just beyond it, the magnificent Cathedral of Notre-Dame. Standing on a small island considered the very heart of Paris—and one of its oldest areas—this is one of the finest examples of French Gothic architecture in the world. To me, it is forever linked with the story of Quasimodo, *The Hunchback of Notre-Dame*. I love that it's so close to where we're staying; we'll be able to pass by and gape at it every day.

'Look at those armed guards,' Darryl says as we near the cathedral.

'Wow, they're really heavily armed, aren't they?' I reply.

It's a sobering reminder of the terrible terrorist attacks France has endured in recent years—most notably the November 2015 Paris attacks, which left 130 dead and nearly 400 injured, and the July 2016 attack in Nice, which claimed 86 lives and injured over 400.

'I wasn't expecting so many guards… and so heavily armed. And they're all so young,' I add.

It's a sight we'll have to get used to—one we will encounter often as we travel further across Europe.

The queue to enter the cathedral is enormous, so for now we settle for circling its perimeter, taking in the intricately carved sculptures and watchful gargoyles that guard the façade. Every angle reveals some new detail—saints, demons and fantastical beasts frozen in stone for centuries.

Behind the cathedral, its gardens blend seamlessly with the banks of the Seine, a green pocket in the city's heart. From here, we wander back towards the Latin Quarter, crossing one of the many bridges alive with tourists, street performers and lovers attaching padlocks to the railings.

It is nearing dinner time and I am itching to try one of the menus du jour I have heard so much about. France is renowned for its food and a set menu is the perfect way to sample a few dishes. We choose a quaint little café just a short stroll from our hotel, complete with red-chequered tablecloths and a cosy hum of conversation. For ten euros, I am served a three-course meal: a steaming bowl of French onion soup with a golden, cheesy crust; tender beef bourguignon and a silky crème caramel. Crusty bread and a chilled carafe of rosé complete the experience. It's everything I had hoped for—simple, rich and full of flavour. It's no wonder everyone raves about French food.

That night, we lie under the heaviest eiderdown I have ever encountered, so thick it feels as if it might pin us to the mattress. The sound of the violin from the busker below is replaced by the wail of sirens—loud, urgent and, as we soon discover, a constant backdrop to Paris nights.

The next morning, our room rate's promise of a continental breakfast lures us downstairs to a small dining room heavy with the smell of fresh pastry. At the sight of huge, flaky croissants, tubs of creamy yoghurt and a generous selection of cheeses, our mouths water instantly. The croissants are among the best we have ever tasted—light, buttery and impossible not to devour. With three more weeks in France ahead of us, we are already celebrating the thought of many more mornings like this.

Today we decide to explore Paris aboard the hop-on, hop-off bus. As we've discovered elsewhere on our travels, it's one of the easiest—and surprisingly cheapest—ways to take in a city's highlights. There's a stop right in front of Notre-Dame Cathedral and here we buy our tickets.

'If you want to pay four more euros each, you can travel for two days,' the attendant suggests.

'I also have this voucher from our hotel compendium,' I reply. 'Can we use it as well?'

'Mais oui, of course.'

'Merci. Deux passes, s'il vous plaît.'

We climb aboard and are happy to find the two front seats on the upper deck have just become free. Plugging in our earphones, we lean back and prepare to be entertained and overawed by the sights and stories of magical Paris. That sense of calm does not last long. The traffic is chaotic and deafening. French drivers seem to treat road rules as optional, relying instead on a constant chorus of blaring horns. Sirens wail almost without pause as emergency vehicles weave through the congestion. It is nothing short of remarkable that our driver manages to steer this large, cumbersome bus through the madness.

From our front-row perch on the upper deck, we have the perfect vantage point to admire the grandeur of Paris—ornate facades, flashes of the River Seine and the endless battle of impatient drivers below. At the Champs-Élysées, we hop off and stroll the wide, tree-lined boulevard, passing iconic cafés, glittering theatres and luxury boutiques. We pause at a makeshift memorial to a policeman killed in a terrorist attack here just two weeks earlier, the site still carpeted with fresh flowers.

Our walk carries us onward towards the towering Arc de Triomphe, the great monument honouring those who fought and died for France. Beneath it lies the Tomb of the Unknown Soldier, its eternal flame flickering quietly against the roar of the city.

Unlike many other ancient cities, Paris feels deliberately and carefully designed. Between 1853 and 1870, an ambitious public works programme transformed it from an overcrowded, unhealthy maze into a city of light and order. Medieval neighbourhoods were demolished, replaced by sweeping boulevards, grand parks and graceful squares. A modern sewerage system was installed, along with new fountains and aqueducts to carry fresh water.

Standing in the wide-open Place de la Concorde, the scale and success of Paris's transformation are clear. Covering 21 acres, the square sits at the intersection of four major landmarks, with symmetry and elegance stretching in every direction. Surrounded by space, beauty and careful design, I realise I may never again see another city planned with such thought, generosity and breathtaking detail.

Being a very highly anticipated bucket list item, our first glimpse of the Eiffel Tower is incredible. From the top deck of the hop-on bus, I spot it suddenly and, in my eagerness to point it out, nearly knock Darryl's sunglasses off. We choose to alight one stop short, giving ourselves the chance to stroll slowly towards the iconic structure—taking in the full view, noting the presence of heavily armed guards and soaking up the atmosphere of its surroundings.

Completed in 1889, the wrought-iron Eiffel Tower was so heavily criticised at first that it nearly faced demolition. Today, at 324 metres, it stands as Paris's tallest structure and one of the most recognisable landmarks in the world. While visiting, it was firmly on our bucket list, our plan was not to climb it but to picnic on the lawns in front— just as some good friends of ours once did. One of them, Big Bird, has since passed away far too young, but we still remember the photos and stories of him and his wife, Anne, enjoying wine and baguettes under the summer sun. We had promised ourselves that when we visited, we would do the same. Unfortunately, the weather today is against us and a picnic is out of the question.

'How about we get a coffee and baguette from that vendor instead?' I suggest.

'Coffee sounds great. And it's the thought that counts,'

Darryl replies.

So we stand together, coffees in hand, in front of one of the most famous structures in the world, quietly remembering Big Bird and thinking of Anne.

Our journey back takes us through the red-light district of Montmartre, past the glittering lights of the Moulin Rouge and on to the Palais Garnier, birthplace of *The Phantom of the Opera.*

That night, we choose another quintessential French café and indulge in a rich, velvety cheese fondue, followed by warm apple pie and a carafe of rosé. Around us, Paris hums—music drifting from nearby bars, laughter spilling from tables on the pavement, though often interrupted by the wail of sirens. Touts weave between couples, offering armfuls of brightly coloured roses, while groups of animated Sorbonne students chatter their way along the street. It's everything I had imagined Paris to be—and more.

With the heaviest eiderdown in the world now relegated to a nearby chair, we sleep soundly and wake to another gourmet breakfast. Today, we will make full use of our second-day hop-on bus tickets and this evening we will visit the Louvre—where seeing the Mona Lisa tops our list.

'I can't get used to those armed guards. They're so young,'
I say again as we pass Notre-Dame Cathedral.

'It's good to see so many other tourists about, though,' Darryl replies.

'Yes, the terror attacks haven't stopped people from visiting Paris.'

'Safety in numbers?' he suggests.

'Exactly,' I nod, though I admit to feeling a faint undercurrent of apprehension.

Using our hop-on bus to reach or pass by the many sights, Sacre-Coeur, Les Invalides, the Musée d'Orsay, Sainte-Chapelle, Jardin du Luxembourg, the day slips past in a blur. There is simply so much to take in. By the time we climb off the bus, we are exhausted, our senses overwhelmed.

'Let's be pigeons and have a drink and something to eat in that café,' Darryl suggests.

And so we join the rows of other pigeons, sipping our drinks and watching the steady stream of life pass by.

The Louvre is only a ten-minute stroll from our hotel. With early evening approaching, we cross the famous Pont Neuf—the oldest bridge in Paris—and soon find ourselves standing before the iconic glass pyramid. Once a royal palace, the Louvre is now the world's largest and most visited art museum, home to over 360,000 artefacts and more than 35,000 works of art. None is more famous than Leonardo da Vinci's Mona Lisa, and it is her we have come to see.

'The queues don't look too bad,' Darryl remarks.

'Waiting until 5 pm on a wet Friday evening was obviously a good idea,' I reply.

We had put some thought into our visit today. As we were already discovering—and would continue to discover—queues in Europe can be horrendous. The line to see the Mona Lisa is probably only rivalled by the one for the Crown Jewels at the Tower of London, an ordeal we endured years ago and had no desire to repeat. This time, we gambled on two things: that a wet spring day and a visit after 5 pm on a Friday evening might work in our favour. It seems we were right. Having pre-purchased our tickets online, we bypass the entry line entirely, glide through airport-style security, take the elevators down and suddenly, we are in the heart of the Louvre. Clear signage points the way, and just ten minutes after stepping inside, we are standing before Leonardo da Vinci's masterpiece.

Although the rest of the museum may be thinning out, here the crowd is thick, everyone jostling for a clear view or the perfect photo of the most famous, most expensive and most visited painting in the world. I am surprised—pleasantly so—by its size; larger than I'd imagined, a luminous half-length portrait. Then I see her properly. The Mona Lisa's expression is serene yet knowing, her gaze following you in a way that feels almost alive. I can do nothing but stand and take her in.

'No wonder this is the most famous painting in the world,' I breathe. 'It's so much more than I was expecting.'

Of course, it is far too crowded to linger, so after taking my own photos, I step aside, quietly savouring the satisfaction of another bucket list dream fulfilled. The Louvre, arguably the most impressive museum in the world, is impossible to take in during one visit, but we devote the next few hours to exploring a small fraction of its treasures. In this brief time, we stand before works by Raphael, Veronese, and Caravaggio, pause in admiration at Michelangelo's sculptures and end with the pièce de résistance—the timeless beauty of the Venus de Milo.

Extremely happy and replete with culture, we meander through the lively streets of the Latin Quarter, enjoying the evening's energy before returning to our hotel. Dinner is another enticing menu du jour—this time pâté, coq au vin and crème caramel, all for just nine euros.

On day four of our six in Paris, we take the train to the outer suburbs to visit the Palace of Versailles. Originally built as a hunting lodge in 1623, it was transformed into a royal palace in 1660 and soon after became the seat of political power in France when the royal court relocated here. Over the next century, staggering sums of money were poured into its expansion, culminating in perhaps the largest and most opulent building we have ever seen. Crafted from beautifully decorated stone, adorned with mosaic wood floors, mirrored walls and the world-famous Hall of Mirrors, it was here that Marie Antoinette was captured. The gardens of Versailles are equally legendary—so vast and meticulously designed that it would be easy to spend an entire day exploring them alone.

The train ride from the city is quick and inexpensive and before long, we are stepping onto the platform at Versailles. There's no need to ask for directions—we simply follow the tide of people. Despite having pre-purchased tickets, we're met with a daunting sight: the entry queue stretches for what must be 400 metres. This is one of

BUCKET LISTS AND WALKING STICKS

those moments, however, when Darryl's walking stick comes in handy. Guests with mobility challenges are ushered directly to the front and soon, we are at the information desk.

As at Hampton Court Palace, we're handed small wireless audio guides and moments later, we're wandering through the palace, wide-eyed, as a calm voice in our earpieces feeds us its extraordinary history. Versailles is pure excess: more than 2,100 windows, 1,200 fireplaces, 700 rooms, 76 staircases and gardens sprawling across 2,000 acres. At today's values, its construction cost would top two billion US dollars. It's not hard to see why the French people eventually rebelled against such a staggering display of wealth—the sheer opulence is breathtaking, but also impossible to justify.

It's been another incredible day and we end it as we have before—being pigeons. Sitting with our drinks, watching the passing parade, I discreetly record snippets of the Paris sirens on my iPhone. From now on, those sirens will always be the soundtrack of Paris for me—loud, relentless and everywhere.

Our final full day in Paris dawns bright and clear. We begin with an early visit to the beautiful yet solemn Notre-Dame Cathedral before following the Seine towards the distant suburbs. Cutting through the nearby Luxembourg Gardens, we emerge not far from the Pantheon, the grand secular mausoleum that houses the remains of notable French citizens. Outside, as in so many places we have visited, young soldiers stand guard, their weapons at the ready.

As we wander through the quieter suburbs, the soundscape changes—or rather intensifies. Sirens seem to wail even more persistently than usual, and above us the steady thrum of helicopters fills the air. France has just elected a new president, Emmanuel Macron, and today, May 14th, marks his inauguration. Between the news crews, the security presence, and the energy in the streets, Paris feels electric. It is a day we know we will never forget.

It is a leisurely start to our last morning in Paris. With our train not departing until 11 am, we linger over one final delicious breakfast in the little dining room. Darryl braves the tiny lift one more time and we exchange farewells with the staff, who have been unfailingly helpful and friendly. Not once have we encountered the aloofness we were warned to expect in Paris.

At 10 am, our Uber pulls up to take us on the short, 20-minute drive to Gare de Lyon. From here, a six-and-a-half-hour train journey will carry us south, to the Dordogne region and the town of Sarlat.

CHAPTER 12

South West France

Extract from Darma Travels Blog-
Originating in the ninth century, Sarlat has the greatest number of classified monuments per square km in the whole of Europe.

After validating our paper tickets at one of the little yellow machines found in every French train station, we locate our platform, board, and depart Paris. In just over three hours, we'll cover more than 600 kilometres to Bordeaux aboard a TGV high-speed train, the flagship of France's rail network. The carriage is spotless, the seats comfortable and each one has a handy phone-charging port. As we speed south, the scenery grows more distinctively French.

'Look at the vineyards,' I squeal to Darryl. 'And those lovely little stone houses!'

Bordeaux is simply a stop for us to change trains; we plan to return at the end of the week to explore it properly. For now, though, we have about 15 minutes to find our connection to the Dordogne region.

'Look for a screen with platform numbers.'

'There aren't any.'

Anxiety creeps in when we realise that, due to maintenance work, the usual platform screens are missing. Resorting to my high school French, we finally track down our onward train with minutes to spare.

'That's probably the tightest change we'll have,' I sigh in relief. 'From now on, there's a bit more time between trains.'

There's a problem, however, and 20 minutes later, we find ourselves still sitting at Bordeaux Station.

'What's the problem?' I ask in faltering French to some ladies across from us.

'This train has been cancelled and replaced by buses,' we eventually gather.

No explanation is given, but our planned two-and-a-half-hour train trip to Sarlat has now become a four-hour bus ride. With daylight still ahead, we are not too concerned—if anything, we hope the slower pace will give us a better look at what is already shaping up to be stunning countryside.

Leaving the coastal, flatter region of Bordeaux, our bus heads east towards the greener, more mountainous Dordogne. The lowlands are lined with endless vineyards, while the higher country is dotted with castles. The farther we travel and the higher we climb, the narrower the roads become—so much so that at one point the driver must execute a three-point turn to make it around a bend. Only later do we discover the reason for our winding route: the Tour de France is due through shortly, and many main roads are closed in preparation.

At one stop, I see from my window young men greeting each other in the traditional French way and can only muse on how customs differ. Kissing alternate cheeks is definitely a far cry from how the young men in Australia greet each other. Finally, at eight-thirty that evening, the bus pulls into Sarlat station. I phone Pierre, the owner of our B&B, and he arrives a short while later. The late spring sun is still high as we pull up outside a 500-year-old building—our home for the week ahead.

We have chosen to spend the week here after being inspired by a series of books. Martin Walker's *Bruno, Chief of Police* novels have long been a favourite of mine, and his vivid descriptions of the scenery and rhapsodies about the food in this region convinced us we had to see it for ourselves.

Sarlat is a medieval town dating back to the ninth century. Its early prosperity as a trading hub, coupled with the wealth and influence of the church, led to the creation of magnificent sandstone buildings, a maze of cobbled laneways, and tucked-away squares. Unlike many other French towns with similar heritage, Sarlat escaped heavy modernisation, preserving its medieval charm. Today, it boasts the best-preserved medieval architecture in France and holds the highest number of classified monuments per square kilometre in all of Europe.

Pierre, a proud Sarlat local, leads us to our room at his 500-year-old B&B, *La Maison du Notaire Royal,* pointing out features along the way.

'This was once three separate houses, joined together in the 17th century. There used to be a road here, but it was built over. The floorboards in your room are more than 600 years old,' he tells us.

We are awed by the age of everything, but two things please us most: the location—right in the heart of Sarlat—and the balcony off our room. Through authentic French doors, we can step from our large open-plan space, with its four-metre-high ceiling, onto a balcony that looks directly down onto the 800-year-old cobbled town square. We are within a stone's throw of cafés where people linger like pigeons, and on Wednesdays and Saturdays, the market stalls will spring to life below us.

'It's fantastic, Pierre. Merci. Thank you,' we say.

'Tout bon. Breakfast is from seven until nine in the room next door,' he replies.

Unlike Paris, where restaurants and cafés stay open late into the night, here in the heart of the French countryside, kitchens close much earlier. Tonight, that means we must forgo dinner. After quick showers in the claw-footed bath, we collapse into bed. The warm glow from the town square seeps through our windows, as does the hourly chiming of the town clock—both things we will simply have to get used to.

By morning, we are ravenous and the first to arrive in the nearby breakfast room. Pierre has been up early, and our table is laden with freshly baked croissants and crusty baguettes. We slather both with creamy butter and generous helpings of his homemade cherry jam, quickly declaring it the best we have ever tasted. A large pot of coffee completes the feast.

'Pierre, is there a laundromat nearby?' we ask in faltering French.

'Oui, there is one very close by.'

The rest of the morning is spent mastering the quirks of a French laundromat and finding space in our room to hang the washing. Darryl, even on holidays, refuses to use a dryer.

As we have found, when staying put for a while, the days begin to slip into a comfortable rhythm. After stuffing ourselves with croissants, baguettes and jam, we set out to explore Sarlat's winding streets. The town is a maze of beautiful honey-coloured cobblestones, and we manage to get lost every single time. Ancient sandstone buildings tower over us, and the cathedral is every bit as impressive as we'd hoped.

Watching our budget, we resist the temptation of the mouth-watering *menu du jour* each night, choosing instead to dine on our balcony overlooking the square. From the local supermarket, we feast on fresh baguettes, local cheeses, tomatoes, strawberries, chocolate mousse and a chilled bottle of rosé—all for no more than nine or ten euros.

'I'm not going to bother with my 6–1 diet while we're in Europe,' I finally admit. 'The food's far too good to be missing out.'

'I'm finding it impossible to stick to anyway,' Darryl laughs. 'I'm happy to stop for a while.'

In the early hours of Wednesday morning, we are woken by the sounds of stallholders setting up their wares beneath our balcony. Excited to explore a genuine French market, we eat breakfast quickly and head outside, where trestles groan under the weight of fresh produce. Huge wheels of cheese, steaming pots of paella, olives in every shade imaginable, foie gras for which the region is famous and piles of glorious fruit and vegetables fill the air with irresistible aromas.

'Look at the size of that nougat!' Darryl exclaims.

'I've never seen anything like it,' I reply.

'Oui, merci,' Darryl tells the shopkeeper in answer to his question. 'We'd like about five euros' worth.'

The nougat turns out to be the best we have ever tasted, and for the rest of our stay in Sarlat, buying some becomes a daily ritual.

The Dordogne region, named after the mighty river that runs through it, is one of France's most beautiful and popular areas. Dating back to prehistory—around 500,000 years ago—it has seen more than its share of upheaval. History records marauding Arabs, Vikings, Crusaders, English, Catholics, and Protestants. Today, their legacy is a landscape rich with heritage, caves, castles, and culture.

'Let's visit the caves today,' I suggest, referring to the nearby Lascaux caves. 'Pierre says they're well worth it.'

Estimated to be over 17,000 years old and discovered as recently as 1940, the Lascaux caves prove to be incredible. Although the original caves are closed to protect them from damage caused by carbon dioxide, the replica is more than enough to inspire awe. Over 600 wall and ceiling paintings have been recreated here, part of a total of more than 6,000 figures—mostly large animals.

Later that evening, still talking about the Great Hall of Bulls—where one painted bull measures over five metres long—and other remarkable sections of the cave, we nod in total agreement when Pierre says,

'The caves are known as the prehistoric Sistine Chapel.'

'Pierre mentioned a good tour that leaves from the information office,' I suggest one morning.

'It's called *Villages of the Dordogne*, and it visits three places that sound interesting. We could do it today.'

After breakfast, we stroll to the nearby office and discover we are the only two booked in.

'Personalised service,' jokes Darryl.

Our first stop is La Roque-Gageac. Ranked among France's most beautiful villages, it clings to the north bank of the River Dordogne, a row of handsome stone houses fronting the water and backed by towering cliffs. From a pathway lining the water's edge we spot troglodyte caves and an ancient stone church tucked into the rock face. The church is open, but the caves are closed for safety reasons. Later, ice-creams in hand, we wander narrow lanes before boarding a *gabarre*—a traditional flat-bottom boat—for a ride along the fast-flowing river. We pass ancient castles, arched bridges, and dramatic cliffs, all while hearing tales of the region's often bloody past.

Next is Domme, a fortified medieval *bastide* (town) perched high on a cliff. The views are simply breathtaking: castles, stone bridges, winding rivers, green fields, deep forests, and rolling hills that stretch to the horizon. It is easy to see why Domme, too, is counted among France's most beautiful villages.

We end the day in Beynac, a small hamlet overshadowed by its imposing 12th-century castle. Perched on a limestone cliff, the fortress still stands in remarkable condition, a silent witness to centuries of history.

That evening, as we spoil ourselves by feasting on pizzas sprinkled with truffle oil in one of the many nearby restaurants, we marvel at the beauty and the history here.

'It makes Australia seem so young,' I say. 'It's incredible that the Europeans did and left so much. Aboriginal people have inhabited Australia for the past 65,000 years, yet there is so little to show for it. I don't know if that's a good or a bad thing.'

Our final days in Sarlat pass in a relaxing haze of eating nougat, exploring the surrounding countryside, and reading on our balcony. Someone has left a Harry Potter book behind, and I devour it in no time. The weather remains unpredictable—some days reach 30 degrees, while others bring rain and temperatures in the mid-teens. I find myself looking forward to heading further south, where the climate will be more consistent.

Eventually, our week in Sarlat comes to an end. Early on Wednesday, 24 May, we make our way to the train station. This time, there are no hiccups, and two and a half hours later, we arrive in Bordeaux, home to that world-famous red.

Bordeaux could not be more different from Sarlat. Where Sarlat is a small, enclosed medieval town nestled in the lush Dordogne hills, Bordeaux, with its 750,000 residents, sprawls across the banks of the River Garonne. Its coastal proximity means it's also noticeably warmer.

Google Maps tells us our hotel is a half-hour walk, but Darryl is feeling a little sore today, so we summon an Uber instead. As we head towards the centre of Bordeaux, we travel along grand boulevards lined with majestic 18th-century limestone buildings, some stretching the length of an entire block. Between them run a modern tram line and wide cycling paths, while open parklands and expansive squares break up the cityscape. It's an elegant mix of old and new, and it's little wonder we are instantly impressed by Bordeaux.

Our original plan was to spend just one night in Bordeaux, but maintenance work on the rail line—and the resulting cancellation of some services—has turned it into two. We are not at all unhappy about this; Bordeaux is, after all, the world's wine capital, and we both love good wine. Onward travel remains unaffected.

I have booked us into the Hotel des 4 Soeurs, right in the heart of the city. Housed in an elegant 18th-century building, it once served as the residence of the German composer Richard Wagner.

'Look, is that a Gordon Ramsay restaurant across the road?' Darryl says as we step out of the Uber.

'It looks like it,' I reply. 'I'll Google it—maybe we can have dinner there one night.'

Our room is on the fourth of five floors, with a view over tiled rooftops and genuine pigeon roosts. To get there, Darryl squeezes into yet another tiny lift—a feat in itself, considering these old buildings were constructed long before lifts even existed.

That afternoon, I leave him resting while I explore the neighbourhood. I have been itching for some retail therapy, and Rue Sainte-Catherine, Europe's longest shopping street, is right next to our hotel. At Kiko, I update my lipstick; at Etam, my underwear.

Dinner is a supermarket picnic: cheese, fruit, and fresh baguettes eaten on our beds with the plastic cutlery we have been carrying since Malaysia. Dessert is an enormous tub of ice cream, which I work through while browsing and then booking a half-day wine tour for tomorrow.

Breakfast is not included at our hotel, so we wander to a nearby café early the next morning for flaky croissants and large mugs of coffee. Next door, at the tourist information office, we meet our guide.

'Our tour today will take us to two renowned Classified Growth Châteaux—Cru Classé and Cru Bourgeois,' she explains.

'You'll learn how the wines are made and have the chance to sample them.'

Joining us are a young Slavic couple and an older British couple. While the British pair, like us, are happy to sit back and listen, the Slavic couple can't seem to stop interrupting, asking endless questions, and generally being a noisy distraction.

Heading northwest towards the Médoc region, home to thousands of hectares of Cabernet Sauvignon and Merlot vines, we visit two renowned châteaux. At each, we stroll through the vineyards, noting the stony soil and tiny new grapes, before moving on to the sheds where fermentation bubbles away in huge stainless-steel tanks, and the cool cellars lined with hundreds of barrels quietly ageing. Both visits end with refined tastings—more measured sipping and thoughtful analysis than the enthusiastic chugging we have known on some Australian wine tours.

On the return journey to Bordeaux, reflecting on what I have learnt—that vines thrive in poor soil and that climate change is already casting a shadow over the industry's future—I spy from our bus window two sights that bring home just how far we are from Brunswick Heads. The first is a group of pilgrims, small packs on their backs, walking along the roadside.

'Pilgrims on the Camino,' our guide explains.

The second is far more sobering—an enormous, grey concrete structure looming near the River Garonne.

'A Nazi submarine base from the war,' she adds.

The day, while informative, hasn't been strenuous, so that afternoon we wander further through Bordeaux. Our path takes us along the mighty Garonne, where long river cruise vessels line the banks. A two-week cruise along one of Europe's great rivers has been high on my wish list for years. We stroll through parklands, pause at intriguing sculptures, and marvel at the city's vast, imposing buildings.

'Apparently, 20 years ago these were filthy,' I read from my phone.

'In 1995, they began a programme to rejuvenate the city.'

Indeed, according to my research, just over 20 years ago, Bordeaux's buildings were dark and neglected. Abandoned warehouses crowded the riverfront, town squares were clogged with cars, and the view of the Garonne was blocked by a grim port. Today, it is a different city. The port has been moved, the façades scrubbed clean, the centre pedestrianised and a sleek tram network installed. The result is a city that's grand, easy to explore and a place I could return.

'I haven't booked, but let's see if we can get a seat at the Gordon Ramsay restaurant,' I say to Darryl as dinner time approaches.

'It'll probably cost a fortune, but the experience will be worth it,' he replies.

'Bonsoir. Do you have a reservation?' asks an immaculately dressed, slightly supercilious waiter.

'Um, sorry, no.'

A pause, a thoughtful hum.

'Oui, we can fit you in—if you don't mind eating outside.'

It's a cold, windy evening, hardly ideal, but it seems our only option.

'Merci. That's fine.'

The table we are given is wedged tightly among a long row of others. As we sit, we spot the noisy Slavic couple who have annoyed us all day, walk in.

'Oh, please don't let them sit next to us,' Darryl mutters—vainly, as the waiter starts leading them directly to the table beside ours.

'They obviously don't want to sit next to us either,' I laugh, when a few quickly muttered words see the waiter turn on his heel and seat them at the back instead.

Our waiter returns with water and menus, and for a few quiet minutes we study what's on offer.

'There's a lot of seafood,' I say, dismayed.

'Apart from a chicken burger for 33 euros, offal and lamb shanks, it's all seafood.'

'The lamb shanks look good, but I'm not sure I'm that hungry,' Darryl replies.

'And I'm not paying 50 Australian dollars for a burger.'

Annoyed at the limited choice, we do something rather embarrassing—we get up and leave. As we pass through the main doors, I can feel the eyes of everyone in the restaurant, including the Slavic couple, following us.

'That was really embarrassing,' I admit a short while later, 'but I'm glad we did it.'

'Please don't tell anyone,' is all Darryl says.

Although humiliating, it shortly proves to be the right decision. Tucked away in a small alley off Rue Sainte-Catherine, we stumble upon a cosy Italian bistro. For just 15 euros each, we are served heaping plates of spaghetti, enormous bowls of crisp salad and glasses of chilled rosé.

'I don't think we're going to forget tonight in a hurry,' says Darryl, as he finishes his meal.

'And I don't think we'll ever hear the name Gordon Ramsay again, without thinking of his restaurant here,' I laugh.

Our train does not depart until 11 am the following morning. Darryl is feeling rested, so with our bags trundling alongside us, we stroll down Rue Sainte-Catherine and turn left at Place de la Victoire, passing a funky bronze statue of an enormous tortoise. From here, it is only a short walk to the station. Our next destination is Arles—the town that inspired Vincent van Gogh and where some friends from Mullumbimby have recently relocated.

CHAPTER 13

Finding Vincent in Provence

Extract from Darma Travels Blog-

Arles is the town where Vincent van Gogh came in 1888 for inspiration. With its plethora of ancient monuments, pollution-free environment, and vibrant colours, he was able to produce an abundance of work here.

The journey ahead will take six hours, carrying us from the coastal reaches of western France south-east towards Provence and the Mediterranean. Before boarding, we search for the little yellow validation machines for our paper tickets—not as easy to spot here in Bordeaux as they were in Paris. Once underway, the hours slip by. My phone contains some books I have downloaded specifically for these journeys, but I find myself more often than not gazing out at the changing landscape. Vineyards gradually give way to drier fields, and the neat rows of brown stone houses shift to brighter, more colourful buildings. It is an easy, pleasant trip, and before we know it, it's early evening, and our train is pulling into Arles station.

Arles, population 52,000, was founded in the 7th century BC. Its position on the River Rhône made it a thriving trade hub, eventually growing into a major Gallo-Roman city. Today, many Roman remnants still stand, earning it UNESCO World Heritage status. We have chosen to spend five nights here for three reasons: it's a convenient stopover on our way to Italy, one of my favourite artists—Vincent van Gogh—lived and painted here and some friends of ours now live nearby.

Only a handful of passengers step off the train, and as most head in the same direction, we fall in behind. Leaving the station, we soon find ourselves walking along the banks of the mighty Rhône.

'Look—this is where Van Gogh painted *Starry Night Over the Rhône*,' I say, pointing excitedly to a small plaque.

'I'm more interested in how those huge riverboats fit under that bridge,' Darryl replies, eyeing the long vessels gliding towards the low span.

We follow the water a little further before turning sharply into what appears to be the remains of an ancient wall and gate—later we learn they are part of the Roman fortifications that once enclosed the entire city. Before long, we are thoroughly lost in a maze of narrow streets winding between centuries-old buildings. This feels like another of those medieval cities that are impossible to navigate.

'Time for Google Maps,' I say, pulling out my phone.

The Hotel du Forum, partly built in the 17th century, has appealed to us not only because of its excellent central location but also because of its outdoor pool area, where we can sit and linger over flaky croissants and coffee for breakfast. It is family-run, and after a warm welcome, Darryl rides a slightly more generous lift up to the second floor while I take the broad, ancient stone staircase. Our room is large, bright and airy. The notes of an expertly played piano drift in through the windows, mingling with the chatter of diners enjoying their evening meal. Hungry, we head straight back out in search of our own.

Just steps from our hotel entrance, patrons sit beneath the awning of a vivid yellow café. We somehow missed it on our arrival, but it is the Café du Forum—the very one made famous by Van Gogh's *Café Terrace at Night*.

'It looks almost exactly like the painting,' I say, unable to hide my delight.

The place is packed, so we wander on and soon settle at a nearby café, where steaming bowls of beef bourguignon are set before us. Under the stars, in this ancient town square, we savour each bite and watch the world go by, soaking in a scene that words cannot do justice.

As promised on the hotel's website, the outdoor pool is set in a leafy garden, enclosed by ancient stone walls that rise nearly 20 metres high. The next morning, we enjoy breakfast here while deciding how to spend the day.

'We need to catch up on some laundry,' Darryl says.

'There's a tourist pass from the information office that gives entry to one museum and four monuments for eleven euros,' I add. 'We could get one and use it whenever we want during our stay.'

'When's lunch with John and Alex?' Darryl asks.

'Tomorrow.'

Clean clothes are the priority, so shortly after breakfast, we set off through the narrow, winding streets in search of a laundromat. The sky is a glorious, cloudless azure, and our route takes us past Roman treasures, the theatre, the amphitheatre and the Cloître Saint-Trophime, making us look forward to later buying a pass.

Unlike the Sarlat laundromat, presided over by a large, friendly French woman, this one is entirely self-serve and has a distinctly dodgy feel.

'I think we should stay with our washing this time,' Darryl says.

'I agree.'

Our earlier wanderings took us past a supermarket, so with the washing now drying on our room fittings, we head back out to find it and pick up something for dinner. An hour later, thoroughly foiled by the labyrinth of Arles' streets, we give up and opt for refreshments instead.

'How about an ice cream or coffee at that café?' I suggest, pointing to a lively spot near the Place de la République.

'What's that?' Darryl exclaims moments later, as the waitress sets down the largest ice cream sundae I have ever seen.

'It looks ridiculous.'

'I didn't know it was going to be so big,' I protest. 'We can share it.'

Hot and hungry from trudging under the fierce Provençal sun, I had ordered this instead of a coffee like Darryl. Served in something that could pass for a glass bucket, it's piled high with ice cream, jelly, fruit, nuts, and cream. It's totally over the top and utterly delicious. We demolish it together, laughing the whole time at just how outrageous it is.

Fortified by our sugar hit, we succeed this time in finding the supermarket and happily load up with brie, baguettes, grapes, strawberries, water, biscuits, tomatoes, chocolate and wine. Walking back to our room, we notice that most shops, cafés and restaurants have shut for the afternoon siesta. Over the coming days, we learn just how much this affects our plans. The shops closing from noon to 2 pm is no great inconvenience, but the cafés and restaurants closing from 2 pm until 7 pm certainly is. Used to a late breakfast, we often do not think about lunch until well after 1 pm—only to find everything closed by the time we are ready to eat. More than once, we end up waiting until 7 pm, turning dinner into 'linner'—a combined lunch and dinner feast.

That afternoon, while Darryl rests in our room amongst the drying laundry, I set off to explore more of Arles. The Roman Amphitheatre—looking in better condition than the arena we saw in Rome years ago—immediately captivates me. Still in use today, this largest and best-preserved monument in Arles dates back to the first century. For now, I must be content with walking its perimeter, but I am already looking forward to returning with Darryl to explore its interior using our tourist passes. Outside the entrance, the usual souvenir shops line the street, and I amuse myself browsing through the kitsch on offer. I even buy a shopping bag decorated with Van Gogh's *Café Terrace at Night*.

Leaving the amphitheatre, I make my way towards the Roman Theatre. Along the way, a small picture of a scallop shell stops me in my tracks. The scallop shell is the iconic symbol of the Camino de Santiago, and I wonder if its presence here has something to do with the epic pilgrims' walk. It reminds me of the pilgrims I'd seen from the bus window back in Bordeaux, and I can't help but wonder if they, too, pass through this place. A quick Google search confirms it—much to my delight, I am walking along a section of the Arles Camino.

The Camino de Santiago, also known as the Way of St James, is the centuries-old Catholic pilgrimage to the cathedral in Santiago de Compostela, Spain. For over a thousand years, pilgrims have walked its routes, and the Arles Camino is one of the four main ones. My interest began years ago after seeing a film starring Martin Sheen. It wasn't a hit with critics, but I loved it. The idea of walking day after day on a path trodden by pilgrims for more than a millennium—staying in humble gîtes or albergues, discovering local towns and villages along the way—has never left me. I do not know if I will ever walk the entire Camino; the Arles route alone is nearly a thousand kilometres. But today, I am thrilled just to see the scallop shell in situ, to walk even a few steps along the path that begins here in Arles.

As often happens in communities, friendships sometimes begin through one's children. I first met Alex over 20 years ago, in a sandpit while collecting Pierce from day-care. She was there for Sam, the third of her four boys. Over the next decade, Alex, her husband John, Darryl, and I became regular weekend companions, cheering from the sidelines as Pierce, Sam, and the rest of the team played their local football matches. As the years passed and football faded from our children's lives, our catch-ups became less frequent, but the camaraderie forged on those sidelines never disappeared. So, when we learned Alex and John were building a new life in France, living out one of our own long-held dreams, we reached out.

This morning, Alex and John meet us in the square outside our hotel and drive us the 17 or so kilometres to Saint-Rémy-de-Provence, their new hometown. It has been a while since we last saw them, so the journey passes quickly as we catch up on everything—most notably, their decision to sell their Australian property and pursue a long-held dream of renovating a home in the South of France. They have bought a rundown 17th-century barn and are in the midst of transforming it into a residence, with part of it planned as a gîte to provide rental income. The property's olive orchard and ancient well only add to its appeal.

Before heading to their new home, we make a brief detour and come across a graceful building surrounded by manicured gardens. Alex and John tell us this is the asylum where Van Gogh committed himself after cutting off his ear. From his room here, he painted my favourite of all his works, *The Starry Night*.

Continuing into the French countryside, we pass orchards of apple and olive trees beneath a flawless blue sky. The scorching sun feels worlds away from the damp chill of London. In Saint-Rémy-de-Provence, we stop to buy baguettes and pastries for lunch, stretching our legs in the process.

'This building here is where Nostradamus was born,' Alex informs us casually.

Conversion of their new home is only partially complete, so after a thorough inspection, we drive the short distance to their current abode. Alex has prepared a feast of crusty baguettes, fennel salad and barbecued lamb, followed by delicate local pastries for dessert, all washed down with generous pours of rosé.

The afternoon drifts by in a warm haze of nostalgia as we sit on their patio swapping stories. Later, our drive back to Arles takes us within sight of the Alpilles, a small but striking mountain range of bare limestone, rock and scrub, where Alex and John often go hiking. It has been a wonderful catch-up, leaving us both envious of their new life and deeply grateful they have shared it with us.

Our third day in Arles finds us up early again, but this time, instead of lingering poolside, we head straight out onto the busy streets. We breakfast at a tiny café on a bustling footpath, people-watching as we enjoy the usual flaky croissants, fresh orange juice, and large mugs of coffee. At only three euros each, it feels like a bargain, and we agree we will return. The tourism office is close by, and before long, we have our passes in hand.

'Look at that sign. They offer free Van Gogh walking tours of Arles,' Darryl says, nodding towards a notice in reception.

'A fully guided tour visiting ten places connected to Van Gogh,' I read aloud. 'Sounds great. We could do it one evening before we leave.'

Today's plans keep us busy, starting with the Arles Amphitheatre and later the Cryptoporticus, or Arles Crypts. As I suspected from my earlier wanderings, the amphitheatre, built to seat 21,000 people, is in remarkable condition. The two-tiered structure is almost entirely intact, and we spend hours exploring its covered passages and both the outer and inner rings.

Our visit to the Arles crypts is both fun and enlightening. Like most Roman cities, Arles once had a Forum—a public square and meeting place—and our hotel, the aptly named Hotel du Forum, stands on its former site. The crypts are underground tunnels built as the Forum's foundation, meaning we have been sleeping directly above them.

A narrow staircase winds down into the depths, leading us into a long, cool, and gloomy stone chamber that branches into more shadowy rooms. Apart from the occasional tourist emerging unexpectedly from the dimness, there is little to see, but the excitement lies in wandering these ancient subterranean passages.

We end the day back at the Café Terrace at Night, where we feast on coq au vin, crisp salad and apple tart, and feel as if we are dining inside a page of history.

Our final days in Arles are spent browsing the sprawling local market and making full use of our tourist passes. At the Van Gogh Foundation, we are somewhat disappointed to find only a couple of small examples of his lesser-known works on display. The Saint Trophime Cloisters, dating back to the 12th century, are far more rewarding—especially the view from the roof. We linger there for ages, watching the shifting clouds and counting the number of vapour trails streaking the sky.

But our favourite site turns out to be the Départemental Museum of Ancient Arles. Housed in a strikingly modern building, it offers an extraordinary collection: sarcophagi, fragments of ancient, tiled floors, artefacts dating back more than 2,500 years, and even a 2,000-year-old Roman cargo boat, dredged from the Rhône River only six years ago. Walking among these treasures feels like stepping through a portal into the layers of Arles' long, remarkable history.

On our final evening, we take advantage of the free van Gogh walking tour—and it proves well worth it. Over the course of the evening, we visit ten sites around the city where the artist once set up his easel and created some of his masterpieces. Each is marked with a plaque, explaining, at last, the one I had spotted on the riverbank the night we arrived. Our guide is witty and engaging, brimming with knowledge not only about van Gogh but also about Arles itself. By the end, we feel as though we have seen the city through the artist's eyes, and we finish the day with even more appreciation for this remarkable place.

Up early the next morning, we have just enough time to duck back to the laundromat so I can give my only pair of walking shoes a much-needed wash. They are looking rather shabby, and this way they will have the entire day to dry while we make our way to Nice, our stop for the night.

As we wait for them to finish, the laundromat gradually fills. By the time the machine beeps, two or three people are hovering, clearly waiting for a turn.

'Why aren't they using my machine?' I whisper to Darryl.

'Once they saw you'd put shoes in there, they changed their minds,' he whispers back with a grin. 'They probably think you stepped in something.'

We both dissolve into laughter, still chuckling as we head back to the hotel to collect our bags. Soon after, we are walking to Arles station. We may not have spent quite a full week here in Provence, but I am happy to consider another bucket list item well and truly ticked.

The train from Arles to Nice is scheduled to take four hours, including a half-hour stop in Marseille. As we leave Arles, the view from our window is mostly green, scrubby bushland. The closer we get to Marseille, the more industrial it becomes, and by the time we roll into the station, my first impression is that this is a squalid industrial city. Graffiti is everywhere, and the buildings look tired and grey.

While we wait for our onward train, I need to use the station toilets and am horrified to find it costs me about $1.50 in Australian money for the privilege.

Something that has consistently fascinated me on our train journeys are the departure boards. They list destinations I have long dreamed of—Budapest, Milan, Warsaw, Naples—and they never fail to stir my imagination. Because trains only appear on the boards 20 minutes before departure, we stand with the crowd at Marseille station, scanning the list of far-flung places as we wait for our platform number to appear. Heavily armed guards patrol among the passengers, their presence a reminder that not all travel moments are as carefree as they seem.

Leaving behind dismal Marseille, the scenery improves with every kilometre. Soon the train is hugging the fabled Côte d'Azur, and we are lucky—our seats are on the seaward side, where the best views unfold.

The first flash of the Mediterranean draws an involuntary gasp. It feels like a lifetime since we last saw the sea, and I realise how much I have missed it. When the train pauses at Cannes, the name alone sends a ripple of excitement through me. We really are travelling through the French Riviera now.

It is still early afternoon when our train pulls into Nice Station. A quick Google search shows our hotel, the Best Western Alba, is only a ten-minute walk away. Exiting the station, we follow Avenue Jean Médecin, a wide boulevard lined with shops and department stores, running through one of Nice's main shopping precincts and ending at the Mediterranean. We find our hotel about halfway along and soon check in. Our little room is tucked high under the rafters.

'They've certainly made good use of space here,' Darryl observes.

'And I'm definitely going to hit my head if I need to get up in the night,' I reply.

With plenty of daylight left, we freshen up quickly and head back out. A supermarket across the road catches our eye, and we agree to return later to hunt for dinner supplies. For now, the pull of the Mediterranean is stronger. Knowing it lies just at the end of our street, we bypass the department stores and make straight for the sea.

Standing on the Promenade des Anglais, we cannot help but think of what happened here just ten months ago: 86 people killed and over 430 injured when a truck ploughed into crowds celebrating Bastille Day. The memory casts a shadow, made heavier by the sight of more armed guards. Yet, despite the horror, life has returned. The promenade is crowded with tourists, the beaches dotted with umbrellas, ice-cream stands doing a brisk trade, and people stretched out in the sun. Life, it seems, does move on.

Time slips by as we make the most of our single night in Nice—strolling the promenade, wandering the avenues and side streets, and gazing in awe at the yachts crowding Nice Harbour.

'I've heard about the boats owned by the rich and famous along the French Riviera,' I say, 'but these are beyond even what I imagined.'

As planned, we stop at the supermarket on our way back to the hotel. Our trusty Malaysian cutlery proves its worth once again as we feast on croque-monsieurs, yoghurt, biscuits and strawberries in our little room under the rafters.

It is with some regret that we check out of our hotel early the next morning. With its wide avenues, beautiful blue sea, elegant buildings, handy tram lines and near-perfect weather, Nice has been an unexpected surprise. Another night here would have been welcome. We stroll back to the station, stopping for freshly brewed coffee and two enormous almond croissants to sustain us through the day.

Today will be our most demanding train day yet—seven hours to reach Lucca, in Tuscany, with three train changes. Our first change is at Ventimiglia, and the view along the way is spectacular. We pause at Monte Carlo, where passengers board with their dogs—allowed on trains here—and then continue along a track so close to the Mediterranean it feels like we could trail our fingers in the water. The sparkling cerulean sea is just metres away, dotted with swimmers, sunbathers and the occasional stretch of black sand. Passing such legendary beauty from the comfort of our train seat feels surreal.

Departing Ventimiglia, our train comes to an unscheduled 20-minute stop. The change of crew makes it clear we have crossed into Italy, and the point is underlined when armed Italian guards and their sniffer dogs methodically move through each carriage. Our second change, in Genoa, is thankfully straightforward.

'Italy seems to have a lot more signage in English than France did,' I observe.

'That's good—we know even less Italian than French,' Darryl replies with a grin.

The final leg of our seven-hour journey takes us inland from Florence. Leaving the coast behind, the train glides past green fields, the occasional vineyard, glinting streams and neat rows of walnut orchards. Beyond them, to our surprise, rise substantial snow-topped mountains.

'Crazy that we can see snow—it's hot here,' I remark.

After a long day on the move, stepping off the train feels like a relief. We have arrived in Lucca, tucked within Tuscany's footprint, and will call it home for the next eight nights—another long-held bucket list dream, finally realised.

CHAPTER 14

Under the Tuscan Sun

Extract from Darma Travels Blog-
Whilst full of winding cobblestone streets and known as the city of over 100 churches, Lucca has shown itself to be a quirky, fun city with great food and great shopping.

As we step out of Lucca's train station, the view stops us in our tracks—a vast, unbroken expanse of brick stretching into the distance. From ground level, it appears to be crowned with trees, their green canopy stretching towards the horizon. This is the city's remarkable Renaissance wall, built in the 16th and 17th centuries to encircle and protect the historic centre. Eleven bastions and numerous gates punctuate its four-kilometre circuit, and passing through one of these gates, we find ourselves transported back in time.

Dating back to the Roman era, Lucca is the birthplace of composer Giacomo Puccini and one of Italy's best-preserved Renaissance cities. Within its walls lie medieval churches, graceful towers, and sunlit piazzas, each adding to the city's charm. We are here on the recommendation of my sister Michelle, along with advice from friends Big Bird and Anne. Michelle first came for the wedding of an old high school friend and returned to Australia full of praise for the place, insisting we include it in our travels. We have booked a room with a balcony for the next eight days and we are looking forward to watching life in Tuscany unfold below while soaking up the gorgeous weather.

Firing up Google Maps once again, we are guided deeper into the heart of Lucca. Our bags rattle over the cobblestones, each jolt making me wince for the wheels. At one busy junction, the strap on my lightweight sandal gives way.

'Well, if I'm going to have to buy new shoes, I'm glad it's here in Italy,' I laugh.

'Maybe we can get it repaired,' Darryl suggests.

'I need a new handbag as well,' I remind him—my current one broke just a few days ago.

'How convenient that you arrive in Italy needing new shoes and a new handbag,' Darryl quietly grumbles to himself.

A little further on, he asks, 'How much further? I thought you said it was close to the station entrance.'

'Well, it's meant to be,' I reply, glancing down at my phone.

It turns out that, for the first time on this trip, Google Maps has let us down. We about-turn and trundle back through Lucca, retracing our steps over the cobblestones. This time, with new shoes in mind, I pay more attention to the shopfronts we pass—gorgeous leather goods displays, inviting delicatessens and cosy little cafés spilling onto the street. We weave through a couple of buzzing piazzas and admire the façades of impressive churches.

'It's another one of those cities where we're going to get lost, but everything looks great,' I say.

'It definitely feels like we're not in France anymore,' Darryl replies. 'Everyone seems a little friendlier, and it's a bit cleaner.'

When we finally reach our accommodation, we discover it is only a few hundred metres from the entrance gate. We have, quite unnecessarily, walked the length of Lucca—though, given the city's small size, it has hardly been a long trek.

'They are expecting us,' I say to Darryl after pressing the bell several times with no response.

'What is this place anyway?' he asks, glancing around. 'It doesn't look like a hotel.'

'It isn't. I wanted somewhere with a balcony, and this is what we could afford,' I reply.

A few more presses later, the door suddenly swings open.

'Welcome to Residence il Duomo,' announces a young Italian man in halting English. 'I am Andrea. My wife, she is not here but she soon will be.'

As if on cue, a petite woman bursts into the room.

'Welcome to Residence il Duomo! I am Benedetta,' she practically shouts, her smile beaming. 'We are so glad you are here. Come, I will show you your room.'

What follows is a comedy Darryl and I will never forget. Benedetta sweeps us through a comfortable, slightly ageing apartment with a large kitchen, separate lounge, huge bedroom and—of course—the balcony. The facilities are more than we were expecting, but because of Benedetta, there's barely time to take them in. The volume of her voice is nothing short of ear-shattering, her words fly at supersonic speed, and every syllable is accompanied by a fine mist of enthusiasm.

We trail behind her in shell-shocked silence, nodding at intervals, until the door finally closes behind her. Darryl collapses onto the sofa.

'I don't think I've ever heard anyone speak so fast or so loudly,' he says, exhausted. 'I understood maybe half of it.'

'Half? I didn't catch a quarter,' I laugh. 'But I can't believe we have all this for the next eight nights. I thought we were only getting a room with a balcony. This is huge. We can cook. We can even catch up on all our washing.'

It's been a long day, so while Darryl rests, I head out in search of a supermarket and return laden with supplies: baguettes, brie, wine, strawberries and water. I also grab coffee (there are no fewer than three different coffee machines in our apartment), butter, juice, jam, yoghurt, some prepared hot roast vegetables, a couple of dips and washing powder.

That evening, we dine on the balcony, looking down onto a mosaic courtyard where a heavily laden orange tree dominates the space. The evenings are long here, with the sun setting well after 10 pm, and the spring air is perfect. Tuscany, so far, is everything we had hoped for.

The following morning, I'm up early for yoga. While I've managed a few sessions since arriving in Europe, there's been no real routine—something I plan to fix this week with all the space our apartment offers. Darryl is still sleeping when I finish, so I slip out in search of breakfast. Just around the corner, I find an irresistible bakery. The bread and pastries all look tempting, but it's the sight of a huge tray of vanilla slice on the counter that stops me in my tracks. Both of us love vanilla slice, and this one—oozing thick, creamy custard between perfect layers—might be the best I've ever seen.

'Due, per favore,' I manage.

'Grazie.'

Back at the apartment, I experiment with two of the coffee machines, the Moka pot and the automatic drip machine. I've never used a Moka pot before, and I want to see if I like it. We drink the copious quantities of coffee I have produced while feasting on fresh baguettes, jam, and thick slabs of vanilla slice.

'Where was that bakery?' Darryl asks, wiping a smear of custard from his mouth. 'I definitely want more of this.'

Our first day in Lucca is spent roaming the streets, trying to get a feel for the layout. It's hopeless—we give up on the idea of mastering it and accept that getting lost will just be part of the experience. When it happens, we simply keep walking, knowing that sooner or later we'll stumble back to our room.

At the tourist office, we're directed to a cobbler who repairs my broken shoe on the spot—and for free.

'Bugger. I was looking forward to buying a new pair,' I pout.

My handbag problem is also quickly solved when I find an almost exact replica of my current one, only larger and far nicer, in one of Lucca's many leather shops.

In a piazza just metres from our room, workers are busy erecting security fences and assembling a large stage. A banner announces that Green Day will be performing here—three days after we leave.

'It's so close to our room, I'm sure we would have been able to hear them,' Darryl says.

'It would have been good,' I reply, 'but I'm glad we'll miss the crowds. The town is going to be packed.'

That evening, deciding to spoil ourselves and eat out, we wander the streets, scanning menus and peering into doorways in search of the right Italian restaurant. We both love Italian food, so we want our first meal out here to be memorable.

We finally settle on a tiny place tucked among others on a lively piazza.

'I'm going to have the carne with spaghetti. I think that's spaghetti bolognese,' I say.

'I'll have lasagne,' Darryl replies.

When we place our order, we hit a problem over the salad.

'Yes, we'd like a salad,' I tell the waitress.

'I will bring it after,' she says.

'Could we have it with our main dish?' I ask.

'You want it with your lasagne? Not after?' she says, eyebrows rising.

'That's right—together with the spaghetti and lasagne.'

'Okay,' she says with a small tut, eyebrows still raised.

The food, when it arrives, is delicious—rich, comforting and perfectly paired with the wine we order. After so many days of cheese and baguettes, it is a welcome change. Full and happy, we make our way to the counter to pay. The space is crowded, so Darryl steps aside to make room.

'They just heat up the food in a microwave,' he splutters when I rejoin him.

'What?'

'Look. There's no kitchen. The waitresses just take the food out of the fridge and heat it up,' he says, nodding towards the space behind the counter.

'You're kidding!'

'No, I'm not.'

I watch in disbelief as a waitress pulls a dish from the fridge, pops it in the microwave, and then plates it up.

'Maybe let's not tell anyone about this,' I say at last. 'It's embarrassing how much we enjoyed it.'

While Lucca alone could easily keep us busy for our entire stay, it has some rather famous neighbours. Pisa is just a 25-minute train ride away, while Florence can be reached in around 80 minutes. Today's destination is Pisa, home to one of the biggest items on our bucket list—the Leaning Tower. I'm sure most people have heard of it, and many dream of seeing its famous tilt for themselves. This morning it's our turn. After a quick breakfast on the balcony, we are eager to be on our way.

The journey from Lucca to Pisa takes us along a different route from the one we arrived on, and the time passes quickly as we watch the scenery change. At Pisa, we fire up Google Maps—though there's really no need. Pisa station is heaving with tourists, all heading in the same direction. It feels almost like a pilgrimage as we join the steady stream moving through the streets, everyone wearing the same mix of eager and reverent expressions.

Taking 226 years to complete, construction of the Tower of Pisa started in 1173 on ground too soft to properly support the structure's weight. This, combined with inadequate foundations, caused the tower to tilt and consequently become the famous tourism icon it is today.

Our first sighting of this oddity catches us completely off guard. We turn a blind corner, and there it is—suddenly, unmistakably, in front of us, and instantly obvious that all the photographs in the world have failed to do it justice. It is so much more beautiful and leans so much more than I was expecting. Rising from a lawn of vivid green, the 56-metre white-marble structure gleams in the hot Tuscan sun.

'I didn't realise the Tower of Pisa was surrounded by so many other beautiful buildings,' I say to Darryl, taking in the striking white-marble cathedral and the great circular baptistry nearby.

'It all looks so gorgeous,' I add, and we stand for a while among the crowd, taking the obligatory photos before retreating to a shaded bench.

'This whole area is called the Field of Miracles,' I read from my phone. 'Apparently, Galileo was baptised in that baptistry—and both it and the cathedral are sinking too.'

'It's definitely been worth the journey,' Darryl replies.

We have been in Lucca for three days now and still have not set foot on the four-kilometre wall that encircles the city. The next morning, after breakfast and putting a load of washing on, we set out to find our way to the top of this imposing structure. A nearby ramp leads us up, and to our surprise, we find a broad avenue running along the wall—wide enough for a single-lane road. Rows of trees line each side, their shade falling over benches where people sit and chat. There are almost no cars here; it's mostly cyclists gliding past. In places, the wall widens into open spaces, and at one such point, we find a small café. We stop for morning coffee, watching children laugh and chase each other in the playground beside us.

Many of the eleven bastions can be explored, some housing photographs or sculptures by local artists. At one, we pause to watch water rushing through a wide channel, its steady current carrying a surprising force. Darryl, ever the former plumbing inspector, decides he will look into Lucca's water supply once we're back at the apartment. Further along, something else catches my attention.

'Look—The Rolling Stones are performing here in September,' I say, pointing to a stencilled sign marked with the band's unmistakable red lips.

'Imagine the crowds.'

We take our time along the tree-lined path, resting often on the plentiful benches, gazing out at the Tuscan countryside and the city's rooftops. The day slips by slowly, easily, and well.

One of the reasons my sister Michelle loved Lucca was the chance to attend a Puccini concert here every night at 7 pm. Giacomo Puccini, born in Lucca in 1858, is the town's most celebrated son and, after Verdi, arguably Italy's greatest composer. That evening, we take our seats in a nearby church and listen to selections from *Tosca*—one of his most famous works alongside *Madame Butterfly*, *Turandot*, and *La Bohème*. The soaring arias echo through the high stone arches, each note carrying with it the weight of history and the unmistakable beauty of Puccini's music.

The following morning, we set out with the idea of exploring the countryside. Darryl, still digging into Lucca's water supply, has discovered a nearby viaduct that has caught his interest. At first glance, it looks like something the Romans might have built, but in fact it is merely two centuries old. Completed in 1851, it carried water from mountains south of the city along a stone channel supported by more than 400 arches—a striking, if seldom visited, landmark.

'We'll find a spot on the way to buy some rolls and cheese,' I suggest.

'If we take a water bottle, there are places along the viaduct where we can fill it,' Darryl replies. 'Apparently, the water from the fountains here is fine to drink.'

I am not entirely convinced, but we toss an empty bottle into our pack.

According to Darryl's research, the viaduct starts not far from the station. Heading in that direction, we stumble across a tiny, solitary shop—the only one in sight—and somehow manage to emerge with everything we need: a slab of cheese, two crusty rolls, and a couple of apples.

'Amazing,' I remark. 'No other shops around, and yet we get exactly what we were looking for.'

Hoping we are on the right track, I show the shop owner a photo of the viaduct on my phone. His eyes light up and he starts nodding vigorously, arms flailing for emphasis.

'Si. Quel modo,' he calls. 'Là! Là!'

We take his enthusiastic pointing as confirmation, and sure enough, less than five minutes later, we come upon a large, round neoclassical structure of brick and stone. It looks like a holding tank, and from its side stretches a line of interconnected brick arches, each towering around 20 metres high, reaching towards the horizon. A narrow, well-worn path runs alongside the arches, and following it soon has us deep in the Tuscan countryside. Mid-spring has left the fields and scrub around us fresh and green, though there are hints of the dryness that summer will bring.

'There's a water fountain,' Darryl says, pointing to a metal spout pouring a steady stream into a stone basin. 'Let's fill the bottle.'

I take a sip and stop in my tracks.

'Wow. This is the best water I've ever tasted.'

And it truly is—cold, pure, and almost sweet. Later travels will show us that Europe's city fountains often provide water just as incredible, but this first taste remains one of the most memorable.

It takes us about 90 minutes before we come to the last of our brick arches, punctuated by another large, round brick holding tank. We have enjoyed plenty of stops along the way, captivated by fields of olive trees, meandering clear streams and the general beauty of the

Tuscan region. Crossing a small bridge, we have even been able to challenge one another to a few games of 'Pooh Sticks'.

There's a slight incline to reach the base of this holding tank, and from here, the views of the surrounding green countryside are breathtaking. Our simple picnic—slabs of cheese, crusty rolls, and crisp apples—tastes exceptional, washed down with the cold fountain water. Sitting here, legs stretched out in the sun, I can't help feeling like I've stepped into an Enid Blyton story, where the picnics are always perfect and the settings unforgettable.

Our return walk takes a little under an hour—there are fewer distractions this time. Back in our room, while Darryl rests, I turn on the television for the first time in days. Every news channel is covering a terror attack in London the day before. A van had ploughed into pedestrians on London Bridge before its occupants began stabbing people at nearby Borough Market. It is chilling to watch, and with both our children currently living in London, I do not relax until I have spoken to them and know they are safe.

After days of uninterrupted sunshine, we wake to a cold, blustery morning. Today we are bound for Florence, and after being so impressed with Pisa, we are eager to see what awaits us. I have long had a soft spot for Florence—birthplace of the Renaissance and home to extraordinary art, marble-clad basilicas, fresco-filled churches, elegant palaces and world-class museums—despite never having set foot there before.

Arriving at Florence's train station, our plan is to use Google Maps to navigate, but within minutes of stepping onto the narrow, cobblestoned streets, we realise this is wishful thinking. The city is swarming with tourists, many of whom move in tight clusters, their eyes fixed on the placards held aloft by their guides. With footpaths barely wide enough for two people and the constant shuffle of large groups, progress is slow. For Darryl, walking stick in hand, it is especially frustrating. I eventually pocket my phone and duck into a nearby boutique hotel, emerging with an old-fashioned paper map. Top of our must-see list is the Galleria dell'Accademia, home to Michelangelo's masterpiece, David—one of our most anticipated bucket list sights.

Our map shows the gallery is close, and pushing through the crowds, we soon reach the tail end of what looks like yet another impossibly long European queue.

'Should we bother?' I ask Darryl.

'I'm not going to manage that queue, and I'm not sure we can skip it,' he replies.

'I think I read that there's a replica of David in the spot where the original once stood,' I say. 'We could go there instead.'

'That sounds much better,' he agrees.

Any lingering disappointment fades the moment we turn away and see just how far the line stretches—snaking around corners and disappearing into the distance. We would have been standing there for hours.

Heading toward the Piazza della Signoria, where the replica David is said to stand, our way is suddenly claimed by one of the most extraordinary buildings I have ever seen. Rising 114 metres into the sky, clad in panels of pink, green, and white marble, is the 800-year-old Cattedrale di Santa Maria del Fiore—the Duomo. With its intricately carved Gothic façade, towering marble bell tower, and vast red-tiled dome, it stops us in our tracks. We wander slowly around its perimeter, taking in every detail, as do the many other visitors wandering awestruck beside us. Among the crowd, I notice a number of heavily armed guards.

'There are a lot of guards here,' Darryl observes.

'After what happened in London this week, I think there needs to be,' I reply.

Indeed, visiting this highly touristic destination so soon after another terrorist attack has made me feel slightly anxious. With its beautiful buildings and flocks of tourists, Florence feels like a place where an attack could very likely happen.

Lunch is at a tiny sidewalk café, where a steaming plate of spaghetti bolognese not only warms us but gives us the energy to face Florence's crowded streets again. That walking stick tip I convinced Darryl to buy back in Malaysia has finally disintegrated on the cobblestones, and, as we leave the café, we spot a shop that seems like an answer to our problem.

'Look—this place sells things for the elderly and disabled,' I say in surprise. 'Those tips from Malaysia are useless. Let's see if they have a better one.'

Inside, we find exactly what we need. At 22 euros for two (a far cry from the 70 cents we paid for the others), the shopkeeper assures us these tips will survive Florence's streets.

'Well, I never thought I'd be buying a walking stick tip in Florence,' Darryl laughs as we step back outside. 'At the very least, it's a memento of our day here.'

We eventually find the replica David and decide it's a worthy stand-in for the original, happily ticking off another item from our bucket list. Not far away, we pass the entrance to the Uffizi Gallery, its striking façade a promise of the treasures within. I would love to wander its halls and see Botticelli's *Birth of Venus* in person, but this trip has taught me that I can't do everything. The Uffizi will have to wait for another time.

From here, we stroll alongside the River Arno until we reach the Ponte Vecchio. Believed to date back to Roman times, this medieval stone bridge—its closed arches lined with jewellers and souvenir shops—has starred in more than a few films. We make it perhaps 30 metres before the crush of people becomes too much, and we turn back.

Having seen some of Florence's most beautiful sights, we make our slow way towards the station. The crowds have been exhausting at times, but there's no denying it—Florence is breathtaking. It's the kind of place we could return to, given more time, to immerse ourselves fully in its galleries, museums and remarkable architecture.

Our last days in Lucca drift by in an easy rhythm—browsing little Italian shops, lingering over coffee in sidewalk cafés, and taking life at a slower pace. The kitchen and balcony get plenty of use, our meals, a mix of delicatessen treasures and supermarket finds, eaten with a view of the orange tree in the courtyard below. While we return to the little bakery shop many times, it never again stocks that incredible vanilla slice.

On our final evening, we choose a small restaurant beside the church where the Puccini recitals are held. From our table, we can hear the soaring notes for free, the music drifting across the square as we dine. And early the next morning—after one last booming farewell from Benedetta—we wheel our bags back to Lucca station, reluctant to leave but ready for what lies ahead. Venice is calling.

CHAPTER 15

Towards the Sound of Music

Extract from Darma Travels Blog-
 So, this has been Venice, where the senses are assaulted on every level. It's been tacky but beautiful. Smelly, crowded and noisy but also mystical, romantic and an enigma. It's a place that we have enjoyed visiting but have no need to return.

Today's journey takes us eastward across Italy to Venice, our home for the next three days. We change trains at Florence, where the incoming service demands a photo—gleaming red, with an elongated bullet nose that looks fast and futuristic. It promises to cover the distance in just two hours, and it does. Time slips by, and as we approach the causeway linking Venice Island to the mainland, our excitement builds.

 Venice is made up of more than 100 small islands scattered across a lagoon of the Adriatic Sea. Since childhood, I have been enchanted by tales of this floating city where gondolas glide along canals instead of cars driving along roads. Stepping into Venice's Santa Lucia Station, a large, rather modernist structure, we pass through its wide exit and are met instantly by a scene that feels plucked from a painting: canals, bridges, and historic façades stretching away before us. Our immersion into this waterbound wonderland is immediate.

I have booked a hotel nearby, and once again, we fire up Google Maps to guide us to the Residenza al Doge Beato, our home for the next two nights. It doesn't take long to realise that Venice is not going to be particularly kind to Darryl. Not having given much thought to the fact that if you rely on waterways, you must have bridges, we are dismayed when we are constantly presented with them. It's not so easy lugging a suitcase up a flight of stairs and down the other side, especially with a walking stick. Add in the glare of the Italian sun, and the whole exercise becomes not just tiring but hot and exhausting.

We are relieved when Google Maps announces we have reached our destination after 20 minutes, yet there is no sign of anything resembling a hotel. The meandering, narrow, water-lined alleys we followed here have opened onto a small square with a well-stocked supermarket, a fantastic little bakery, and a scattering of cafés—but no accommodation in sight.

'Maybe give them a call,' Darryl suggests.

'Hopefully they speak English,' I reply.

To my relief, the call is answered immediately by someone whose English is fluent. After a brief exchange, they inform me that the entrance is through a small door in a large wall directly behind us. Only then do we spot the discreet plaque marking the place.

'Well, this is different,' Darryl remarks.

Pushing open the small but solid door, we step into a dim, musty corridor. To reach the Residenza al Doge Beato, we climb a flight of crumbly, ancient stone steps—there is no lift. Bernard, the proprietor, greets us warmly and shows us to our room: spacious, lined with floor-to-ceiling gold wallpaper, and furnished with pieces that have clearly seen better decades. The balcony we chose has come at the cost of an en-suite, our bathroom located a few metres down the corridor. Still, when I push the curtains aside and see gondolas gliding along the nearby canal, it feels like a worthwhile trade.

After a quick rundown of the area—and the revelation that we are staying in a 600-year-old building, part of which is home to Venetian locals—Bernard hands us a map and heads off. He does not live on site. We are on our own.

As on our arrival anywhere, our first priority is to locate the nearest supermarket and stock up on supplies. While Darryl rests—climbing so many sets of stairs has taken its toll—I head back to the store we spotted earlier. I load up on our usual staples, adding a concession to Italy with a few slices of pizza. On the walk back, I notice a water fountain; a quick sip confirms it is nearly, though not quite, as good as Lucca's. With plenty of goodies to choose from, delicious water to drink, and our trusty Malaysian cutlery once again proving its worth, we enjoy a late lunch on our lovely little balcony.

Despite Venice being at the top of our bucket list, now that we are here, we do not feel the need to tick off an endless list of sights. For us, the excitement lies in finally arriving—in seeing with our own eyes a city without streets. The few places we do hope to visit are the Rialto Bridge, Saint Mark's Basilica, and the Piazza San Marco. According to our map, they are all within easy walking distance.

Rested and replete from our late lunch, we set out into the cooling evening. The streets are alive with chatter, the cafes and footpaths packed with both Venetians and visitors.

'Everyone seems to be drinking that orange drink,' I say to Darryl as we stroll, recalling that I had first noticed it in Lucca. 'I definitely want to find out what it is and try one.'

'Let's just get to St Mark's Square first,' Darryl replies. 'There's a sign pointing to the Rialto Bridge—this way.'

It is fortunate that clear signage points the way to Venice's most popular sights, because navigating its labyrinth of footpaths quickly becomes more challenging the further we walk. Without obvious landmarks, our map is useless, with the paths twisting into a confusing maze. Adding to the challenge are the heaving crowds, sudden dead ends where a lane meets a canal, and the constant need to haul ourselves over yet another bridge.

After what feels like hours, though in reality it is barely 30 minutes, we finally step onto the Rialto Bridge. Lined with shops, this marble, single-span bridge has stood since 1591 and offers some of the best views of the Grand Canal from its summit. Yet, despite the stunning view, the pushing and shoving from the crowds eager to claim the same vantage point quickly curtails our stay. Feeling slightly battered, we follow a sign towards Piazza San Marco.

'I didn't know what to expect in Venice, but I never imagined shop-lined footpaths jammed with this many people,' I remark.

'And so many dead ends,' I groan, as we once again retrace our steps to avoid a canal with no bridge.

'There's no way we could find our way back to our room without the phone.'

'Well, this looks pretty good anyway,' Darryl says when we finally arrive at Venice's most famous square. We are standing in the Piazza San Marco, surrounded by some of the most ornate and beautiful buildings I have ever seen. From the riot of domes and arches crowning Saint Mark's Basilica to the vast Gothic landmark of the Doge's Palace, it is easy to see why this square is considered one of the finest in the world. Built in the Venetian Gothic style, the Doge's Palace was once the residence of Venice's military leader. Today, it is not only one of the city's most iconic landmarks but also a museum.

We take our time wandering the vast area, admiring the architecture and enjoying the live music drifting from a few of the elegant cafés. Unsure how long it will take to navigate our way back, and lacking the energy for deeper exploration, we decide to leave further sightseeing for another day and begin the journey home. Along the way, we browse a mix of kitsch souvenir stalls and glittering fine-glass boutiques.

The glassware, with its vibrant colours and flawless craftsmanship, holds our attention. For centuries, artisans on the Venetian island of Murano have been perfecting their techniques, creating everything from delicate figurines to ornate sculptures, tableware and wine stoppers. Wanting a keepsake of our time here, we settle on a small Murano glass wine stopper featuring a tiny orange 'Nemo' fish. It is cute, sturdy enough to survive the rest of our travels, and—thankfully—within budget.

Although breakfast is included in our booking, when we wake up the following morning, there is no sign of it, so we wander down to the little bakery we spotted yesterday. Darryl chooses a generous slab of cheesy pizza while I try what the waitress describes as a cheese-and-spinach–filled strudel. Large, fortifying coffees complete the meal.

We eat outside in the small square, watching the morning traders go about their work. Conversation drifts to some of the differences we've noticed here.

'Did you notice there's no garbage bin in our room?' I say. 'Just a sign telling us to leave it for the housemaid to sort.'

'They seem to take recycling more seriously than we do,' Darryl replies, nodding towards men wheeling refuse in large trolleys.

'I suppose on an island surrounded by water, you have to think carefully about waste,' I say. 'Even the straws are paper, not plastic.'

Darryl points out a couple walking their dog. 'Poor things—no parks, no trees. They'll never get to pee on a tree or roll in the grass, just the cobblestones.'

'Same for kids,' I add. 'No grass to kick a ball on. And with all those bridges and steps, pushing a pram here would be a nightmare.'

A large part of the afternoon is spent wandering along the Grand Canal, ducking into quiet little squares and soaking up the atmosphere.

A small market draws us in with its mix of quirky stalls, and a pair of brazen seagulls puts on a show, swooping in to steal a tourist's lunch.

'Look at the size of that seagull,' I exclaim. 'It's the biggest I've ever seen!'

'They're all that size,' Darryl replies. 'They can't be the same breed as ours back home.'

Lunch comes from a tiny takeaway stand serving fresh pasta. For just five euros each, we watch our spaghetti bolognese cooked before our eyes and packed into cute cardboard boxes. If we were not leaving tomorrow, I suspect we would be here every day—it's that good.

'I know one should have a gondola ride when they visit Venice,' I reflect as we pause on a bridge, watching a steady stream of them glide beneath our feet.

'It's something I always imagined doing, but at $120 Australian for just half an hour, I'm not sure it's worth it.'

'I don't want one either, but I will if you do,' Darryl replies.

'Look at how crowded the canals are, and how slow they're moving. Half an hour won't get you far—you'd spend most of it stuck in a gondola queue.'

He's right. As we watch, we see gondolas waiting their turn to pass under bridges, stalled at busy junctions, or drifting along in convoys five boats deep. It's nothing like the romantic vision I've carried here—the one painted by films, TV, and stories.

'I think I'd rather put $120 towards a good meal or another experience,' I conclude, a little regretfully.

Not far from our room, I spot a cluster of lively cafés, their tables full of people acting like contented pigeons—perched and sipping that vibrant orange drink. That evening, after a short siesta, we wander back and choose one to settle into.

'What are those orange drinks called?' I ask our waiter, discreetly nodding towards a nearby table.

'Aaah… Spritz,' he says.

'Sorry, a what?'

'Aperol Spritz,' he repeats.

'Aperol Spritz. What's in it?'

'Prosecco, Aperol, e soda,' he replies.

'That sounds perfect. I'll have one, please.'

And so begins my affair with this slightly bitter but wonderfully refreshing drink. One sip, and it is easy to see why it's so popular in the heat of a European summer.

'You should try one,' I say to Darryl.

'I'll stick to beer,' he answers without hesitation.

Our two nights in Venice are over. With our train not leaving until just before noon, we retrace our steps to St Mark's Square for one last look, capturing a few final photos before returning to check out. Bernard greets us with an apology for not warning that breakfast is no longer provided and knocks a sizeable amount off our bill. While we have thoroughly enjoyed our stay, the constant battle with the crowds has taken its toll. So it's with a touch of relief that we board our train bound for Austria. By tonight, we will be among the Austrian Alps, in the town of Villach.

The journey from Venice to Villach takes three and a half hours. The first hour is spent crossing the drier plains of northern Italy before the train begins its gradual climb into the Alps. We hardly notice the incline itself, but the change in scenery is unmistakable.

Craggy, snow-covered peaks appear on the horizon, their bases thick with dark green conifers. Long tunnels throw us into sudden darkness, only to bring us out into views of steep gorges and fast-flowing icy rivers. Each time, the landscape feels more dramatic than the last.

Our book and sudoku are soon forgotten. With noses pressed to the window, we sit quietly, taking in the incredible views—a welcome release after the crowded, enclosed atmosphere of Venice.

At the border between Italy and Austria, the train comes to a halt and armed guards with dogs make their way through the carriages.

Just a few seats in front of us, three young men, who appear to be of African origin, are heavily questioned. When it is discovered that they are not carrying passports, they are escorted from the train. From my window, I watch as more armed guards close in around them. Heated arguments follow, but the guards seem to win. The last I see of the men is them being led away through the station.

It's around 5 pm on an exceptionally warm Saturday evening when we disembark at Villach station. We have chosen to pause our journey here, partly to give Darryl a rest, but also because the only train leaving Venice for Salzburg on a Saturday does not arrive until very late. We would prefer not to be hunting for our accommodation in the dark.

Villach, with its population of about 61,000, lies on the Drava River. In summer, it draws hikers and cyclists, while in winter it is a gateway to ski fields and the Villach Alps. Midway between Venice and Salzburg, it seems a sensible place to break the journey—and we can only hope our decision proves a good one.

Our accommodation is only a few hundred metres from the station. As we walk towards it, it is immediately clear that we have left the relaxed flamboyance of Italy behind and arrived in a more conservative, far cleaner Austria. Although it is still early evening, the surrounding shops are already closing—something unheard of in Italy or France.

The Altstadt Hotel Mosser, our hotel, turns out to be a large, sprawling building in the Austrian style. After a quick and easy check-in, we enter our room and make two discoveries. The first is the bedding arrangement: while we are familiar with two single beds pushed together to make a queen or double, here we also find two doonas, one for each of us. Later, we learn this is standard practice in Austrian and German hotels.

Our second discovery is less welcome. Though the room has air conditioning, there is no remote control to use it. With Europe gripped by an unprecedented heatwave and our room's tiny windows barely opening, the air feels stifling.

'Excuse me, but we can't find the remote for the air conditioning in our room,' I ask at reception a short time later.

'No, we only put them in for heating during winter,' comes the reply.

'But the room's really hot—we'd like to turn the air conditioning on.'

'The air conditioning? But we never use that,' the receptionist responds, surprised. After a pause, she adds, 'But I expect we can find one and have it delivered to your room.'

That evening, we take a long walk around Villach. Despite its size, the city centre feels compact, the highlight for us being a small park that has an area set aside for bees.

Not far from our hotel, the wide Drava River meanders through town. As we stroll along its banks, we witness the most spectacular sunset. With the Austrian Alps looming around us, the sky shifts through deep reds and golds before softening into a glowing pink. I had not expected the mountains to feel quite this breathtaking.

None of the restaurants we pass appeal, so we return to our hotel, whose on-site restaurant offers a solid menu of Austrian dishes. Darryl opts for a hearty wiener schnitzel, while I order beef goulash, finishing with a slice of warm apple strudel.

The following morning, after a leisurely breakfast in the hotel dining room—already busy with summer hikers—we return to Villach Station for the next stage of our journey.

We have been looking forward to this leg. Weeks earlier, we had received an email, written entirely in German, advising that part of the route was closed for track maintenance and that a bus would replace the train. With our German limited, it took some deciphering, but we eventually understood the gist. Hoping the transfer point would be obvious, we board the train, find our seats, and soon begin what turns out to be the most breathtaking ride yet.

Clinging to the mountainside, the track winds ever upward. Far below, an icy river snakes its way through a fertile valley, while scattered across the slopes are neat Austrian houses and fields of contented cows. Towering above it all are snow-capped peaks, brooding and beautiful.

'It looks like an advert for chocolate,' I sigh, unable to look away.

'I'd love to see this in winter,' Darryl adds.

To our relief, the transfer point for buses is well marked, and we are quickly on our way again. The detour carries us through tiny Austrian villages, each one picture-perfect in its own right.

'We wouldn't have seen this from the train,' Darryl points out, and he is right.

An hour later, we rejoin the train, and before long, Salzburg Station comes into view.

Salzburg, whose early wealth came from the salt (salz) mined nearby, is famous for three very different exports: Red Bull, which originated here; *The Sound of Music*, which was filmed here; and, of course, Mozart, who was born here. The city itself is divided not only by the icy, fast-flowing Salzach River but also in style—its medieval and baroque old town on the left bank facing the more orderly 19th-century streets of the right.

Our hotel, the Hotel Krone 1512, sits on the right bank, directly across from the churchyard where the Mozart family graves are found. At check-in, the receptionist greets us warmly.

'You are on the third floor, and we have a lift,' she says. 'We also have croissants each morning for one euro. And you will soon get used to the clock.'

'What does she mean by the clock?' Darryl whispers as we head towards the lift.

'No idea,' I reply, laughing.

Of all our accommodation so far, the Hotel Krone 1512 is the dingiest—yet certainly not the cheapest—reinforcing the idea that Salzburg is an expensive city to visit. With little desire to linger in our room and our stomachs growling after the early morning adventure across the Austrian Alps, we drop our bags and set off in search of lunch. The streets are a gallery of Gothic, Renaissance, Baroque, and even modernist architecture, each style layered upon the next. But no matter where we look, our eyes are inevitably drawn upward to the formidable Hohensalzburg Castle, its medieval bulk looming over the city like a watchful guardian.

Constructed from 1077 onwards, Hohensalzburg Castle is one of the largest medieval strongholds in Europe. Perched 500 metres above Salzburg, it dominates the skyline and leaves an unforgettable impression. At a cheerful little café near the river, with the castle looming above us, we ease our hunger with generous wiener schnitzels, creamy potato salad and tall steins of lager.

Tired from a long day in the hot sun, we collapse into bed early that night. Almost immediately, the mystery of the receptionist's 'clock' remark becomes clear. Three bell towers sit close to our hotel, and instead of chiming just on the hour, they strike every 15 minutes.

'My god. I'm glad we're only here two nights,' Darryl mutters as the cacophony begins.

'We'll get used to it,' I reply, fingers crossed under the covers.

Salzburg is a city where what you choose to see depends largely on your musical taste. If you favour *The Sound of Music*, you can visit the sites where the film was shot or even take a dedicated tour. If Mozart is more your style, the city is overflowing with places tied—sometimes loosely—to his life. With Darryl having no preference, he goes along with mine, which in this case is Mozart.

By mid-morning, we are wandering among the tombstones of the nearby Saint Sebastian Cemetery in search of the Mozart family grave. While Wolfgang Amadeus himself is buried somewhere in Vienna's St Mark's Cemetery, many of his family members rest here. It doesn't take long to locate their tomb—we simply follow the cluster of photo-snapping tourists.

From the cemetery, we make our way into Salzburg's Old Town, once again simply following the stream of tourists. Before long, we are standing outside a striking yellow house. This, we learn, is where Mozart was born and spent part of his youth. Now a museum, it holds personal items such as his childhood toys and even some of his original keyboards.

Our wanderings eventually lead us to Café Sacher, an elegant hotel café long favoured by celebrities including Tom Hanks and the Dalai Lama. Here we indulge in generous slices of Sachertorte, the city's famous chocolate cake layered with apricot jam and coated in glossy chocolate. It is every bit as rich and indulgent as its reputation suggests.

The afternoon is spent resting in our room in preparation for the evening ahead. Much to Darryl's dismay, I have booked a 'Night of Mozart' tour, which involves a boat ride along the Salzach, then dinner followed by a Mozart concert. The only reason he has agreed to attend, is because both dinner and the concert will take place in the incredible Hohensalzburg Castle.

While the boat ride is fairly mediocre, the rest of the night more than makes up for it. To reach the castle, we board the 120-year-old Festungsbahn funicular, which climbs over 100 metres in under a minute. Stepping out at the top, we are greeted with a breathtaking panorama of Salzburg and the surrounding countryside. With the sun beginning to slowly sink over the far horizon, we couldn't have timed our arrival here more perfectly, and eyes and cameras are kept busy as we take in the mesmerising sight.

After a decadent three-course dinner, we climb to the very top of the castle. Sitting in a darkened hall with the moon rising through the nearby windows, lulled by the music of Mozart, Haydn and Strauss, the night is truly unforgettable.

For a second night, our sleep is broken again and again by the relentless chiming of the nearby clocks. By the time morning arrives, we are simply grateful that our stay at the Hotel Krone has come to an end. Salzburg has been educational and its scenery is nothing short of spectacular, but we are ready to move on. Ahead lies Vienna—just two and a half hours east by train across Austria.

CHAPTER 16

A Theme Park Called Prague

Extract from Darma Travels Blog-
It's nearing the stage where we constantly need to keep asking, where are we? what day is it? Four months of constant travel can obviously result in total disorientation.

While not quite as dramatic as our earlier journey over the Austrian Alps towards Salzburg, today's trip has still been spectacular. The endless sweep of lush green meadows dotted with fat, contented cows has kept us entertained for hours. So too has the unexpected sight of a group of little kids glued to a television in what must be the first—and perhaps only—play area I have ever seen on a train. Lunch is simple: a sandwich and coffee picked up from the buffet car.

Once again, our accommodation—the Motel One Wien Staatsoper—is within walking distance of the station, and we are relieved to find it large, modern and spotlessly clean. After the shabby, noisy nights at the Hotel Krone, this feels much more to our liking. We pause only long enough to drop our bags and freshen up before heading back out. With late afternoon settling in, it is the perfect time to begin our exploration of Vienna's city centre.

According to my phone, the centre is only a short walk away, and our route will take us past the Vienna State Opera. We have chosen Vienna for several reasons. Attending an opera is certainly one, but so too is tracing the footsteps of musical greats such as Mozart, Beethoven, Haydn and Strauss. Add to that the chance to eat more schnitzels and to see for ourselves why Vienna has been voted the world's number one city for 'quality of life' eight years running.

It is easy to recognise the Vienna State Opera when we come across it. It's the beautiful 1869 Renaissance structure with enormous modern audio-visual screens mounted on its façade showing Rigoletto. With no hurry to be anywhere, we slip onto a vacant bench and, like dozens of others gathered, sit back to enjoy the performance. Knowing that we can repeat this over the next two nights, we surrender our seats at intermission and wander deeper into Vienna's city centre.

The centre of Vienna has been given over to pedestrians and, known as Stephansplatz, is now one vast dining and shopping mall. Rising proudly at its heart is the extraordinary Gothic-inspired St Stephen's Cathedral. First completed in 1160, it is remarkable that it still stands at all, having been almost destroyed during World War II. Reaching it, we stop in awe before stepping inside for a quick look. The vast interior leaves us marvelling at the 18 ornate altars, the intricately carved stone pulpit and the strange, almost mischievous faces peering out from the walls. As we walk across the ancient flagstones, it is impossible not to think about the remains of more than 10,000 people lying in chambers beneath our feet.

Feeling hungry after our meagre lunch, we decide to skip any further exploration of Vienna and instead turn to the *Find Near Me* app to locate a supermarket. Before long, we are wandering the aisles, stocking up on supplies. Along with the customary bread, we pick up a container of fresh salad, some crumbed chicken and a couple of generous slabs of cake that look far too good to leave behind. Back in our room, after hand-washing a small load of laundry, our supermarket dinner goes down exceptionally well.

After a traditional Austrian breakfast, our plan for the day is to make our way slowly towards the Natural History Museum. The museum is home to the Venus von Willendorf, a tiny stone figure of a curvaceous woman carved around 29,500 BC. At nearly 30,000 years old, it is one of the world's oldest known pieces of art, and I have been eager to see it. According to Google Maps, the walk should take just over 20 minutes—but distracted by all we encounter along the way, it ends up taking us several hours.

We wander along Vienna's spacious footpaths, passing one grand museum or palace after another. Every so often, the streets open into beautiful squares, and everywhere we look, the city seems seamlessly linked by what is often described as the world's best metro system. Well-preserved Roman ruins catch our attention, and we pause to refill our bottles at fountains pouring out cold, fresh water. Adding to the atmosphere, strains of music drift from open windows or rise from the instruments of street performers, while elegant horse-drawn carriages clip-clop past. Many of these features can be found in other cities such as Rome or Paris, yet here it is the spotless streets and the sense of order that, to my mind, set Vienna apart.

Arriving at the Natural History Museum—an imposing building that houses more than 20 million objects—we spend the better part of the day exploring its vast collections. Afternoon tea in the elegant onsite café provides a welcome pause before we round things out with a restful show at the planetarium.

The museum is cleverly structured to take you on a journey from the Big Bang through to space exploration, making it one of the most informative and easy-to-navigate museums I have ever visited. The real meteors, glittering gold cabinet, and towering dinosaur skeletons are all impressive, but it is the tiny Venus von Willendorf—an 11-centimetre stone figure carved nearly 30,000 years ago—that makes my day.

'I need to lie down, but if you want to continue exploring, go ahead,' says Darryl later that afternoon.

'I wouldn't mind,' I reply. 'Apparently, there's a department store a few blocks away. I'd like to see what one here looks like.'

So, while Darryl rests, I wander through what seems to be Vienna's university quarter, full of students and bicycles. A short walk later, I arrive at a large department store. Inside, it feels much like a David Jones or Myer—until I notice one surprising difference. Many shoppers have dogs with them, leads in hand, tails wagging. I have never seen dogs in a department store before, and the sight leaves me quietly astonished.

Following another value-for-our-euro breakfast, we step once more into the streets of Vienna. The heatwave lingers, and a quick Google search has pointed us towards a nearby park threaded by the Danube Canal. Stadtpark, when we reach it, is a calm green haven of shady trees, grassy lawns and duck-filled ponds. We find the canal, a waterway branching off from the mighty Danube, and stroll slowly along its banks, grateful for the faint breeze drifting from its surface.

Continuing along the canal, we pass restaurants set on floating pontoons and even an artificial sandy beach, where we laugh at sunbathers stretched out on deckchairs as if the Danube were the Mediterranean.

'Rather than head back to the hotel, let's be pigeons?' I suggest, hot and thirsty from our wandering. 'We could write some postcards too.'

What begins as a quick beer and an Aperol Spritz soon turns into a late lunch of (more) Wiener schnitzels with chips, eaten at a café in the Stephansplatz while we scribble postcards and watch the world go by.

'They clearly haven't introduced no-smoking laws in restaurants here,' Darryl grimaces, waving away a drifting cloud of smoke.

'Yes,' I agree. 'Strange how Europe is so far behind Australia in that regard.'

For our final meal in Vienna, we set out in search of Wienerwurst, the traditional pork-and-beef sausage that carries the city's name. We find it at a simple cart in the Stephansplatz and eat standing in front of the Plague Pillar, the 21-metre-high Baroque monument raised in memory of the 75,000 locals who perished during the plague of 1679. The setting feels heavy with history, but the sausages are delicious, and when washed down with cold Ottakringer beer, they become the best meal we have had in Vienna.

The journey from Vienna to Prague, today's destination, takes four hours. In preparation, we revisit a local supermarket on our way back to the central train station and stock up on supplies. While the trains invariably have plenty of food to purchase, we enjoy bringing our own picnic. Most trains we have travelled on so far have had a table between our seats, making it easy to spread things out. We load up on bread rolls, cheese, chicken, and salad, and add a packet of chocolate biscuits. With bottles refilled from one of Vienna's many fountains, we have the makings of a great meal.

Vienna's central station does what so many others have done on this journey: thrill me with its display of far-flung destinations. The platform number for our train soon appears, and we make our way aboard.

It doesn't take long after crossing from Austria into the Czech Republic to notice subtle differences outside the window. Formerly Czechoslovakia, the country only emerged from Communist rule in 1989, after more than four decades under an oppressive regime. The traces remain.

We pass towns where factories of bare concrete stand abandoned, houses that are smaller and more modest, and stretches of land beside the tracks that look less well cared for. Everything feels a little greyer, a little more neglected—and the weather, as if in sympathy, turns colder.

As usual, we have booked a hotel within walking distance of the train station. This time it is in Prague's Old Town, a district inhabited for more than 2,000 years and centred on the Old Town Square, which has served as a marketplace for over a millennium. The area is lined with narrow cobblestone lanes that radiate in all directions without any discernible plan, making it less than ideal for wheeling a suitcase.

'How's HiHo going?' I ask, using the nickname I've given Darryl's silver suitcase.

'My bag's fine, but this is clearly another place where we're going to get lost,' he replies.

'I think this is the worst yet,' I say.

Looking around, Darryl frowns. 'How come all the prices are in koruna? Don't they use euros here?'

'I have no idea. Doesn't look like it—though I don't recall reading otherwise. Anyway, there's our hotel,' I say in relief as the Residence Leon D'oro finally comes into view.

The Residence Leon D'oro turns out to be a gorgeous, elegant hotel in Italian style. Our room is spacious, decorated in gold and red velvet. Already impressed, we are even happier when we discover we have been upgraded.

'Look at the size of this room,' I say, taking in the two king-sized beds, the oversized chairs, and enough floor space left over for yoga.

'Plenty of room for hanging washing,' Darryl replies.

At the far end of our room, heavy drapes hide a wall full of windows and throwing these open, I gaze down on the crowds milling along the cobblestone streets two storeys below.

'I don't think we could have chosen a better located hotel.'

We have come to Prague for three main reasons. The first is to visit my cousin, an engineer who moved here from England some years ago after landing his dream job—travelling the world to troubleshoot for the global Bobcat company. The second is to discover for ourselves what all the fuss and hype around Prague is about. And the third is to watch the Astronomical Clock strike the hour.

I can't remember exactly when I first heard of Prague's Astronomical Clock, but this medieval 15th-century timepiece has long been on my list. Its hourly chiming is brought to life by the parade of twelve apostles and the macabre figure of a skeleton symbolising death—something we have both been eager to witness.

Once again, after dropping our bags, we return to reception for directions to the nearest supermarket.

'It's not far. Turn left out the front of the hotel, then left again and continue toward the Town Square. It's just before you reach there,' we are told.

Armed with what sound like simple instructions, we set off—only to find ourselves baffled within minutes. Prague's Old Town, with its swarms of tourists and winding cobblestone lanes that never seem to run straight, proves to be the hardest city of all to navigate.

'I can't see a supermarket anywhere—but look, there's the Astronomical Clock,' I say to Darryl a short time later.

We have clearly missed the supermarket and wandered straight into the Old Town Square. Incredible buildings and churches line the edges, though many are hidden behind stages, pylons, seating, and scaffolding. It looks as if the square is being transformed into a temporary concert venue, much like the setup we saw in Lucca for Green Day.

Directly ahead stands what can only be the Astronomical Clock—although this too is shrouded in scaffolding.

'It's under renovation,' I read from my phone. 'But it's still operating. We'll just have to come back on the hour.'

Deciding to leave the clock for tomorrow, we wander down one of the cobblestone streets. If we can't find the supermarket, we may as well eat at one of the many cafés. As we search for a place that appeals, it quickly becomes clear that, despite being part of the European

Union, Prague does not use the euro. Instead, the local currency is the Czech crown, or koruna. A quick stop at a nearby exchange solves the problem, where we hand over a few of our emergency American dollars and receive a fistful of korunas in return.

With the right currency in hand, we soon settle into a cosy little café serving traditional Czech fare. The menu looks surprisingly familiar: schnitzels, sausages, and dumplings—much like what we had found in Austria. Darryl orders schnitzel yet again, while I choose the beef goulash, attractively served inside a hollowed-out bread roll.

Both meals come with large glasses of beer from an impressively long list.

'They really like their beer here,' I remark. 'This menu is huge—and on the way, I noticed heaps of places selling beer.'

'I think I've heard something about the Czechs being big beer drinkers,' Darryl replies.

A quick bit of Googling confirms it. Not only has beer been brewed here since 993 AD, but the Czechs also drink more per capita than anyone else in the world. In fact, beer here is cheaper than bottled water.

With dinner behind us, we slowly make our way back to the hotel. Along the way, we pass shops displaying sparkling examples of Bohemian crystal and once again wish we could take some home. At some stage, I begin to notice people walking along eating what looks like a sugary, cone-shaped doughnut filled with cream or ice cream. They look delicious, and I become aware of the many vendors selling these tempting desserts.

Called Trdelníks, they are made by wrapping dough around a fat stick and grilling it over an open flame. Once cooked, the stick is pulled out, the shell is rolled in sugar and walnuts, and the hollow centre is filled with something delicious. I spend ages deciding at a stall and finally settle on one filled with Nutella and ice cream, topped with extra Nutella and strawberries. It's right up there with the best desserts I have ever eaten, and I end up having one every day we are in Prague.

That evening, back in our now laundry-strewn room, I contact my cousin Ewan. He has been living in Prague for the past six years and is one of the main reasons for our visit. We had originally planned to stay at his nearby house, but the recent sale of the property put an end to that idea. Still, he has set aside the next few days for us, and we quickly arrange to meet after breakfast the following morning so he can show us around Prague and the nearby countryside.

'Ewan apparently has a slight problem,' I read on my phone over breakfast the next morning. 'He may be a bit late.'

Half an hour later, another message arrives: 'Ewan's problem is a bit bigger than he realised.'

It turns out he really does have a problem. He had stayed overnight with a friend, and that friend left for the day—unknowingly deadlocking Ewan into a tenth-floor apartment. With no way out, he would be stuck there until at least 8 pm. By way of apology, he sends us an impressively detailed itinerary for Prague and arranges to meet us the following morning instead.

We spend the day more or less following Ewan's itinerary to the letter. Ten am finds us standing alongside hordes of other tourists in front of the Astronomical Clock. Phones at the ready, we film the apostles parading and the skeleton of death striking the hour. From there, we make our way towards Charles Bridge—a span that has stood since 1390, its Baroque statues gazing impassively down as we, along with what feels like half of Europe, struggle to reach the other side.

'This is crazy!' I exclaim. 'This is the thickest crowd yet!'

'It's like a theme park on steroids,' Darryl replies, perfectly summing it up.

Although it's hard to push our way through the crush, the crowds don't stop us from noticing two men fishing from the bridge, their lines dangling into the swiftly flowing Vltava River below.

'Are you fishing?' Darryl asks.

'Yes, this is our hobby. We try to come most days,' one of the men replies.

'Is that a magnet you're using?' Darryl continues.

'Yes. A special one. It lets us fish for the coins people throw into the river.'

'Wow! Do you get many?' I exclaim.

'Yes. This is the second container I've filled this morning,' he says, pointing to what looks like a litre-sized tub.

After chatting a little longer, we walk away suitably impressed. Magnet fishing here seems to be quite a lucrative pastime.

Dominating the Prague skyline, and visible from almost anywhere in the city, are two striking landmarks. One is the Gothic-inspired, treasure-filled St. Vitus Cathedral, among the most richly endowed in central Europe. The other is Prague Castle, the largest ancient castle in the world, still in official use today and currently home to the President of the Czech Republic.

Caught in the crowds, we leave Charles Bridge behind and begin the climb towards these two landmarks. Before long, we're faced with two options: a cobblestone road with a steep incline, or a set of low-rise steps that wind gently upwards. Although I'm not usually in favour of stairs, we choose them—what we can see looks harmless enough.

Five minutes later, with the crowds thinning ahead, we realise our mistake. What had seemed like a modest staircase now stretches endlessly upward, each corner revealing yet another flight vanishing into the distance.

'What do you think? Should we turn back?' I ask Darryl.

'No, I don't want to backtrack. We'll just take them slowly and rest when we can.'

It takes us quite a while to reach the top, and though the climb is tough on Darryl, the views as we rise higher—and the sense of achievement—make the effort worthwhile. With the last step finally behind us, we are confronted once again by long queues, this time to enter the heavily guarded Prague Castle.

More interested in the sweeping views of the countryside from our hilltop vantage point than in joining the line, we content ourselves with strolling along the sections of the castle perimeter that are accessible. As for St. Vitus Cathedral, we somehow fail to find the entrance at all—a shortcoming we decide to blame on Ewan's itinerary.

Thirsty from our earlier exertions, we begin searching for somewhere to rest. The search takes us higher still until we arrive at the Strahov Monastery, where a large sign in the gardens promises food, drink, and the best aerial views of Prague. Sceptical that a monastery could really provide all that, we make our way in—and to our delight soon find ourselves seated at a small cliffside table. With Prague spread out at our feet and uninterrupted views stretching to the horizon, the sign outside had not lied. Over tasting plates, an Aperol Spritz, and a beer, the next hour slips by happily. It is with some reluctance that we finally rise and return to Ewan's itinerary.

Ewan has recommended that from Prague Castle, we make our way back to the river, this time following the cobblestone road. Not far ahead, he tells us, lies the Lennon Wall. With his songs of peace, freedom, and independence, John Lennon became a great inspiration to Czech youth who, during the years of Communism, had none of these. The wall appeared after Lennon's death in 1980, and despite repeated attempts by the authorities to paint over it, it still stands.

From the Lennon Wall, we continue alongside the Vltava until we reach the Memorial to the Victims of Communism. This haunting sculpture depicts a series of ragged human figures, each in a further stage of decomposition. It is both striking and deeply poignant.

To finish, Ewan has suggested we return via Wenceslas Square—a name instantly recognisable the world over thanks to a certain Christmas carol.

Released from his enforced captivity, Ewan meets us early the next morning, and before long, we are heading out of the city in his car. It doesn't take long for the urban signs to fall away, replaced by fields of wheat, rivers where children swim, and rolling, forested hills. We pass through small grey villages of stone houses before pulling up beside a well-trodden walking track. Following it through dense forest, we suddenly emerge before the striking Gothic silhouette of Karlstejn Castle.

Built on a promontory, this castle once safeguarded the Bohemian crown jewels and remains one of the most famous and visited castles in the Czech Republic. The hours slip by as we explore its many rooms and courtyards before heading to a nearby restaurant for a late lunch. Ewan persuades me to try a national dish—beef meatballs in a creamy sauce, served with rounds of bread to soak it all up. It tastes great, as does the generous wedges of apple strudel and cream that follow.

Ewan drops us as close to our hotel as he can, and we say our farewells before heading back into the mayhem of Prague's Old Town. It is Sunday, and if anything, the crowds are even bigger, swelled by large tour groups. Earlier, we had noticed market stalls selling cartons of beautiful fruit—strawberries and cherries that would have made a perfect light dinner. But by the time we go looking, the stalls have just closed.

'Let's be pigeons and have a beer instead,' Darryl suggests, noting that this seems to be a popular Sunday afternoon pastime here.

So our final evening in Prague is spent drinking beer alongside the throngs of tourists not far from Old Town Square. Afterwards, we return to the Astronomical Clock to watch it strike the hour one last time before making our way back to our room. Prague has truly delivered: beautiful, affordable, and memorable—a city every bit worthy of its reputation. Tomorrow, a five-hour train journey to Berlin lies ahead.

CHAPTER 17

Wars and Marijuana

Extract from Darma Travels Blog-
　We have always been conscious of Berlin, its celebrity up there with London, Paris or New York. Because of this, I think we were expecting a city on par with these three. What we didn't expect to see was a city still under reconstruction. In hindsight, I suppose we shouldn't have been surprised: after all, it's been only 72 years since the end of WW2 and 28 years since the fall of the Berlin wall.

Prague's central train station has recently undergone a complete overhaul and is now a large, modern hub with cafés, supermarkets and chemists. With a fistful of loose koruna rattling in our pockets, I decide to spend it rather than carry it around for the rest of the trip. Knowing Darryl needs a few toiletry items, I start by picking up a packet of biscuits from the supermarket before heading into the chemist next door.

Our money stretches far in Prague, so I'm able to stock up easily on Band-Aids and antiseptic cream—both useful for treating the blisters Darryl's foot-brace has begun to cause. Remembering he also needs toothpaste, I spend some time scanning the shelves. Unlike a Band-Aid, toothpaste is not so easy to identify in Czech, and in the end, I simply grab the tube that looks most likely to be the right one.

With the Alps now far behind us, much of today's train journey follows the green lowlands beside the River Elbe. Instead of an open carriage, we find ourselves in a small compartment. While Darryl happily communicates in sign language with the elderly Czech couple sharing it with us, I gaze out the window at the swiftly flowing river and the ruins of castles flashing past.

Lunch is simple: the packet of biscuits we bought earlier, a handful of pistachios discovered at the bottom of our backpack, and Prague fountain water to wash it all down.

The hours slip by, and before we know it, we are stepping off the train at Berlin Hauptbahnhof, the city's central station. A vast glass-and-steel structure, it thrums with passengers from both intercity trains and the subway lines that run through its basement.

Confident we can once again walk to our hotel, I pull out my phone and try to open Google Maps.

'There's no internet here,' I say in frustration.

'Turn your phone off, then back on again,' Darryl suggests.

'Nope. Still nothing.'

For some reason, despite trying both inside and outside Berlin station, we still cannot pick up an internet signal. Unable to find our way to the hotel or hail an Uber, we have no choice but to join the nearby taxi queue.

The temperature is soaring into the mid-30s, and standing on the hot concrete pavement with no shelter quickly wears thin. Even worse, after failing to move forward at all, we realise that our fellow queuers are either ignorant of queuing—or simply extremely rude.

'The people who have just joined are taking the taxis!' I exclaim in disbelief. 'Look—they're not collecting from the top of the queue where people have been waiting the longest. Those at the bottom are stopping them and jumping straight in.'

'Why aren't the people at the front saying anything?' Darryl frowns. 'How come we seem to be the only ones bothered?'

Ashamed as we are to admit it, we eventually give up on the queue as a lost cause and pinch a taxi ourselves. It is either that, or spend the rest of the afternoon queuing and fuming in the hot sun.

Gazing out of the taxi window as we drive through a cityscape of large, grey, low-rise buildings, I recall a recent comment a friend left on Facebook:

'It's so nice to see cities without huge high-rise buildings', written in response to a photo I had posted of Salzburg.

Although I had been aware that many of the cities we've travelled through felt flat and sprawling, it was only when reading that comment that I realised how few high-rise buildings we had actually seen. Berlin, while also broad and low, does have a scattering of taller buildings—the first we have noticed in quite some time.

It's a short taxi ride, and before long, we are once again settling into a hotel room—this time at the NH Berlin Mitte Leipziger Straße.

'Two doonas again, but no room for yoga,' I note to myself.

With a few busy days ahead, Darryl chooses to rest and conserve his energy, while I set off on my usual exploration of the surrounding area. At the top of my list, as always, is a supermarket.

Berlin, one of Europe's most populous cities with around 3.7 million inhabitants, is relatively young by European standards, its construction first documented in the 13th century. Today, it serves as Germany's capital and is divided into 12 boroughs. Our hotel, the NH Berlin Mitte Leipziger Straße, sits in Mitte—the first and most central borough.

BUCKET LISTS AND WALKING STICKS

As I walk the broad footpaths along wide roads, it's clear there is no shortage of things to see and do. The afternoon slips by as I browse the shops on Friedrichstrasse, pause at Checkpoint Charlie, and make a note to return with Darryl to the Memorial to the Murdered Jews of Europe. Underground, drawn by a long corridor with a striking mosaic floor, I unexpectedly stumble upon a supermarket. Delighted, I stock up on fruit, containers of Asian noodle salad, yoghurt, and bread rolls. The leftover biscuits from Prague will do perfectly for dessert.

'What's this?' yells Darryl from the bathroom a few hours later.

'What's what?' I call back.

'This toothpaste. It's brown and tastes awful.'

'It's Prague toothpaste,' I say, hoping that it really is toothpaste.

'It's disgusting,' he mutters—a fact that doesn't stop him, over time, from finishing the entire tube.

Wanting to see as much of Berlin as possible in our three nights here, we decide to make use of the hop-on bus once again. After breakfast, we head towards our starting point: Checkpoint Charlie.

Located close by, Checkpoint Charlie—the famous crossing between East and West Berlin during the Cold War—is one of the images I carried with me long before arriving. Berlin loomed large in my Australian school history lessons, with its role in the Second World War and the later division of the city during the Cold War. I am now curious to see how those classroom impressions measure up against reality.

'There's the checkpoint,' I say to Darryl, pointing towards a wooden structure with an American Jeep parked out front.

'You can have your photo taken with the guard,' Darryl replies dryly.

'Look how many people are waiting—and you have to pay for it!' I add in disbelief.

Checkpoint Charlie, once the scene of an infamous Cold War showdown between the United States and the Soviet Union, is now reduced to a money-making attraction in front of an imitation structure.

Fortunately, I am still so thrilled to be here that I can overlook the disappointment.

As the day goes on, many of my preconceptions about Berlin are challenged. Expecting a large, busy, vibrant city much like London, I am surprised to find it more laid back, more spacious, more open. What surprises me even more are the gaps—the buildings that are missing. Everywhere we go, vacant lots still await development, a strange sight in a major capital. Occasionally, an old survivor stands flanked by newer buildings, or we pass half-restored façades waiting for funds to complete the work. Berlin, unexpectedly, feels like a city still under reconstruction.

Curious for answers, we turn to Google—our school history lessons too distant in memory—and are reminded that at the end of World War II, Berlin was described as a post-apocalyptic wasteland. Subjected to 363 air raids and more than 86,000 tons of bombs, with between 20,000 and 50,000 people killed, the city had been left in ruins. In just over 70 years, Berlin has had to come a very long way. Clearly, my expectations of a fully polished, finished city were ambitious.

With more than 30 stops on the hop-on bus, it's just as well we purchased a two-day pass—we will need it. On our first day, we take in Charlottenburg, KaDeWe and Pariser Platz, along with two of Berlin's most famous sites: the Brandenburg Gate and the Memorial to the Murdered Jews of Europe.

The Brandenburg Gate—*Tor* in German—is Berlin's most recognisable landmark. Once a symbol of a divided city, and the place where Ronald Reagan famously declared, '*Mr Gorbachev, tear down this wall!*'—it has, since reunification in 1990, become a powerful symbol of unity.

As moving as it is to stand beneath the Brandenburg Gate, it is the Memorial to the Murdered Jews of Europe that will stay with me the most. Spanning nearly five acres of undulating ground, it consists of

2,711 stark grey concrete slabs—each identical in footprint but varying in height. Reminiscent of coffins, the effect is haunting.

Opened in 2005 to honour the six million Jewish victims of the Holocaust, the memorial invites visitors to walk freely among the slabs. Climbing them is forbidden, though not everyone obeys. Wandering through the rows—surrounded by the sheer number, the cold colour, the silence—creates an overwhelming sense of reflection and loss.

That evening, relaxing in front of the television with more supermarket goodies, the news is dominated by yet another terrorist attack—this time at Brussels' Central Station. An individual tried to detonate a large bomb and was shot by soldiers patrolling the station. As we are due to arrive there in just four days, the news is unsettling.

'I think we just have to do what everyone else does and go on with our plans,' I eventually say to Darryl.

'I agree. We can't let it stop us. Otherwise, we'd be too worried to do anything,' he replies.

Making use of our two-day pass, the second day on the hop-on bus takes us along the green route. This one winds through much of what was once Eastern, Communist Berlin. Unlike the West, where democratic governments built housing blocks with some comfort and style in mind, the East focused almost entirely on practicality. The result is long rows of low-rise buildings divided into hundreds of tiny, often impractical flats.

The highlight of the day, though, is the Berlin Wall—a guarded concrete barrier that physically and ideologically divided the city from 1961 to 1989. What remains are the famous, much-photographed stretches of wall, and they live up to every expectation I had.

But Berlin is not only about its past. Surprisingly for a capital, nearly one-third of the city is made up of forests, gardens, rivers, canals, and lakes. At one point, we leave the bus and wander through a park, where a group of what look like university students are discreetly sharing a joint.

Berlin, a young person's city with around 40% of its population under 35, has clearly moved with the times. Here, marijuana can be smoked quietly and without fuss, so long as it's done unobtrusively.

Our final stop for the day is Alexanderplatz—or Alex, as the locals call it. Alex is Berlin's, and indeed Germany's, largest and most famous square. Having been largely pedestrianised, it allows us to walk almost the entire way back to our hotel without worrying about traffic.

For such a major square, it is quieter than I expected, and the gaps between surrounding buildings once again challenge my preconceptions of a fully complete city. The walk takes about 40 minutes, during which we pass Berlin's most visible landmark, the TV Tower, as well as the magnificent Berlin Cathedral.

That afternoon, over a much-needed German beer in a nearby pub, I read some blogs about Hitler's Bunker—the place he ruled from during the final weeks of World War II and where he ultimately took his own life. Now destroyed, its site is deliberately kept low-profile by Berliners, who fear it could otherwise become a place of pilgrimage.

It takes some deciphering, but we eventually piece together enough clues to learn that it lies not far from our hotel. Leaving the pub, we soon come across a discreet plaque confirming we have indeed found the spot. Standing there feels strangely surreal—to be on the ground where Hitler once stood and died.

Our walk back to Berlin Central Station the following day takes us under the Brandenburg Gate, where we pause to snap a few farewell selfies of Berlin. In all, it has been an eye-opening city—both physically and emotionally different from what I had imagined. Physically, Berlin is greener, greyer, flatter, quieter and with more buildings still under reconstruction than expected. Emotionally, despite the locals' efforts to move on from their history, it is impossible not to feel the weight of the past. The memorials, the surviving fragments of the wall, and the knowledge of what Hitler once directed from here make me doubt whether Berlin will ever fully escape it.

Germany is famous for its high-speed trains, and today's seven-hour journey—our longest yet—is no exception. We race through flat green countryside, past countless farms dotted with wind turbines. The closer we get to Amsterdam, our destination, the more it feels as though the train is gliding downhill towards the reclaimed land of the Netherlands. Crossing the border, the scenery becomes almost a cliché: iconic windmills and wide expanses of water come into view.

For the first time in our eight weeks of travelling through Europe, our arrival at Amsterdam Central Station coincides with driving rain and cold temperatures. We briefly consider calling an Uber, but a lull in the downpour encourages us to step out onto the flooded cobblestone street, raise my umbrella, and set off in search of our hotel. Fortunately, the walk is short, and we reach the Hotel Rokin just as the squall begins again.

It is with some anticipation that we arrive in Amsterdam. More than 20 years ago, when we were living and working in London, it was a must-visit destination for many Australian travellers—drawn by cafés where marijuana could be smoked legally, nights of endless partying and the curiosity of sex workers sitting in shopfronts. Our early return to Australia meant we missed the chance back then, and so visiting the city's famous Red-Light District has lingered on our bucket list ever since.

Amsterdam, however, is an expensive city to overnight in, and because we wanted to be central, something had to give. We chose the Hotel Rokin—small and basic, but right by the Red-Light District and supposedly offering a great breakfast. There is definitely no room for yoga—and, as we will soon discover, the bathroom floods disastrously.

With early evening approaching and the rain finally gone, we head back out onto the crowded streets in search of food and some orientation. The crowds—mostly young backpackers, by the look of it—all seem to be moving in the same direction, and it's easiest just to join the flow.

It leads us quickly to a neighbourhood where smoking and sex paraphernalia fill the window displays, music pulses from packed cafés, and the smell of marijuana lingers in the air. We have clearly arrived in Amsterdam's Red-Light District—and with it, another bucket list item is ticked off.

We're glad to have ticked this item off so soon after arriving, because our 50-something selves do not much enjoy the loud, pulsing music, the claustrophobic crowds, and we certainly have no interest in getting stoned anymore.

'Let's explore a bit further and then get out of here.'

'Let's head back towards our hotel,' Darryl suggests. 'I saw some cafés nearby where we can hopefully grab dinner.'

It takes time to retrace our steps—going against the flow is no easy task—but the effort pays off when we find a few welcoming little cafés.

'Look. Pigeons!'

'I'm going to miss this back in Australia,' I sigh, settling into my seat.

'I don't think they even have it in England,' Darryl responds.

'It must be a very Continental thing.'

Fortified by a few drinks and a dinner of assorted tasting plates, we fall into bed—only to be woken an hour or so later. The room seems to pulse with heavy music, and although our window is tightly shut, the shouts and laughter of boozy street revellers three storeys below still manage to find their way in. Our hotel, so conveniently close to the Red-Light District, proves perhaps a little *too* convenient. At some point, either the noise dies down or we finally block it out, because we wake the next morning to quietness and sunlight streaming through the window.

The much-hyped breakfast at the Hotel Rokin delivers on its promise, and we feast on waffles, pancakes with maple syrup, cereal, fruit and coffee. Fortified, we set out to stroll the city and perhaps take a cruise along one of its many canals.

It takes barely an hour of wandering to fall under Amsterdam's spell. Like Venice, it is built on a network of waterways, but here they feel more accessible, and more beautiful, lined with flower boxes that brighten the water's edge. The streets are alive with offbeat gift shops, cycle paths criss-cross everywhere, and cafés invite you to linger for hours over a wine, a snack, or something else entirely.

The grand buildings housing art galleries and museums are stunning, but it is the small, quirky houses that truly captivate me. Higgledy-piggledy and leaning forward, backward and sideways, they appeal perfectly to my sense of whimsy. Painted in a rainbow of pastels, they are impossibly photogenic—and it's no wonder they grace so many postcards.

At some point, a tout selling river cruises catches our attention, and soon we find ourselves aboard a small boat with just one other couple for an hour-long canal cruise.

As the boat glides under bridges and through narrow canals, our captain shares snippets of history.

'Artefacts from prehistoric times have been found here,' he explains, 'but Amsterdam itself took shape in the 13th century.'

'There are more than 100 canals,' he continues, 'most dug in the 1700s—and over 1,000 bridges in the city.'

He glances at the water. 'The canals are flushed daily with 600,000 cubic metres of fresh water.'

I raise an eyebrow. 'Really? Judging by the murky colour, I'm not so sure about that.'

At the end of our circuit through Amsterdam's main waterways, we are left with two final facts: the city's population is around 750,000, and the average age of its residents is 42.

Anne Frank, the teenage heroine of her thought-provoking wartime diary, wrote from a house nearby, and after disembarking our boat, we go in search of it. The sight of a queue with no visible beginning confirms we are in the right place, and eventually, we come across both the house and the head of the line.

Now a museum, we had never seriously contemplated going inside. The queue alone would have been discouragement enough, but the steep steps within make it impossible for Darryl in any case.

We had noticed a little Mexican restaurant called *Miss Margarita* just around the corner from our hotel, so later that evening, we head there for dinner. The place is absolutely packed—much like the Miss Margarita in Byron Bay back home. An accommodating elderly waitress beckons us inside, and before long, we are squeezed onto the end of a long trestle table.

With a margarita in hand and nachos disappearing fast, I lean towards Darryl over the din of Mexican music and the jostling crowds.

'Look at the staff behind the bar,' I say. 'They've all got drinks tucked away, and every time the older lady isn't looking, they sneak a quick gulp.'

'Good on them,' Darryl grins. 'The older lady looks like a bit of a dragon.'

'I'm surprised they haven't been caught. They're not exactly subtle about it.'

With stomachs groaning after a great meal, we say goodbye to what must be some fairly tipsy waitstaff by now and head back to our room. The streets are thick with 20-somethings spilling out of hostels, beers in hand, gearing up for the night ahead.

'This really is a young person's city,' I say.

'All party, party, party, isn't it?' Darryl replies.

'I'd hate to be a neighbour here—imagine dealing with this every single night.'

Perhaps it's the long day, or maybe the margaritas, but tonight's pulsating music doesn't bother us nearly as much as the night before.

We sleep soundly and wake to yet another breakfast of waffles and pancakes.

'What time does our train leave?' Darryl asks over coffee.

'Around twelve. It's only a two-hour trip. After the terrorist attack, I'm keen—but also a little apprehensive—to see what Brussels is like.'

CHAPTER 18

The Beauty of Brugge

Extract from Darma Travels Blog-
I must admit that arriving in Brussels, Belgium, four days after another terrorist attack, this time at a main train station here, was a definite reason for concern.

Today's 230-kilometre journey finds us hurtling southwards through cities such as The Hague, Rotterdam and Antwerp. Amsterdam's flat green countryside gradually gives way to Belgium's more industrial landscape as we near Brussels. A little after 2 pm, we glide into Brussels Midi Station—our alternative to the recently bombed Brussels Central Station.

'There's absolutely no one here,' I say in awe, peering out at the empty platforms from my window seat.

'There's no one! I've never seen anything like it,' Darryl replies.

'Look, there are guards,' I say, pointing to a cluster of heavily armed soldiers. 'This does feel pretty heavy.'

Along with the other passengers, we alight and head quickly for the exit. Unhindered by the usual crowds, we move easily down the escalators and into the main terminal. Once again, the spaces that should be bustling are empty, save for groups of armed guards patrolling the area. The effect is eerie and unnerving, and all we want is to get outside as quickly as possible.

When we finally emerge, both of us breathe a sigh of relief.

'That's something we won't forget in a hurry,' Darryl exclaims.

Pulling out my phone to check our location in relation to the hotel, I pause to take stock of my surroundings. We are clearly back in the land of high-rise—grey, concrete and glass towers looming in the distance. Closer by, the streets feel almost deserted, though perhaps that is because it is a Saturday afternoon.

Google Maps tells us it's a 20-minute walk to the Old Town, where our hotel, the Hotel Le Dixseptieme, awaits. We set off under a dismal, overcast sky, passing garbage-strewn streets, grimy buildings, and clusters of homeless people. Groups of young men—foreign nationals, by the looks of it—linger on corners, smoking or kicking a football around.

'I can see why this is considered a recruiting ground for ISIS,' I say quietly to Darryl.

'Yes,' he nods. 'It's not hard to imagine terrorists coming from here.'

At some point, we leave behind the concrete jungle of grimy footpaths and tired buildings and realise we've stepped into Brussels' Old Town. The streets are cobbled now, the architecture transformed into elegant stone façades.

'This is looking better,' I remark. 'And look—there's the Hotel Le Dixseptieme. It actually looks really good.'

And it does. Either Brussels hotels are cheaper than the rest of Europe, or I happened upon a remarkable discount when booking, because the moment we step inside, it's clear this place is in a different league from our previous stays. Marble staircases, glass conservatories, candlelit tables, linen napkins—and a beautiful suite at our disposal. We can only appreciate our good fortune.

'This building has been here since the 14th century, and in the 17th century, it was the residence of the Spanish ambassador,' I read aloud from the compendium in our room.

'Remind me to thank the Darma Travels agent,' Darryl grins. 'She's outdone herself this time.'

'Haha,' I reply with mock sarcasm.

Brussels was a very last-minute addition to our itinerary. Beyond its name, all we really knew was that it served as the de facto seat of the European Union—and that it had great chocolate. Believe it or not, the promise of chocolate alone nearly secured its place, but what tipped the balance was discovering we could catch the Eurostar from here directly back to London. Once the decision was made, the next step was to organise a tour to nearby Bruges, an apparently stunning, once-forgotten city friends had urged us to visit. With that arranged, today would be given over to exploring Brussels Old Town, and tomorrow to a full-day tour of Bruges and its equally beautiful neighbour, Ghent.

Our suite comes well-stocked with a generous selection of hot drinks and biscuits, and after sampling both, we return to the streets well-fortified. Our destination is the Grand Place, only a two-minute walk away, according to our hotel receptionist. The Grand Place is Brussels' central square and its most memorable landmark—a fact that becomes obvious the moment we arrive.

We find ourselves standing in a vast cobblestone market square dating back to the 12th century, surrounded on all four sides by the most eclectic mix of decorative buildings I have ever seen. With the Town Hall, the City Museum and more than 40 guildhalls forming a blend of Baroque, Gothic and Louis XIV architecture, the effect is nothing short of formidable. It is little wonder the Grand Place is considered the finest square in the world.

Being summer in Europe, the square is packed. And while we are still slightly on edge in what has long been a terrorist hot spot, that unease doesn't stop us wandering from building to building, determined to take in as much as we can.

Eventually, with the sun beginning to sink and the sound of music drawing us on, we leave the square and wander into a nearby arcade. It feels enormous, stretching far ahead of us, and is beautifully decorated with delicate cast-iron details. As we stroll through, our attention is soon caught by the sheer number of chocolate shops.

'I know Belgium is famous for its chocolate, but I honestly didn't expect to see this many,' I say to Darryl. 'Did you?'

'No,' he replies. 'I'm surprised as well. How about we try some from here?'

'Well, we can't come to Brussels and not buy chocolate,' I laugh, stepping inside.

Overwhelmed by the choice, it takes us a while to decide, and we emerge a few euros lighter but clutching our spoils. Since this will more than likely count as tonight's dinner, the expense feels entirely justified.

Our tour to Ghent and Bruges leaves early the next morning, so we are up before seven and find ourselves the only diners in the hotel breakfast room. In keeping with everything we've experienced at the Hotel Le Dixseptieme so far, breakfast is exceptional. An ample buffet awaits—bread, pastries, cheeses, cereals, yoghurts, fruit and juices—followed by platters of bacon, eggs, tomato and toast. Served by our own private waiter, eaten by candlelight and accompanied by linen napkins, it feels like a quietly luxurious start to the day.

Confusingly, Brussels street signs are bilingual, displaying both Dutch and French names. Our tour company has given us only the Dutch version of the pick-up point, which leads to some anxious moments when Google Maps fails to recognise it. A quick call to the tour office—and the French name in hand—finally sets us straight, and we locate our group. Unlike our small, intimate tours in Sarlat and Bordeaux, this one is enormous—at least 55 to 60 people. It is going to be interesting seeing the sights as part of a large, noisy crowd rather than as the independent travellers we have been until now.

Belgium is divided into three regions, and today we are exploring the Flemish, or Flanders, region. Our first stop, Ghent—the capital of East Flanders and its largest city—is often overlooked in favour of its more famous neighbour, Bruges. Since the City Centre is the largest car-free zone in Europe, our coach drops us a few blocks away, leaving us to enjoy a pleasant walk in. Much of Ghent's medieval architecture, built on the wealth of its once-thriving wool industry, has survived battles, rebellions and even two world wars.

The first stop on our city tour is Saint Bavo Cathedral, home to the Ghent Altarpiece—a vast 15th-century panel painting regarded as one of the world's great treasures. Unfortunately, since it is Sunday, we are permitted to wander the cathedral but not to view the altarpiece itself.

From there, our guide leads us on a winding walk through Ghent: along canals lined with magnificent medieval stone buildings, over cobblestone streets, past horse-drawn carriages, and by towering churches and grand museums. The tour finishes with lunch in a bustling pub, where we tuck into generous plates of the local speciality—carbonnade of beef.

Back on board the coach, it isn't long before we reach Bruges—a city untouched by the industrial revolution and often called the Venice of the North.

As in Ghent, our guide takes us on an engaging tour through what feels like a fairy tale. We wander beside waterways edged with golden stone buildings and pause before a succession of soaring churches. It is easy to see how Bruges earned its nickname. For some in our group, the highlight is standing before Michelangelo's Madonna and Child in the Church of Our Lady; for others, it is the chance to glide along the canals by boat. Despite the chilly, overcast weather, the ride reveals the city at its most magical.

By the end of the day, we are enriched, exhausted and a little overwhelmed. So much history, so much beauty. Choosing between the two cities proves impossible, but one thing we have learned: navigating crowded streets is far less daunting when buffered by the size of a tour group.

It's after 6 pm when our coach drops us back in Brussels, and we decide to find dinner straight away rather than venture out again later. Our search leads us once more to the Old Square, where we are again left in awe of the sheer majesty of the buildings towering around us.

'I read that there used to be a river, the Senne, flowing beneath Brussels,' I say to Darryl. 'It became so polluted that they eventually covered it over.'

'When was that?' he asks.

'I'm not sure—I'll check later. But isn't it remarkable that they could simply build over an entire river?'

A cafe selling crepes proves impossible to resist, and as we sit tucking into huge plates of freshly made crepes smothered in creamy mushroom sauce, Darryl makes an observation.

'Have you noticed how many groups celebrating their buck's night there are?'

'Yes, I have noticed. I can see two now.'

'I've never seen so many groups of stag and hen parties in one place.'

'I wonder what attracts them to Brussels?' A question to which we never do receive an answer.

Walking back to our hotel room, the chocolate shops once again figure prominently; their window displays are so mouth-watering. We eventually capitulate and, along with a few for our own enjoyment, stock up on some boxes to take as gifts for those back in England.

The following morning finds us reluctantly departing our hotel after one last private five-star breakfast. It feels like a fitting finale to two months in Europe—weeks that not only acquainted us with unforgettable places but also brought unexpected growth. The culture, art and history have stretched our minds, while the endless cobblestones have reshaped our bodies. Darryl is now the strongest he has been since his accident, easing my earlier fears about whether he could cope with the journey.

We have once again elected to walk to the station, this time along a long street lined with free-standing market stalls piled high with fruit, vegetables and all manner of goods. Allowing ourselves plenty of time, we arrive at a virtually deserted Brussels Midi Station, where both British and Belgian customs are handled quickly and efficiently. Darryl faces a few probing questions, but before long, his passport is stamped with another six-month visa, and we are free once more to enter England.

Knowing what to expect doesn't make the journey under the Channel any easier, and it's only when the train bursts back into daylight on English soil that I finally breathe more freely. Quick and convenient it may be, and yes, I would use it again—but that doesn't mean I have to like it.

From London's St Pancras Station, where the Eurostar deposits us, the journey to Reading involves both the Underground and the London Overground. By early afternoon, however, we are unlocking the door to our Caversham home. Eight weeks of European travel are behind us. Now, our exploration of England begins.

CHAPTER 19

Living Life as a Pom

Extract from Darma Travels Blog-
Last week we played Monopoly. Not, as one assumes, sitting around a table throwing some dice but rather traipsing from Piccadilly Circus and Regent Street to Trafalgar Square via Northumberland and the Strand. While they are not on the board, we also landed on Buckingham Palace, Westminster and the South Bank.

After living out of our suitcases for nearly four months, it feels great to finally unpack and give our clothes, knick-knacks and toiletries permanent homes. Having our own washing machine and clothesline feels like pure luxury, and while I am not especially keen to resume cooking, I know our diet will be the better for it.

With everyday arrangements sorted, the television channels memorised and the kitchen deciphered, all that remains is to make ourselves more comfortable in this new, albeit temporary, way of life.

Comfort, however, requires a car, so a few days after our return to Caversham, we set off on foot to a nearby rental office.

'We're after a car for about a month,' we tell the solemn-looking receptionist. 'It doesn't need to be big—we'll do some touring in it, but not much.'

'I have a BMW coming back today, or a Benz tomorrow,' he replies.

'Um, maybe something cheaper. And it has to be an automatic,' I add, since Darryl's injuries mean he can't drive a manual.

'We do have a little VW Golf, but it's a manual. There's an automatic coming back next week—you could take the manual now and swap it later when the automatic is returned.'

'Okay, that sounds good. And could we also get a GPS with it?'

Although the public transport here is phenomenal compared to Australia, we are hoping our little VW Golf will let us slip into the nooks and crannies the trains and buses don't quite reach.

It's been more than 20 years since I last drove a manual, so the trip back from the rental office—through traffic far heavier than I'm used to—is both interesting and a sharp refresher. On the way, we spot an Aldi we'd noticed earlier and stop to fill the boot with groceries and essentials: toilet paper, dishwashing liquid, laundry powder. This small act drives home just how much of a gypsy lifestyle we've been living for the past four months.

To get used to the car and explore our surroundings further, we head westward the next day. While perusing the road maps, the town of Bucklebury catches my attention.

'I knew it sounded familiar,' I exclaim, looking up from my phone. 'It's where Kate Middleton's parents live. Let's go for a drive and have a look. You'll have to help with the navigating,' I add, since yesterday's trip home proved the GPS can't always be relied upon.

Our drive soon takes us out of busy Reading and into the quieter countryside. As we had discovered months earlier, the roads are heavily trafficked, and the hedgerows make it difficult to see oncoming cars. Accustomed to Australia's wide-open roads with good visibility and far

BUCKET LISTS AND WALKING STICKS

less traffic, I find the driving conditions frustrating. The further we go, the narrower the roads become, and more than once, we are forced to reverse to let another car through. Even the GPS seems to give up, eventually falling silent.

Forced to rely on Darryl's navigating, fed up with the constant reversing, and cursing the hedgerows, tension slowly builds until it boils over when we realise we have somehow missed Bucklebury.

'It's on the map in front of you. How could we have missed it?' I snap at Darryl.

'I was too busy watching for oncoming traffic,' he shoots back.

'And the map's useless anyway,' he adds, tossing both it and the GPS into the glove box.

'Oh, great. That's really going to help us get home.'

As first outings go, we later laugh—it is a total failure.

Although he had mentioned it casually during a FaceTime call a few weeks earlier, we are still surprised when Pierce messages the following morning to say he will be moving in over the weekend. After working hard for the past 18 months, he sees our return to England as the perfect opportunity to take a breather. With plans to travel around Europe later with some Australian mates, in the meantime, he is quite content to mooch off us for a while.

Not having had him around for the past two and a half years, we are looking forward to reconnecting with Pierce and making plans for what we might do together in England. Before leaving Australia, whenever friends asked what we most wanted to see, our answer was always the same: Port Isaac, the filming location of the TV series *Doc Martin*. With Pierce now joining us, it feels like the perfect chance to put that wish into action, and so a five-day tour of southwest England is planned to begin within the fortnight.

The days leading up to our planned trip are easy to fill. With the Thames just down the road, we spend many a morning or afternoon strolling its banks, feeding the ducks, and laughing at the swans with their tails in the air as they dive for food. In Caversham, we stumble across a scruffy little pub offering meals for two pounds and soon begin to feel at home, frequently dining on two-pound roasts followed by two-pound treacle puddings. Our sense of comfort wavers slightly, however, when we learn that the pub's locals have taken to calling us the 'Nordic Giants.'

'Nordic Giant? What does that mean?' I ask Darryl, who has uncovered this little detail.

'Not sure. Giant must be because we're tall'—and we are, compared to most Brits.

'And Nordic maybe because we're pale or grey-haired?'

As June rolls into July, England really turns on the weather for us—long, hot days with temperatures hovering in the high 20s and the sun lingering late into the evening. Paige comes for a two-day visit, and it feels wonderful to be a family again. We still marvel that, out of all the pubs in England, the one where she lives and works is less than a 50-minute drive from Caversham. To celebrate her visit, we head to a nearby upmarket pub, where Paige is delighted to discover it belongs to the same chain as hers. Not only does this mean she knows the menu well enough to make recommendations, but it also earns us a 30% discount on the entire bill.

Having swapped the manual car for an identical automatic a few days earlier, and securing a new, fully functioning GPS at the same time, we are more than happy to drive Paige the 40-odd kilometres back to her place. On the way, our conversation drifts to favourite TV shows, and *The Vicar of Dibley* comes up. Starring Dawn French, it is one of the few shows that appeals across both our generations and remains a firm favourite with all four of us.

'I wonder where it was filmed?' I muse aloud.

'Turville,' cries Paige a few minutes later, looking up from her phone. 'It's only about 20 minutes from here.'

'You're kidding!' we exclaim together. 'Well, we definitely have to find it.'

BUCKET LISTS AND WALKING STICKS

By now, we are becoming accustomed to the narrow lanes hemmed in by hedgerows, but the journey to Turville proves to be defined by them. While Darryl and I simply sigh in resignation each time we are forced to reverse for an oncoming car, Pierce and Paige are far more taken aback. Paige's phone has the timing right, though, and 20 minutes later, we crest a rise to see, ahead of us, a windmill perched on a grassy green field. Recognisable from the opening scene of *The Vicar of Dibley*, it gives us all a small thrill to spot it in real life.

Turville—or Dibley, as fans of the TV series know it—turns out to be small, quiet, and wonderfully unassuming. At its centre lies a tiny village green, framed by mossy stone cottages draped with summer roses. A little Tudor pub sits to one side, sadly closed during our visit, and nearby stands Geraldine's church. Dating back to the 12th century, its weathered stone walls and lichen-scarred gravestones exude history and character, making it easy to see why it was chosen for the show.

We linger, wandering among the gravestones and exploring the simple interior before stopping outside the cottage that served as the vicar's home. Cameras in hand, we take our time capturing the moment. Still marvelling at how effortlessly we have stumbled upon a place so familiar from television—something that never seems to happen in Australia—we continue on to Beaconsfield, where we say our goodbyes to Paige.

That evening, with the weather still glorious and the sun not due to set until 10:30 pm, we decide to christen our recently purchased 20-quid barbecue. Back in Australia, barbecuing is one of our favourite pastimes, and here it serves a dual purpose: a taste of home and a way to avoid my aunt Charlotte's spotless, overly complicated oven. For both Darryl and me, it is the first time cooking over charcoal rather than gas, so the experience feels both novel and slightly daunting. Fortunately, Pierce—well practised from the occasional barbecue duty at his Twickenham pub—steps in with plenty of advice.

'You need a chimney or something that shape to light it. Why didn't you buy lighter fluid? No, not like that. I said you need a chimney or something.'

'Well, we haven't got a chimney, and you shouldn't need to buy one just to light a barbecue. And I didn't realise lighter fluid was a requirement,' Darryl replies, a little testily.

'It's never going to work like that. Let's try using that flowerpot as a chimney,' Pierce suggests. 'But really, you should have bought lighter fluid.'

Darryl has no choice but to concede the point when, after what feels like hours, the barbecue still refuses to catch.

'Probably best to give up and cook on the stove tonight,' he admits at last. 'We'll buy lighter fluid and try again tomorrow.'

On one of our many recent walks along the Thames, I spotted a sign advertising river cruises. Waking early one morning, I try to convince Darryl and Pierce that it will be a fun thing to do.

'We'd pass through countryside that inspired *The Wind in the Willows*,' I argue. 'And it goes to Henley-on-Thames—you know, where the regatta is held. Then it comes back.'

'How long does it take?' asks Pierce.

'About two and a half hours each way.'

'Five hours? No thanks,' Darryl and Pierce chorus almost instantly.

'We don't have to come back on the boat,' I wheedle. 'We could catch a bus back—and fit in a pub lunch at Henley.'

Promises of a pub lunch tip the argument in my favour, and an hour later, the three of us are boarding a Salter Steamer. Family-owned since 1858, these former steamers still ply the Thames each summer. We are fortunate that only one other group of five adults is joining us, and before long, we are gliding into our first lock.

England's 2,000-mile system of canals and locks, stretching back to Roman times, has always fascinated me. At one point, it was even a dream of Darryl's and mine to buy a canal boat and spend our days meandering around the country. Today, though, it is enough simply to sit back, watch the scenery drift by, and enjoy the slow rhythm of the river.

At first, Darryl and Pierce share my enthusiasm—especially when we cruise past George Clooney's property and a house that Taylor Swift nearly bought. By the fourth lock, however, boredom has set in. Darryl rallies slightly at the sight of a home featured on *Grand Designs*, but only briefly. Fortunately, Henley soon comes into view, still wearing the remnants of last week's Royal Regatta: striped marquees, festive bunting and boats crowding the banks of this famous rowing town.

After sitting for hours on the boat, it feels good to stretch our legs and wander the streets. The old buildings are beautiful, and while we keep one eye out for a promising pub, the antique shops draw Darryl's and my attention. Pierce, however, is far less impressed—hot and increasingly irritated, especially when some shops are too small to even accommodate his 6'5" frame.

'I can't even fit through the doorway,' he mutters in disgust outside the five-foot-high entrance to Tudor House Antiques. 'Yes, you two go on. Don't worry about me. I'll just wait here in the sun,' he continues, clearly put out.

Laughing, Darryl and I take our time browsing. Antiques have always fascinated us, and we love nothing better than picking up a small bargain—though these days, the best finds are more often in op-shops than antique stores. Eventually, conscious of Pierce waiting outside, we leave the little shop and resume the search for the perfect pub. The 300-year-old Argyll Public House, once used as a filming location for *Midsomer Murders*, proves just the spot. With a pint of ale and a steaming bowl of chilli con carne in front of him, Pierce is finally mollified.

Extremely full and with the unseasonably hot English sun beating down on us, all we want after lunch is to get home as quickly as possible. Our relief at a bus arriving promptly soon fades when we discover there is no air-conditioning and the atmosphere inside is closer to the steamy tropics than southern England. With windows that refuse to open, the ride home is uncomfortable in the extreme. One can only hope that, as climate change makes itself ever more apparent, English bus designers will eventually take such realities into account.

Despite having been back in England for nearly a fortnight, Darryl and I have yet to set foot in London. So, when the weather forecaster finally announces an end to the abnormal heatwave, it feels like the perfect time to remedy that.

With no fixed itinerary, we alight at London's Waterloo Station and emerge onto the South Bank—an unabashedly touristy stretch of the River Thames. Opposite Westminster and home to the London Eye, the National Theatre and the London Dungeon, it proves an ideal place to begin our explorations. As we stroll along the riverside, pausing to admire Westminster across the water and craning our necks at the 443-foot-high London Eye, the crush of people around us feels as though we have been transported straight back to the crowded streets of Europe.

As it happens to be graduation day for a nearby university, the crowds are swelled further by gowned students celebrating with their families, making walking difficult—especially for Darryl. Seeking relief from the mayhem, we cross Westminster Bridge to the north bank of the Thames, where we soon notice recently placed bollards and the faded remains of wreaths—stark reminders of the terror attack that took place here only months earlier. It is a sobering sight, a reminder of how vulnerable pedestrians are in busy, high-profile cities, and for the rest of the day, I cannot help but remain acutely aware of our own fragility.

Nearly a quarter of a century ago, Darryl worked on a building site just 100 metres from Big Ben, and it is here we head next. He has never forgotten the experience—working beside the buildings of Westminster, hearing Big Ben chime the hour, and even once catching

BUCKET LISTS AND WALKING STICKS

sight of the Queen passing by. The building is just as he remembers, and Pierce is suitably impressed to see where his father once worked, though he is quick to claim he can better it.

As we continue along the Embankment, Pierce takes the lead, pointing out places of interest from his own London days. For six months after his arrival here more than two years ago, his workplace was Ye Olde Cheshire Cheese, a historic Fleet Street pub once frequented by the likes of Dickens and Twain, rebuilt shortly after the Great Fire of London and often said to be the city's oldest. Living and working there, buying groceries on Fleet Street, and playing table tennis on the banks of the Thames gave Pierce an insider's view of London that most visitors never gain. He is eager to take us back to the old pub—an ideal spot for lunch.

'It's smaller and much darker than I was expecting,' I exclaim, ducking through the low doorway.

'I did most of my shifts down here,' Pierce says, leading us two storeys underground.

We step into what feels like a cellar: a tiny, stone-walled room, gloomy and close. The walls are lined with old ceramic beer and wine jugs draped in cobwebs, and at the wooden bar—its surface stained by centuries of beer slops—we place our order for pies and chips.

'Didn't you find it a bit eerie, working so far below ground and in such a cramped space?' I ask.

'Not really,' Pierce shrugs. 'The worst part was the bedrooms. They're upstairs, and mine looked straight out onto Fleet Street. The noise from outside used to keep me awake.'

Leaving the pub to further explore London, I can't help but feel a sense of wonder. Our stop at Ye Olde Cheshire Cheese has not only given us a glimpse into our son's working life here but also shown us some of the experiences that helped turn a once slightly naïve Australian lad into the mature traveller he is today.

We wander on to other well-known sights—Piccadilly Circus, Regent Street, Trafalgar Square and the Strand.

'We're playing Monopoly,' I laugh as Northumberland comes into view.

'Only we're not collecting 200 dollars as we pass go—more like spending it,' Darryl grumbles.

By the time we summon enough energy to walk the Mall, the day is wearing on, but the reward is Buckingham Palace. Finding a small stretch of railing, we rest for a while, taking in the home of royalty. The flag is flying, signalling the Queen is in residence, and her ceremonial guards stand perfectly still, happily posing for endless photographs.

Thankfully, the good weather continues, and the days dawn crisp, blue and rain-free—perfect summer weather and ideal conditions for a traditional English fair. Pamphlets scattered around Caversham have been advertising the annual fete to be held this Saturday on the banks of the Thames, in the gardens of Caversham Court, and having grown up on a diet of Enid Blyton, I am eager to see it for myself.

'Are you coming, Pierce? It's a very traditional English thing to do—and there will be food,' I call through his bedroom door.

He's still in bed.

'No. Not interested,' comes the muffled reply.

Caversham Court is an easy walk, and by early afternoon, we find ourselves in its gardens, surrounded by everything I had imagined an English fete to include—apart from a maypole. The Pimm's tent immediately catches our eye, though we decide to save that treat for later. Instead, we try our luck at the coconut shy, but despite feeding it copious coins, not a single coconut falls. The hoopla stall offers no more success, and we quickly realise we are better off as spectators at the egg-and-spoon race than participants. We skip the 'beat the goalie' challenge altogether, though my fortunes improve at the tombola, where I proudly win a packet of biscuits.

Deciding we have had enough of the games, we wander towards the stalls, detouring first through the cream tea tent where we devour warm scones piled with jam and cream. From there, we happily lose both time and money at the white elephant table, the bookstall, and the raffle. To finish our fete experience, we return to the Pimm's tent and, drinks in hand, settle by the river to watch ducks, swans and longboats drift past on the Thames. The day has been everything I hoped for—memorable, nostalgic, and every bit the English fete I had imagined.

Although we know English weather can be fickle, it is still surprising when, after weeks of high temperatures, the days suddenly turn cold and blustery, with no sign of changing. Provided the rain holds off, the cooler conditions do not bother us. In fact, they feel like a welcome respite from the heat and should not interfere with our upcoming trip around South West England. With a rough itinerary mapped out, accommodation booked, and friends and family warned of our impending visits, we are ready. So, shortly after 9 am on the Monday following the fete, we fold ourselves into our VW Golf and point its bonnet west.

CHAPTER 20

Meeting Martin Clunes

Extract from Darma Travels Blog-
   Prior to departing Australia, we were often asked, 'What do you want to do in England?' Our standard reply was always, 'Visit Portwenn (Isaac), you know, where Doc Martin was made.' Well, this week was all about making this a reality. The plan was to jump in our little VW Golf and head southwest. The itinerary: Cheddar Gorge, Dartmoor, Portwenn (Isaac) before finishing up in Glastonbury.

I had read somewhere that there was an excellent view of Stonehenge from the A303, so with Cheddar Gorge as our first overnight stop, we take that route. It's great to have the chance to see Stonehenge again. There's no need to stop and fight the crowds for a closer look—we did that on our last trip to England. This prehistoric monument, standing here since around 3000 BC with stones four metres high and weighing 25 tons each, is unlikely to have changed much in the 25 years since we last saw it.

The road trip has started well with an easy exit through busy Reading. Pierce is happy listening to his music in the back, and we are fast learning that there is no need to use indicators at a roundabout—no one else does, so why should we? The A303 is slow, winding and inferior for such a major road, but, helped by disruptive roadworks, does offer a great view of Stonehenge from our car window.

Our travel distance today is only 170 kilometres and, by our calculations, should take about three hours. To break the journey, we stop for an early lunch in Shepton Mallet, a market town dating back to Roman times and once home to the oldest working prison in England before its closure in 2013. It doesn't take long to stroll the cobblestone high street, pass its 15-metre-tall hexagonal market cross, and enjoy a bowl of hearty soup in a nearby café. With such easy travelling, it's only a little after 1:30 pm when we pull into our Cheddar Gorge accommodation, the Gordon's Hotel, Somerset—giving us ample time to relive childhood memories.

Some childhood memories never fade, and my visit to Cheddar Gorge and Caves with my family nearly four decades ago is one of them. Home to Britain's oldest complete human skeleton, the 9,000-year-old Cheddar Man, the dark, dripping caves lined with stalagmites and stalactites had left a deep impression on me. As a child, I found those dim, echoing chambers both exciting and mysterious, and they likely sparked my lifelong fascination with caves.

Now I am back to share the experience with my son and to see whether the Gorge and its caves live up to memory. Before venturing underground, though, we check into our hotel, where Pierce is delighted to discover he has his own room for once and does not have to bunk in with us. Darryl, weary from the drive and not keen on clambering through caverns, waves us off cheerfully—he will meet us for a scrumpy in a few hours' time.

It's about a ten-minute walk to the caves, leading us into the limestone walls of Cheddar Gorge, the largest gorge in the United Kingdom. With its sheer cliff face to the south and steep grassy slopes to the north, the walk is captivating, and the little souvenir shops along the way only add to the sense of adventure.

The caves are easy to spot: black openings in the cliffside, barred with metal gates from which a breath of icy air drifts out. Beside them sits the ticket booth, where we purchase our entry.

Entering Gough's Cave, where Cheddar Man was discovered, it takes only seconds to realise how different this is from my childhood visit. The handheld audio guide, replacing the chatter of a real guide, is the first clue. The bright fluorescent lighting is the second. Forty years ago, we were led slowly into the cave's mouth by an enthusiastic guide, straining our eyes to make out the shapes in the gloom. Today, the cave is lit up like a museum, every detail on display.

Doing as instructed, Pierce and I spend about 50 minutes exploring Gough's Cave, guided by the voices from our handheld devices. The wealth of stalagmites and stalactites is undeniably impressive, but it is the sight of large rounds of locally made Cheddar cheese, maturing in the cave's crannies, that leaves the strongest impression this time. I come away slightly disappointed that technology has dulled the thrill of walking through a dark, dank cave, though I can appreciate the safety and clarity it now offers.

As promised, and well rested, Darryl joins us in the early evening, and together we set off in search of scrumpy, the rough, strong cider native to this part of England's west coast. A nearby pub with a sprawling beer garden looks inviting, and before long, we are seated with generous glasses of flat, cloudy cider in front of us.

'Yuck. That's disappointing,' is Darryl's immediate reaction to his first mouthful.

'I don't find it that bad,' I counter, 'although I didn't expect it to be so flat. Do you think it's usually this flat? And warm?'

'I don't think much of it either. It is a bit warm,' Pierce adds.

'Well, I'm not sure I can drink it,' Darryl admits after a few more grimace-inducing sips.

True enough—when the round is finished, his glass is still half full.

'I'll finish yours, and you and Pierce can get something else,' I offer, to Darryl's relief.

Dinner of roast beef, Yorkshire pudding and vegetables follows in the beer garden, and with stomachs uncomfortably full, we are grateful for the short walk back to our hotel.

At each stop on this quick tour of southwest England, we've made sure breakfast is included, so the following morning finds us sitting down to the ubiquitous full English breakfast before our mid-morning departure. Today's destination is Ashburton, in Devon, on the near side of Dartmoor, but first we are stopping in the village of Ideford for lunch with some very old family friends.

I first met Bill and Ann when I was living on a houseboat at St Katharine's Docks in London. I was ten at the time, and they were the parents of Joanne, a girl my age on the neighbouring boat. My father and stepmother, Patma, had decided that a year living and travelling in England would be a good idea, and so had taken Michelle and me out of school. My aunt Cherry owned a barge moored at St Katharine's Docks near Tower Bridge, and it was here that my father and Patma relocated us. The barge was spacious, home to three of my cousins as well as us.

Bill, Ann and Joanne ran a restaurant from their own barge, and I spent countless hours there, helping Joanne with her chores. When Bill and Ann decided to race their barge up the east coast of England, they asked us to join them. That once-in-a-lifetime experience is something I have never forgotten.

Fast forward a few decades and both my father and Joanne are gone, but correspondence with those left behind has continued. Today is the first time since then that I will see Bill and Ann, and it carries a sadness, knowing that Joanne, my age, lost her battle with cancer only last year.

We meet at the tiny 16th-century Royal Oak pub, with its thatched roof and flagstone floors unchanged by time. Bill and Ann, too, seem little altered, while I am a far cry from the ten-year-old they once knew. Their warm exclamations make that clear. This is their local, as their easy banter with the publican shows, and any lingering awkwardness quickly dissolves over a glass of wine.

Lunch is waiting back at their home, and the hours slip past in reminiscence and catching up on the intervening years. It is a beautiful yet poignant visit, and we part with promises to meet again when Bill and Ann travel to Lennox Head, Australia, to visit Bill's sister the following Christmas.

Our accommodation for the night is Dartmoor Lodge, perched on the very edge of Dartmoor, with a view from our window of rolling green hills, grazing sheep and hedgerow fences. It is a picture-perfect outlook, made even more atmospheric by the evening drizzle. The hotel's large dining room is clearly a favourite with coach groups, and that night we dine on the curry buffet while the lively chatter of a busload of pensioners fills the room. It is a relief to retreat to our quiet room afterwards. By morning, the view has dulled beneath damp skies and low, overcast clouds.

Today we are heading further west, leaving Devon behind and entering Cornwall. At Truro, we plan to meet a cousin of mine for lunch before turning north to finish the day at Port Isaac. After yet another sizeable English breakfast, the weather has only worsened, and we wonder what the drive across Dartmoor will bring.

Dartmoor National Park covers nearly a thousand square kilometres of protected moorland, steeped in myths and legends—among them the Headless Horseman and spectral hounds. It is also famed for its granite hilltops, the tors, which we hope to see, though the weather makes that unlikely.

The road climbs steadily, bleak vegetation and rocky outcrops soon giving way to swirling mists. By the time we level out along the spine of Dartmoor, visibility has shrunk to little more than the glow of oncoming headlights. On the descent, the mist lifts just enough for us to stretch our legs and photograph some damp, grazing sheep. Disappointing as it is not to glimpse the famous tors, the drive itself is atmospheric and memorable.

At the foot of the moor, we reach Tavistock, where, despite the rain, we stop to explore before continuing easily along the A390 to Truro, where my cousin Lesley awaits.

Lesley has organised lunch at a nearby thatched pub, the Punchbowl and Ladle, parts of which date back to the 15th century. Over hearty food, we catch up on family news before following her suggestion for the afternoon: a visit to the National Trust property of Trelissick. Its 375 acres of grassland and woodland provide ample opportunity to walk off lunch, while the estate also contains Trelissick Mansion, once home to Spencer Copeland, the last of the Copeland family whose firm produced Spode china. Although the house itself is not open to the public, the setting alone makes the visit worthwhile.

With the afternoon well underway, we bid farewell to Lesley and head north. The drive along the A39 takes us through rolling green hills, past grazing cattle and the occasional line of wind turbines, before reaching Pendoggett where tonight's accommodation, the Cornish Arms, awaits. A former 16th-century coaching inn, it sits close to the roadside, its white limestone exterior giving it an appealingly timeworn character.

We are in North Cornwall for one main reason: to visit the town of Port Isaac, where the television series *Doc Martin* is filmed. Both of us are devoted fans, and seeing Port Isaac—known as Portwenn in the show—has long held a place on our bucket list. Since accommodation in the town itself is prohibitively expensive, we have based ourselves in nearby Pendoggett, just four kilometres away.

'Can you advise the best way to get to Port Isaac from here?' I ask our landlord once we have refreshed ourselves in our room.

'Here to see where *Doc Martin* is filmed?' he asks knowingly.

'Yes,' we reply.

'They're actually filming the next series at the moment,' he tells us. 'A few of the production team are even staying here.'

'You're kidding!' I practically yell, unable to hide my excitement. 'And Martin Clunes—the Doc—he's around?'

'He's not staying here, but yes. They're due to wrap up this Friday when the school holidays start. You may just see him.'

So excited am I by what we have just learnt that I barely register our landlord's instructions on the best way to reach Port Isaac and instead put blind faith in the car's sat nav. A mistake. Given multiple routes, it chooses the worst of all: a road barely wider than a goat track, riddled with blind corners, hemmed in by towering hedges, and skirting, at times, sheer cliffside drops.

With Darryl at the wheel and me beside him, eyes squeezed tightly shut, it falls to him to edge us through the madness—reversing for oncoming traffic, wincing as hedges scrape the car, and keeping us from the drops. Somehow, he gets us there in one piece.

'I am never trusting that sat nav again,' I declare as we finally pull into Port Isaac's car park. 'That was an experience I do not want to repeat.'

We find ourselves at the top of a sprawling village clinging to the Cornish coastline like it has been dropped onto the sides of a chasm. A narrow road threads down through grey stone houses and walls before spilling out at the sea. These seaside towns, built long before cars were imagined, offer little in the way of parking, so we heed the advice to stop as soon as we find a space and continue on foot. Locking the doors, I take in the view around us. It is starting to look uncannily like the show, and my excitement begins to edge out my still fast-beating heart.

The walk down into the heart of Port Isaac, where most of *Doc Martin* is filmed, is punctuated by cries of recognition.

'Look, there's the Doc's house! And there's the school! And the Portwenn chemist!'

Each corner seems to bring another familiar landmark. At the bottom of the hill, the rocky beach comes into view—so instantly recognisable—and the sight of a film crew confirms that filming really is underway. The Doc himself is absent, but his ever-cheerful secretary Morwenna is there, and like the rest of the tourists crowded into the tiny open-air pub nearby, we settle in to watch her run through her scenes.

It's a totally unexpected, exhilarating experience, only surpassed a short time later by the arrival of Martin Clunes himself. His appearance is met with cheers from the happy crowd, who cheer even louder when he kindly offers himself up for photos. Of course, I jump at the chance—this moment has been one of the big reasons for coming to England.

'Where are you from?' he asks as I stand beside him, Darryl happily snapping away.

'Byron Bay, Australia,' I reply. (No one ever knows Brunswick Heads.)

'Ah. Are you a hippy?'

'I was brought up as one.'

'And near the town of Clunes,' he adds with a grin.

I am impressed at how well he knows our faraway patch of the world, and we chat a little longer before it's time to let someone else have their turn.

While Darryl and I could easily have stayed there all evening watching the filming unfold, Pierce, unfamiliar with the show, is bored and hungry. So, after another wander through the village, we finally leave Portwenn/Isaac, still buzzing. The whole experience has been an incredible high, one of those rare bucket list moments that feels every bit as special as you had imagined.

Staying in a former coaching inn, once a resting point for weary men and their horses, means, of course, being close to the road. What once served the horses now serves the traffic, and its constant roar interrupts our sleep throughout the night. We wake a little groggy, but the copious supply of coffee, sausages, eggs and bacon soon shakes us awake.

'I think I'm getting a bit sick of all this meat and eggs for breakfast,' I groan.

'Well, I'm not,' says six-foot-five Pierce.

'I like them too,' adds Darryl, 'but they're not doing my waistline any favours.'

Today's destination is Glastonbury. Beyond knowing it as the site of the huge Glastonbury Festival, we know little about the town. We have also heard mention of something called the Glastonbury Tor, though we are not quite sure what it is. A few of my former workmates at the Crystal Castle were drawn here too, and we are curious to see what pulled them in.

We have all day to cover the 200-odd kilometre journey, and since Tintagel lies just up the road from Pendoggett, we decide to stop and explore the reputed former home of King Arthur. Darryl and I have been before, though our strongest memory is not of legends but of the delicious Cornish pasties we bought here. What we had forgotten is just how bleak and forlorn this stretch of the Atlantic coast can be. Today, the mood is only sharpened by low, heavy clouds and a freezing wind whipping in from the rough sea. Pierce is reluctant to leave the warmth of the car for what, from a distance, looks like little more than a pile of carefully placed rocks clinging to the edge of the escarpment. With some persuasion—and promises it will be worth it—we coax him out.

Tintagel, like the Cheddar Caves, has changed markedly since our last visit. A bitumen road now leads to a souvenir shop and ticket counter, serviced by a shuttle car. While Darryl opts for the easy ride, Pierce and I walk. From the counter, the only thing visible ahead is a steep set of steps clinging to the rocky promontory, climbing towards the stone ruins of the castle.

Built in the 13th century, Tintagel Castle is rumoured to be the place of King Arthur's conception. From the base, the steps look daunting, and although Darryl buys a ticket, he decides to attempt only what feels safe. Pierce and I, however, set off upwards and, some time later, find ourselves wandering through the stone remnants of this former stronghold. The view over the Atlantic is spectacular, and the bleak weather only heightens the atmosphere—until the clouds finally break. What had been bearable in the dry becomes miserable in the wet, and our descent back to the shop is far quicker than the climb.

By the time we reach the car, a nearby café boldly proclaiming 'World's Best Cornish Pasties' feels like an invitation. With the rain easing, we dry off inside while tucking into a pasty each.

'I've had better,' Darryl declares once he finishes.

'Yes,' I agree. 'Definitely not the world's best—the pastry's too thick.'

'Well, I liked it,' says Pierce.

Early afternoon finds us pulling up at our B&B for the night, the Covenstead. Centrally located and opposite an abbey, its appeal had been the promise of four-poster beds in a generously sized room. What we had overlooked was its main selling point—that the entire place is decked out in a pagan theme. We are therefore pleasantly surprised to find ourselves stepping into somewhere quite unlike anywhere we have stayed before. Brimming with unusual objects and curious artefacts, most with Gothic or pagan associations, the house is quirky yet comfortable. I would not, however, envy whoever is tasked with the dusting.

With plenty of daylight still left, we head back out and quickly see why Glastonbury appeals to people from our part of the world. In complete contrast to most of the English towns we have seen so far, the shopfronts along the main street are splashed in purples, reds, pinks and blues—very hippyish, and very reminiscent of Nimbin and

Byron Bay back home. Like those towns, the shops here lean heavily towards the New Age with meditation, massage, tarot and books dominating the offerings.

'No wonder so many of the girls from the Crystal Castle visit here,' I say. 'We could be back home. Everything looks so similar.'

'It reminds me a lot of Mullumbimby,' Darryl replies. 'Same health food and hippy clothes shops.'

With Glastonbury's main street explored, we make our way to the tourist office in search of information about the famous Tor. We assume it must be the structure perched on the intriguing cone-shaped hill that dominates the skyline and forms such a striking backdrop to the town.

'The Tor is actually the hill itself,' explains a friendly woman behind the counter, 'and the structure on top is St Michael's Tower. Artefacts dating back to the Iron Age have been found there. There was once a church on the summit, but today only the tower remains. You can walk all the way up.'

'Can you show us where the path starts?' I ask, accepting the map she hands me.

'I'll walk with you to the base,' says Darryl a little later, 'but I'm not sure I'll make it all the way to the top.'

The walk from ground level to the summit of the Tor is only about 160 metres, but with every step on a steep incline, it feels far longer. Gruelling though it is, the effort is rewarded. While Darryl makes it partway and chooses to wait below, Pierce and I press on, following the well-laid path that cuts through rolling green fields. With no fences, we find ourselves climbing among grazing sheep, pausing now and then to turn back and take in the ever-widening panorama unfolding behind us.

At the summit, I step through the roofless shell of the 14th-century St Michael's Tower and stand in awe at the sweeping 360-degree view. The countryside stretches in every direction, soft hills and farmland giving way to distant horizons.

'I wonder where the Glastonbury Festival site is?' Pierce interrupts my reverie. 'Do you think it's bigger than the Byron Bay Blues Festival site?'

Clearly, the mystique of this place is lost on him.

Our descent brings us back to Darryl, who is happily communing with the sheep as if they are old friends, and from there we wander down into town. The walk ends at a supermarket on Glastonbury High Street, where we collect a simple dinner—sandwiches, apples and a drink—for the princely sum of three pounds. Back at the Covenstead, we stretch out on our enormous, canopied four-poster beds and tuck in, content with our bargain feast.

Today marks the final day of our whirlwind tour of southwest England, and to round it off, we decide to stop in Bath on our way back to Caversham. Bath is a stunning city full of beautiful honey-coloured stone buildings, churches and bridges. Dating back to 60 AD, when the Romans built baths and a temple around the hot springs here, it has always been a favourite English city of mine. When Darryl and I first visited in 1990, we left deeply impressed, and now we are eager to share it with Pierce.

The complex is built much as you would expect of an ancient Roman bathhouse, full of large stone columns, carved stone statues and even a Gorgon's head. The centrepiece of the complex is the Great Bath, a large rectangular pool of green water fed by hot springs. With tiers of steps rising on all four sides, it was here that notables such as Jane Austen once sat to 'take the waters'.

Purchasing our tickets, we are handed self-guided audio devices—like at the Cheddar Caves, today's tour will be a do-it-yourself affair. The first instructions direct us towards the terrace, where we can stand beside a row of formidable stone statues and look down upon the Great Bath. Once at ground level, two thousand years of history have placed this pool some 20 metres below the streets of modern Bath, making the terrace the perfect vantage point.

But as we step outside, the words of our landlord back in Pendoggett—'*Friday, when the school holidays start*'—echo immediately in my mind. Any hope of a clear view is blocked by a mass of holidaying families. With little choice but to weave our way into the throng, the next hour delivers fascinating commentary and glimpses of pools, spas and ancient lounging rooms, but also an atmosphere that feels more claustrophobic than contemplative.

'School holidays are obviously not the time to visit attractions in England,' Darryl mutters.

'I know. This is crazy,' I agree. 'I suppose it's because every school here goes on break at the same time over summer—and plenty across Europe too. Imagine the numbers, all holidaying at once.'

'Well, lesson learnt,' Darryl sighs. 'Next time we'll steer clear of anywhere likely to attract hordes of school kids.'

Disappointed that the crowds have clouded our visit to one of the best-preserved Roman sites in the world, we leave Bath and begin the journey back to Caversham. Instead of the motorway, we choose the smaller A4. Partly it is to avoid the holiday traffic, but mostly because the A4—known as the Bath Road—has been here since Roman times. To end our whirlwind tour travelling along such an ancient route feels like a fitting conclusion: the road itself a reminder of how deeply history runs through this part of the world.

CHAPTER 21

Living in London

Extract from Darma Travels Blog-
Formerly a Bible printing factory, the three-storey conversion, located in a crazy, noisy Hackney Borough, was an adventure in London living we won't forget for a while.

Our month of car hire has come to an end, and with more train travel ahead, we decide to return the car rather than extend the rental. Beyond the convenience of grocery runs, most of what we want to do is easily reached by public transport.

Our next journey will take us along England's east coast by rail, but for now, there is plenty nearby to explore. My aunt Charlotte had mentioned that Windsor Castle is not far away, so a few days after returning from Bath, Darryl and I set out to find it.

At Reading Station, we are struck by the sight of fellow commuters dressed in their finest. Ascot Racecourse lies on the same line, and today, it seems, is a race day.

'Look, you can buy drinks on the train,' I point out as we watch racegoers begin to celebrate.

'How convenient,' Darryl muses. 'No need to drive, and you can have a few drinks on the way to the races. No chance of that back home.'

Not really knowing what to expect, our first glimpse of Windsor Castle from the train window is startling.

'Look at the size of it—it's huge,' I say in awe. 'It looks fantastic.'

Realising it might be wise to learn a little about the place before we arrive, I quickly pull up Google and read aloud a few facts as the train nears Windsor Station.

'It's the Queen's preferred residence,' I discover. 'Parts of it date back to the 11th century, making it the longest-occupied palace in Europe. King Henry VIII is buried in the chapel here, the Queen and her sister lived here during the war, and apparently we must see Queen Mary's Dolls' House.'

Windsor Castle dominates the small town of Windsor, and from the train station it's only a short walk to the entrance—already clogged with long queues. While Darryl waits on a nearby bench, I join the end of the line, passing the time by chatting with the Canadian tourist behind me.

'My sister and I have been in London for the past five days,' she tells me. 'Windsor Castle is the last on our list to see.'

'What else have you seen—or would recommend?' I ask.

'Whatever you do, try to visit the Soane Museum in London. It's not very well known, but it's really worth it.'

Tucking away that suggestion for the Soane Museum, I buy our tickets, collect the now-familiar audio devices, and rejoin Darryl. Between the two of us, castles are more his passion, but I still find plenty to enjoy over the next few hours. I file past Queen Mary's Dolls' House—the craftsmanship is remarkable, though I quickly decide it is not worth the extra queuing; I have never been fond of dolls. I wander through the State Apartments, their walls crowded with paintings and treasures from the Royal Collection, and admire the sheer opulence. The gardens, too, are worthwhile, but it is St George's Chapel that holds us longest. A stunning 15th-century building in the Gothic style, its atmosphere is steeped in history—royal weddings, burials, centuries of ceremony. It feels like a place worth lingering in.

'It's also where Queen Elizabeth will be buried,' I remark.

Back in Caversham, with our east coast trip fast approaching, we spend the following days wisely. One day takes us back into London by train to meet our niece, Pierce's cousin Tayla. Fresh from a four-week whirlwind Contiki tour of Europe, she flies home to Australia tomorrow. As it is her first trip abroad, we are eager to hear her impressions, and so we arrange to meet at the Serpentine Café in Hyde Park. She arrives looking confident and completely at ease in London, which is lovely to see. The fairly awful meal we are served is quickly forgotten in the fun of swapping travel stories. With the rain holding off, we walk together along the Serpentine, our conversation still flowing, until we find ourselves outside Kensington Palace.

'Home to Kate and Wills,' I say, peering through the gates, 'and heaps of other royals.'

Another day, we set out for Oxford, just a 25-minute train ride away. Beyond its famous university—where my aunt Cherry once studied—and the breaking of the four-minute mile, we know little else about the city. The train deposits us in an area that feels nothing like the Oxford we imagined: industrial, plain, and decidedly short on historic charm. A quick chat with an employee at a nearby kebab shop points us in the right direction, and within ten minutes, a very different Oxford emerges—one of spires, quads, and the beauty we had expected all along.

Oxford's story stretches back to Saxon times, but the city we see today began to take shape around the 10th century. Its university—the oldest in the English-speaking world—was first recorded in the 12th century, and from there Oxford's collection of beautiful buildings, representing almost every English architectural style, grew rapidly.

Our wanderings soon lead us to a more touristy part of town, where modern-day Oxford proudly celebrates two fictional residents. Alice, of *Alice in Wonderland* fame, was inspired by the daughter of the dean of Christ Church College, where Lewis Carroll once taught. And Harry Potter fans flock to the same college, whose Great Hall provided the model for Hogwarts' dining hall in the films.

The city's pride in these two characters is impossible to miss—posters, signs and touts everywhere urge us to join Alice- or Harry-themed walking tours. We decline and choose instead to explore at our own pace.

Much of our wandering is naturally drawn to the university and its cluster of magnificent buildings. The highlight comes when we stumble upon a striking circular structure in the neo-classical style. Built between 1737 and 1749, the Radcliffe Camera is often described as Oxford's most iconic building. Though now a library for scholars, its name puzzled us until we learned that *camera* simply means 'room' or 'chamber' in Latin.

At the Eagle and Child pub, we pause to peek inside, picturing the days when literary giants like J.R.R. Tolkien and C.S. Lewis gathered here with their writing group. Every antique and op shop we pass also draws us in for a browse.

'Did you know Oxford was spared heavy bombing in the war because Hitler planned to make it his capital once he conquered England?' I read aloud from my phone. 'And that monument we just passed—the Martyrs' Memorial—honours three men who were burned at the stake here for their religious beliefs and teachings.'

Before leaving Oxford, we decide refreshments are in order. Currently standing outside a department store advertising high tea in its upstairs restaurant, the choice of where and what to eat is made for us. The store turns out to be Boswells of Oxford, a family-run institution that has stood here since 1738. The high tea they serve is as decadent as it is lavish—and it finally breaks me.

'No more scones, jam and cream. I've had enough.'

Awakening early the next morning, the house quickly becomes a hive of activity. Today we will be farewelling Pierce, who tonight boards a bus to Amsterdam with his mate Matt. The two of them plan to spend the next two months backpacking around Eastern Europe, and the next time we see him will be back in Brunswick Heads.

Having lived in England for the past two and a half years, Pierce has accumulated far more than can fit into a single backpack, so much of the morning's bustle centres on sorting and prioritising what to take.

By mid-morning, with Pierce's backpack finally sorted, the house tidied, and our own cases in tow, the four of us make our way to Reading Station. There we bid farewell to Pierce and Matt before boarding our train, which, with a few changes along the way, will deposit us later that evening at a station near Southwold in the county of Suffolk. Unlike the rolling green hills and postcard paddocks of England's west and south coasts, this eastern side is flatter, wilder, more unkempt. For reasons I can't quite explain, I find it more appealing, and spend most of the journey with my nose pressed to the window.

Southwold is where Charlotte, Derek and Fudge have escaped while we use their Caversham home, and they have invited us to join them here to experience life in an English seaside resort town.

With its working lighthouse, rows of brightly painted beach huts, famous pier, busy harbour and long beach, Southwold is a popular holiday spot, and the next few days pass quickly. We soon come to appreciate the flat, open countryside, and with an abundance of walking tracks on offer, each day brings a new exploratory walk. One such jaunt takes us along a seaside estuary where families line both banks, shoulder to shoulder. At first glance, it looks like they are fishing, but none of them are holding rods.

'What are you doing?' we ask.

'We're crabbing,' replies the father of a young boy.

'Crabbing?' we echo.

'You just tie a bit of bacon to a piece of string and drop it in the water. The crabs grab hold soon enough. The tricky part is shaking them off the string and into the bucket.'

From Charlotte and Derek's house, the famous beach huts of Southwold are in clear view, and our walks often lead us past these pastel-painted little buildings. Despite the cold, damp weather, many are in use, their doors flung wide open. Inside, hardy locals huddle over gas burners or sit wrapped in coats, reading newspapers on deck chairs. I admire their dedication, but the thought of sitting in a bare wooden hut, fully clothed and surrounded by the chill sea air, holds no appeal for me.

Not far from the huts stands the award-winning Southwold Pier, where we spend one afternoon exploring before stopping for lunch. Stretching 190 metres into the cold North Sea, this early-1900s pier is thriving rather than fading, unlike many of its counterparts across Britain. With its mix of modern coin-operated novelty machines, cafés, and souvenir and chocolate shops, it has enjoyed a welcome resurgence in popularity.

On our final evening in Southwold, we decide to forgo Charlotte's wonderful cooking and treat them instead to fish and chips. As the shop is within walking distance, I happily volunteer to collect the order. Standing in line for the 40 minutes it takes to cook, I cannot help comparing Southwold to Brunswick Heads. Both are small, popular seaside towns, both attract the same mix of locals and tourists, and both demand equally long waits at the fish and chip shops.

Before leaving Southwold, Charlotte and Derek surprise us with a gift that is as thoughtful as it is unique: a personalised wall tile made by a local artisan. Brightly coloured and titled *Darma Travels*, it features a large cruise ship, a fiftieth birthday banner, a lighthouse, and the Union Jack. Every detail seems to capture a chapter of our journey. Once hung in pride of place at home, it will forever remind us of this adventure.

Today's journey is again by train, first to Colchester and then on to Clacton-on-Sea, where we have booked a B&B for the night. The train that pulls into the unmanned station is just two carriages long, another glimpse into how England's public transport manages to remain viable.

We are heading to Clacton because it is the town where I was born, and via Colchester because it is where my father went to school. With a gift for storytelling, Dad often filled my childhood with tales of his school days here, of the castle, and of treasures he once dug from the fields. While no treasure reveals itself on this visit, we do explore the still largely intact Norman castle and pause at the house where the nursery rhyme *Twinkle, Twinkle, Little Star* was written.

The last time I set foot in Clacton-on-Sea was nearly 40 years ago, and my memories of it are faint. With no family here now, our visit is purely nostalgic: to see the hospital where I was born, the house where my father and Aunt Cherry grew up, and to get a sense of Clacton as it is today.

Switching on Google Maps as the train rolls into Clacton Station, we weave our way through the main streets towards our accommodation. The walk quickly recalls conversations we had aboard the *Arcadia* on our way to England.

'Clacton is not what it was,' people would say.

'Really? Why?'

'It's gone downhill. No one wants to holiday at the English seaside anymore—it's cheaper to go abroad.'

'And what's that done?'

'Many of the boarding houses and hotels are now cheap bedsits. With fewer tourists, there's far less work, and far less money in the town.'

Our B&B for the night, the Chudleigh, sits only a short stroll from the foreshore. It is only when we arrive that I notice it stands just five doors down from the address listed on my birth certificate. Having grown up on the opposite side of the world, with no nearby family or tangible links like this, the discovery thrills me. I cannot resist sharing it.

'I was born in Clacton,' I tell the elderly lady at reception. 'And my grandparents lived in the house three doors down.'

'Ah, Scattergood,' she replies, glancing at our reservation. 'I remember them.'

We are only in Clacton for one night, so the afternoon and following morning are devoted to seeing as much of the town as possible. Our first stop is Clacton Pier. Built in 1871, it is almost twice the length of the one at Southwold.

With its dilapidated roller coaster and tacky amusement rides, it lacks the charm of Southwold's pier, but its saving grace is the view from the end. From here, we gaze out across the cold North Sea at hundreds of wind turbines, standing to attention like sentinels in the water. We have seen many wind farms on land, but never one at sea, and the sight of so many towering structures rising from the waves is both strange and mesmerising.

Dinner that evening is Mexican, enjoyed at a restaurant overlooking Clacton Pier. The next morning, fortified by yet another hearty full English breakfast, we set out to see Clacton Hospital, a few former family homes, and one of the amusement arcades for which the town is known. With school holidays still in full swing, we do not linger long. Before midday, our list is complete, and after a final photo in front of Clacton Hospital, we return to the B&B, collect our bags, and make our way to Clacton Station.

BUCKET LISTS AND WALKING STICKS

Today's destination is the London borough of Hackney, where my cousin Emma and her husband Simon have generously offered us their house for the next eight nights. While they holiday in St Ives with their young son, Gabriel, the house will be empty, and they have urged us to make the most of it. We certainly intend to, given its central location. We have also arranged for Paige and a close friend from back home, Karen, to join us for a few days while we are here.

Dalston, the district of Hackney where the house is located, is a real eye-opener. Exiting Dalston Kingsland Station, we are immediately swept into a riot of humanity and sound. The throngs of mainly Afro-Caribbean locals, the relentless traffic, and the sheer cacophony could not be further from sleepy Caversham or Southwold. Across the road, the vibrant Ridley Street Market adds another layer, with reggae music and an eclectic jumble of stalls, giving the whole scene an almost electric charge.

Emma and Simon's house, when we find it, is equally surprising. Once a Bible-printing factory, it has been transformed into a three-storey loft within a gated community, and we can hardly believe it is ours for the week. Within hours, we have settled in, stocked the fridge from a nearby supermarket, and are enjoying coffee on their cleverly designed balcony, already feeling at home.

It feels like a stroke of luck to be living in Central London, and we waste no time drawing up an ambitious list of things to see and do. First on the list is the Museum of London. To get there, we alight at Barbican Tube Station, a stop very familiar to me. Twenty-five years ago, when I worked in a large travel agency here, this was where I stepped off each morning—Evening Standard newspaper in one hand, Polo mints and a large bottle of water in the other.

The Museum of London lies only a short walk from St Paul's Cathedral, so after immersing ourselves in its stories of plagues, fires, famine and wars, we wander towards the great cathedral. The wedding venue of Princess Diana and final resting place for Nelson, St Paul's, is not only awe-inspiring in its beauty but also seems to pulse with history.

We are near St Katharine's Docks, a place I spent much of my childhood, and curiosity about how it looks today makes it the perfect spot for lunch.

'We can get something at the Dickens Inn,' I suggest to Darryl.

A short Tube ride takes us to Tower Hill Station, the nearest stop for both Tower Bridge and the Tower of London. Being Sunday, the crowds are heavy, but as we have visited both before, it is enough simply to stroll past and admire their splendour again. From here, the Shard also rises into view—a modern addition that, surprisingly, seems to sit comfortably alongside its much older neighbours.

St Katharine's, when we arrive, still carries a resemblance to the dock I remember, though today it has clearly been modernised. Once-abandoned warehouses have been converted into stylish apartments, and the Dickens Inn looks larger than I recall. The food ends up being disappointing, but the atmosphere more than makes up for it—sitting here on this Sunday afternoon surrounded by chattering Londoners is a pleasure in itself.

Back in Dalston, one of the things we appreciate is its connection to the London Overground. Much of our travel is done above ground rather than in the hot, narrow tunnels of the Underground, and with Oyster cards in hand—London's version of Australia's Opal or Go cards—getting around Zone 2 is both practical and affordable. No tickets to juggle, just a quick tap on and off.

Today, we set out for Greenwich, keeper of time as we know it, with Greenwich Mean Time originating at the Royal Observatory nearby. We are not here for time, however, but because Darryl is eager to relive one of his most vivid London memories. Years ago, one of his jobs required him to walk to work each day through the Greenwich Foot Tunnel, and the experience has never left him.

The tunnel itself is a 370-metre cast-iron passageway, just 2.74 metres in diameter and sitting 15 metres below the Thames. In Darryl's day, its tile-clad walls constantly dripped river water, and the lifts down to it were creaky, wooden contraptions attended by an operator.

'I used to only start breathing properly once I reached the middle of the tunnel,' he recalls. 'Then I'd bolt like crazy until I got to the other side. The floor was always wet, and it was so gloomy.'

To reach the Greenwich Foot Tunnel, we first catch the Docklands Light Railway—an above-ground system that feels straight out of Harry Potter, like the rickety ride to his vault at Gringotts. I can't help but laugh as we are thrown about in the small, two-carriage train as it thunders around tight corners, high above ground level.

'That was totally unexpected and fun,' I grin as we step off. 'Almost like a roller coaster.'

Slightly to Darryl's disappointment, the tunnel has been tidied up since his time—the lifts are now self-operated, and most of the notorious leaks have been sealed. While it may not match his memories, I find the experience oddly exhilarating. Stepping out of the lift, the long, tiled wormhole stretches ahead, empty and echoing. The air is cold, damp, and still. Like Darryl once did, I hold my breath and hurry through the first half, head down, determined to reach the midpoint—just in case I have to sprint for my life. By the second half, my pace slows, and I notice the trickles of water and the strange, otherworldly atmosphere. Emerging into daylight brings a small surge of triumph.

'That was fantastic,' I say, grinning. 'No wonder you never stop talking about it—and kept pestering Pierce to try it.'

'You should have tried it when it was wet and dark,' Darryl replies.

With several ways to leave Greenwich, we decide the most appealing is a river cruise along the Thames that will carry us all the way to Westminster. The next couple of hours slip by as we glide past some of London's most famous landmarks, each steeped in history. What makes the trip even more memorable are the tongue-in-cheek money-saving tips offered by the boat's captain.

'Don't pay 25 quid to see London from the London Eye—you can see it for free from the Tate Museum's balcony,' he calls out.

'And don't waste money going up the Shard. Just tell them you're heading for a drink at the bar on top.'

What amuses Darryl most on this Thames cruise isn't the commentary but the sight of treasure hunters scattered along the muddy banks. With the tide out, wide stretches of riverbed are exposed, and people wander across them, metal detectors sweeping steadily through the silt and debris.

'Look—there's another lot with detectors,' Darryl points out. 'Who'd have thought so many people do this?'

'And just imagine what's been found here,' I say.

'Thousands of years of history and treasure,' he answers, half wistful, half envious.

Westminster is eventually reached, and we linger along the Thames, taking in Big Ben, the Houses of Parliament and the soaring Gothic presence of Westminster Abbey. For a breather, we slip into the neighbouring Victoria Tower Gardens, where Rodin's famous *Burghers of Calais* statue stands solemnly amid the greenery.

Thanks to our Oyster cards, travel is effortless—no fumbling for change—so when a bus pulls up, we simply hop on, caring little where it goes. To our surprise, it rumbles straight across the Thames and soon delivers us past one of cricket's most hallowed grounds, the Oval. By then, the day's sights have caught up with us, and when Vauxhall Station comes into view, we disembark and eventually make our way back to Dalston.

It's great to have Paige arrive the following day, and even better when Karen joins us the day after. Fresh off a long flight from Australia and determined to outpace jet lag, she throws herself straight into our plan to explore Camden Market. Just a few stops away on the overground, it's an easy trip, and by lunchtime, the three of us are seated above Camden Lock, tucking into steaming bowls of dhal, rice and vegetables. Darryl, less enthused by the prospect of more shopping, has opted to stay back and rest.

The market is lively but crowded, and with so many stalls echoing those back home, we decide to push on into Central London. Harrods, the world's most famous department store, is calling. Each of us is determined to leave with a small memento, and we have also agreed it's the perfect excuse for a celebratory glass of champagne. Soon enough, we are perched in the Harrods Champagne Bar, sipping champagne cocktails and sharing camembert croquettes, our shopping bags tucked neatly at our feet. To round off our visit, we seek out the Princess Diana Memorial—which, somewhat disconcertingly, turns out to be tucked away in the men's shoe department.

With Paige back at her Beaconsfield pub, the next few days are spent exploring London with Karen. The British Museum keeps us engrossed for hours, and having so recently stood at the Parthenon in Athens, I am especially eager to see the Elgin Marbles. Removed from the Parthenon in 1805 and shipped to England under the pretext of preservation, the marbles have remained here ever since. Since the 1980s, as restoration of the Acropolis monuments has progressed, Greece has repeatedly called for their return—a debate that still stirs strong feelings. Controversy aside, I am simply glad for the chance to see up close the missing pieces of a monument I had admired only a few months earlier.

The Soane Museum, recommended by the Canadian tourist I met while queuing for Windsor Castle, more than lives up to her praise. Once the home of architect Sir John Soane, it has been preserved exactly as he left it almost 180 years ago. Wandering through its rooms feels like stepping back in time—a kitchen, a bedroom, a lounge, each space offering an authentic glimpse into domestic life two centuries ago.

To balance out what had been a string of fairly cerebral days, we wander through Hamleys, the world's largest toy shop, stroll along Oxford Street, and finish at Selfridges, another of London's grand department stores. Our final day with Karen takes us to Portobello Road Market, arguably the world's most famous and certainly its largest antique market. I pick up a few keepsakes—an antique spoon and an old bottle opener—while Karen, after spilling coffee down her front, is forced into buying a beautiful new top. As we prepare to leave, I catch sight of a burnt-out high-rise in the distance. It takes a moment to register that it is Grenfell Tower, the site of the devastating fire just weeks earlier that claimed 72 lives.

It has been fun exploring London with Karen, and we bid her farewell the next morning with a mix of regret and envy. She is off to join her parents on their longboat as they cruise the English canals, before continuing on to the Continent. To console ourselves, we decide a visit to West Ham is in order—home of Darryl's beloved English Premier League football team. That afternoon, we set off for this storied East End suburb.

Whilst Pierce follows Arsenal in the English Premier League, Darryl has always been a loyal West Ham supporter. He had hoped to attend a match while we were here, but both cost and timing got in the way—tickets are so expensive you could almost buy a small car back home, and our visit happened to coincide with the League's summer break.

Today, though, the season has just recommenced, and our plan is simple: find a pub full of West Ham fans and watch the game with them. Easier said than done. West Ham itself is heaving with teenagers heading to a nearby music festival, and it takes some time before we finally settle on what seems like the right spot.

'West Ham are playing today. Could you put them on the TV?' we ask the barmaid hopefully.

'Sorry,' she shrugs. 'They don't broadcast the 3 pm Premier League game!'

Our nine days in London are up, and while we've seen and done plenty, there are still so many places I would have liked to visit. These will have to wait for another time. Today we are heading back to Caversham.

CHAPTER 22

Circumnavigating Ireland

Extract from Darma Travels Blog-
Never, in all the countries we have passed through, have we been so totally blown away by the cheek, hospitality and fun of a nation's occupants. For a population forever shrouded in grey clouds, whose economy has taken its fair share of blows, whose youth flee to other lands on graduation, they are an amazingly resilient lot.

After such a hectic few weeks, it's a relief to return to the serenity of our Caversham home. With laundry to catch up on and cupboards to restock, the first few days fly by. Midweek finds us walking along the Thames into Reading, hoping to pick up a new lock for my backpack—Pierce took my previous one to Europe.

Unlike other days, when our only walking companions along the Thames are ducks and swans, today the path is heaving with people—and we seem to be walking against the tide.

'There's a lot of people around,' I mutter, squeezing past a pack of teenagers.

'There's more than a lot. There are thousands,' says Darryl. 'And they're all young.'

The further we go, the harder it becomes to push through. By the time we reach our local Aldi, the scene stops us in our tracks. Teenagers are sprawled across gutters, footpaths, and gardens, empty bottles at their feet, refilling plastic water bottles with whatever alcohol they can find. Inside, the supermarket shelves have been stripped bare, the store itself almost impassable.

'It must be a music festival,' we exclaim together.

It turns out to be the Reading Festival, held here each year along the Thames. With more than 100,000 festivalgoers descending, Reading and Caversham are overrun like a swarm of locusts. Supermarkets are stripped bare, trains and buses packed to bursting, and pubs slash their menus while hiking prices. We discover this the hard way when we head to our local, hoping for another bargain two-pound meal, only to find the menu cut down and the prices tripled.

'Come back after the festival,' the barmaid advises.

'But we won't be here,' we groan.

The reason we won't be here is that we've managed to find a way to see some of Ireland. Time and cost had always dictated whether we could make it there at all, but the discovery of a cheap cruise leaving from Southampton this Friday has given us an unexpected solution. Ideally, we would have explored Ireland by car or campervan, but this P&O cruise aboard the adult-only *Oriana* not only promises a good taste of the country, it also comes with the welcome bonus of removing all the stress of planning.

Ireland, with its leprechaun legends, warm people and rolling green countryside, is a country we've both long wanted to visit, and we're extremely happy it's finally happening. We also have a couple of bucket list items to tick off—one being the downing of an authentic

Guinness. In fact, it will be the first Guinness either of us has ever tried.

'I always said I'd have my first Guinness in Ireland,' Darryl insists.

'I just never had the chance to try one,' I admit.

It feels good settling into our cabin aboard the *Oriana*, memories of our last cruise sparking back to life. Our bargain fare means no balcony, just a large window—but knowing Irish weather, that hardly seems a loss. A wise decision, as it turns out: it takes about 30 hours to sail down the English Channel and into the Celtic Sea, and rain lashes against our glass the entire way.

In the meantime, we fall easily into familiar routines. Three-course meals with wine are happily welcomed, the evening shows enjoyed, and the guest speakers prove interesting. What truly surprises—and pleases—us, however, is the captain's first announcement.

'Hello, this is your Captaaaain speaking.'

It's Captain Ashley Cook—Captain Cook—the very same man who carried us halfway around the world four months ago.

'What are the chances?' we exclaim.

'It's brilliant,' I add. 'Now I really feel we're in safe hands.'

Our 30 hours of wet cruising finally deliver us to Cobh, a small Irish seaside town best known as the last departure port of the ill-fated *Titanic*. It is also the gateway for visitors to nearby Blarney Castle, and I wake tingling with excitement. Kissing the Blarney Stone has been a lifelong wish of mine, and today, I will finally make it happen.

I first heard about the stone as a child. Back then, I knew nothing of the legend—the promise of eloquence, or the gift of charming deception, bestowed on those who kiss it. Instead, the story painted for me was of a simple headstone-shaped rock in a field, inexplicably kissed by passersby. Today, I will discover what the reality truly looks like.

The *Oriana* pulls into Cobh Harbour a little after 7 am, and my first glimpse of Ireland is a granite-grey port town wrapped in mist. Rising above the rooftops is a hulking cathedral, barely visible through the haze, while beyond it, fat, low clouds hang over rolling emerald hills. It is exactly as I had pictured Ireland.

Blarney Castle lies only 30 minutes away, and we have chosen a ship-organised excursion that also takes in nearby Cork and, temptingly, includes a warming Irish coffee. It feels like the perfect way to begin.

Our past experience with pre-organised excursions has taught us that much depends on the host and driver, and this time we strike gold. From the moment we board, Maura, our warm and witty Irish guide, keeps us entertained with legends and history. When her voice finally rests, Bill, our leprechaun-like driver, bursts into one ribald Irish ditty after another, filling the bus with laughter.

With such company, the ride passes quickly, and soon we are stepping into the misty gardens of Blarney Castle. Hidden within them is a 600-year-old fortress, and high in its battlements, 80 metres above the ground, lies the famous Blarney Stone. Unlike the childhood image I once held of a simple rock in a field, kissing it requires effort—and some daring contortions. Darryl decides to sit this one out.

'I'm eloquent enough already,' he grins.

As expected, there's a queue, and as we inch closer to the Blarney Stone, I chat happily with those around me. The first stretch leads into a cramped spiral staircase, 120 narrow stone steps twisting upward. A fraying rope offers some reassurance, though it hardly inspires confidence. Emerging at the top, I step onto the parapet, where two men await—one with a camera permanently trained, the other there to stop me from tumbling headlong 80 metres to my death.

My task is clear: sit with my back to the ledge, lean out over the dizzying drop, grip the iron railings and kiss a smooth grey slab of stone. I must do all this quickly and, with the camera aimed squarely at me, as elegantly as possible. Heart thumping with excitement, exhilaration and fear, I manage it—and tick off another bucket list item.

'That was brilliant,' I beam to Darryl. 'A little dodgy in parts, but great.'

With the fat grey clouds we'd seen earlier finally breaking, we don't linger in the castle gardens for long. Instead, we make our way to the café and souvenir shops where our promised Irish coffee awaits.

'That was by far the best Irish coffee I've ever had,' I say, licking the last of the cream from my lips.

'It was definitely the best I've ever had,' agrees Darryl.

'How do they make it taste so good?' I wonder aloud.

'Apparently it's all in the whisky—and the way they whip the cream.'

'Well, I'm going to have one every day while we're in Ireland,' I declare.

It's still raining heavily when we reach the university city of Cork, and with it being Sunday, the place looks half asleep. Rather than wrestle with the downpour, we decide to head back to Cobh instead. The town's towering cathedral begs investigation, and surely there will be a café or pub to shelter in. It proves a good choice: as we drive into Cobh, the rain eases at last, and the mist that has clung to the town all morning begins to lift.

The next few hours pass quickly and eventfully. We never do discover why Cobh boasts such a towering cathedral, but we learn its name—St Colman's—and that it is among the tallest buildings in Ireland. Strolling along the harbourfront, we stumble upon a band playing lively Irish tunes in the rotunda of a small park. We sit to listen, and soon strike up a conversation with Larry Parsons, the cheerful little man beside us.

'I had my own house and business in England,' he tells us, 'but lost it all when the business went broke. Luckily, I'd been left a patch of land on the north coast here. I built a small house and have lived there ever since—over 40 years now.'

'And what brings you to Cobh today?' we ask.

'To earn a bit of money, I drive people around,' he replies. 'I've brought a group of tourists to the Titanic Experience. They're in there now. We'll head back later this afternoon.'

Larry encourages us to visit the Titanic Experience, so we step inside to wander through replica cabins of the ill-fated ship and examine some of its surviving artefacts. We learn that 123 people boarded the ship's tenders here at Cobh, from the very building in which we now stand, and through an interactive game, we discover the fates of two of those passengers. While it is a fun way to engage with the Titanic's story, it feels a little gimmicky, and the sight of a pub across the road, alive with Guinness drinkers and loud Irish music, proves far more tempting.

'I'm waiting until Dublin before I order a Guinness, so I'll have a lager now,' Darryl decides.

'Well, I'm having another Irish coffee,' I declare.

It's a fitting end to our first day in Ireland, and by 6 pm we are back on board, watching as the ship weighs anchor and turns toward Dublin, tomorrow's port of call.

Dublin, the capital of the Republic of Ireland and home to James Joyce, author of Ulysses, is often described as a literary city. Trinity College, Ireland's oldest, counts Oscar Wilde, Bram Stoker and Jonathan Swift among its alumni, and it also houses the incredible illuminated Book of Kells. Many from our ship will be queuing to see it today, but we will not. For us, Dublin is less about libraries and more about life on the streets—firstly, mingling with the locals, and secondly, finally trying a Guinness. Since the beer was born here, what better place to tick another item off our bucket list?

To achieve our objectives, we decide once again to rely on a trusty steed: the hop-on hop-off bus. Disembarking the Oriana, we find one conveniently waiting at the harbour. The cheeky—if somewhat rude—welcome from the driver makes for an odd start, and things soon become even more interesting when it dawns on us that we've boarded a bus with a decidedly erratic, theatrical driver. While the following few hours introduce us to many examples of his eccentricities, the more memorable ones include:

Causing the double-decker bus, while hurtling down busy streets, to sway from side to side in time to the song Black Velvet Band.

'We're dancing,' he cackles.

To pull up just in front of a group of waiting tourists, leave the door closed and keep the bus inching forward each time they draw level.

'Ha ha.' He finds this hilarious.

To toot his horn loudly, wave and point at a young lady walking peacefully along the footpath.

'Eyes left, lads. Isn't she a corker?'

And finally, to pull his bus up well short of a very large gentleman waiting to cross the road.

'We don't want to get hit by that, do we?'

So entertaining is he that we stay on the bus far longer than intended, even forgoing the Guinness Storehouse tour we had considered.

'Someone said it covers seven floors and is self-guided. They don't even brew here anymore, you just see the process. We'll get our Guinness at the Temple Bar Pub instead,' I placate Darryl.

Temple Bar Pub, set in the heart of Temple Bar, a lively, cobbled, pedestrian quarter on the south bank of the River Liffey, was recommended to Darryl years ago by some Irish workmates when he was in London. He had always intended to follow up on that recommendation, and after reluctantly farewelling our unforgettable bus driver, we go in search of it.

With its vibrant red frontage and overflowing baskets of flowers, the 1840s-established Temple Bar Pub is easy to spot. Ducking through its low wooden doors, we step into a dark, dusty warren. Its crowded interior is proof of its popularity, but we are lucky and immediately secure a recently vacated seat. Perched on our stools amidst the milky darkness with live Irish music washing over us, we take our first mouthfuls of Guinness and thus complete another bucket list item.

'Yum. That's really good!' I exclaim. 'It's much creamier than I expected, and I like that it isn't cold.'

'It's warmer than I thought it would be,' says Darryl. 'It's not bad.'

After two beers each, we head back out onto the streets. The afternoon drifts by with antique shops, a wander through the 800-year-old St Patrick's Cathedral, a browse of market stalls and the purchase of small gifts for family back home. Claddagh rings, the traditional Irish symbol of love, loyalty and friendship, prove the perfect choice, and there is no shortage to pick from.

Before reboarding, we stumble upon a little place advertising great Irish coffees. Remembering my vow to have one each day in Ireland, we step inside. Once again, it is every bit as enjoyable as the ones before.

'They really do make the best Irish coffees here,' I say with a happy sigh.

Overnight, as we reacquaint ourselves with the P&O Headliners dance troupe, the Oriana edges further up Ireland's eastern coast, leaving the calmer Irish Sea for the noticeably rougher North Atlantic.

'This ship isn't as smooth as the Arcadia,' I remark.

'I did hear something about that,' Darryl replies. 'Apparently, the Arcadia is one of P&O's smoothest ships.'

Our port today is Killybegs, in County Donegal. Ireland's largest fishing port, yet home to barely 1,200 people, it is also one of the smallest inhabited ports we have visited. The town has laid on a warm welcome—banners strung across the streets, tables of cake, scones and tea, and even a little craft fair put together by the local women's association for our benefit. Killybegs is charming, but it is the wild landscape beyond that draws most of us here. With a local tour already arranged, we are soon tucked into a minivan and on our way.

Inland, the climate is harsh, and from the windows we see bleak, close-cropped fields, scattered white cottages and wind-battered shrubs. It may be spring now, but I can only imagine how cold and desolate it must be in winter.

As we climb higher, the greenery thins into rocky hillsides and peat bogs, with sudden glimpses of ocean flashing between the slopes. We are on the narrow, unnerving road to the Slieve League Cliffs, among the tallest sea cliffs in Europe. Rising 609 metres above the Atlantic, the views when we reach the top—the pounding ocean below, the Sligo Mountains behind us, Donegal Bay stretching out ahead—make the vertiginous journey more than worthwhile.

Our journey back to Killybegs takes us first to a weaving factory and then to a tiny, dark-roomed pub where, with a peat fire glowing and a local lass playing accordion and singing haunting Irish songs, we savour today's Irish coffee. Back in town, eager to support the community's efforts, we wander the little craft fair where Aran sweaters and Irish tweed dominate the stalls. We find a beautiful handwoven scarf, but have no luck at the cake and tea table—every crumb has been devoured.

Killybegs, with its stark, unforgiving landscape and its warm, generous people, leaves us with memories we will not soon forget.

As does the Oriana a few hours later. Tomorrow's destination is Galway, and our current trajectory down Ireland's rugged western coast and through the North Atlantic Ocean is shaping up to be our roughest night of sailing ever. Dinner is ignored as, feeling slightly the worse for wear, we lie on our seesawing bed, listening to the creaks and groans of the ship, and, in my case, praying we don't sink overnight.

'Oh, thank God the rocking has stopped,' I greet the morning. 'That was the worst night ever.'

'I don't know why, but I didn't feel very well,' admits Darryl.

'You were seasick,' I reply.

'No, I wasn't. I've never been seasick before. It must have been something else.'

'Sure,' I say, with all the sarcasm I can muster.

Apart from being the birthplace of actor Peter O'Toole, we know very little about Galway. So today, forgoing organised excursions, we simply set out to walk the town and get a feel for it.

'I wouldn't mind buying a pub T-shirt if we see one,' Darryl suggests.

'That's a great idea,' I reply. 'Let's make it our mission to buy a T-shirt from a pub before the day's out.'

Galway, lacking a dock, must be reached by tender, so it's midmorning by the time we set foot on its cobbled pedestrian high street. The street, alive with buskers playing uplifting Irish music, feels like the perfect place to begin our T-shirt hunt, and so our exploration of Galway begins—through the doorway of one pub after another.

Our quest takes us on a winding circuit that also includes notable sights like the Long Walk, the Spanish Arch, Eyre Square and the River Corrib. At pub number 15, we pause for today's Irish coffee, where Darryl questions our so-called mission.

'I thought we would have visited all the pubs and found one with a decent T-shirt by now. How many pubs are there in Galway?'

'Seventy-seven,' I read out a few minutes later.

'Seventy-seven! You're kidding!' Darryl exclaims.

With no real grasp of how a city could still sustain seventy-seven pubs, we call an end to our hunt and buy the very next T-shirt we see, decent or not. The rest of our time in Galway is spent more leisurely—sitting on park benches, chatting with locals, browsing op shops and poking through souvenir stalls. I manage to find a pair of Irish knot earrings moments before the realised threat of impending rain drives us back towards our ship's tenders.

With Galway, the last of our four Irish ports, the evening is given over to reflection on our whirlwind tour. As hoped, we leave in awe of its people. Of all our travels so far, the Irish stand out as the most accommodating, the friendliest, the cheekiest. And although the land is breathtakingly beautiful, no country deserves such dreadful weather—which only makes its grand, craic-loving inhabitants all the more remarkable.

As on the Arcadia, we have done a poor job of spending our onboard credit, so the 30 hours back through the Celtic Sea and English Channel to Southampton slip by in a happy flurry of last-minute indulgence. At Southampton, we self-disembark once again, surprised that no one bothers to check a passport, and begin the journey back to Caversham.

CHAPTER 23

Hong Kong and Home

Extract from Darma Travels Blog-
It was with some anticipation that we were awaiting our sojourn in Hong Kong. Home to the most skyscrapers in the world (over 2000), ranked as the freest economic and competitive entity in the world, the world's most popular international traveller destination.

It's early September now, and after enjoying the pleasures of an English spring and summer, we are lucky enough to catch a fleeting glimpse of autumn. Leaves fall quickly from the trees, the temperature rarely climbs above 18 degrees, and the once 10:30 pm sunsets have slipped back to 8 pm. With Charlotte and Derek soon needing their house back, and Jordie, our dog in Australia, eagerly awaiting our return, our adventure is drawing to a close. For so long, we were undecided about how we would make our way home, but plans have finally fallen into place. This time next week, we will be boarding a plane from Heathrow, bound for Brisbane via Dubai and Hong Kong.

Sad to be leaving but excited at the thought of travelling once again, we make the most of our final days in England. One day, we take the bus to High Wycombe, where we bid farewell to Paige over lunch at a vegetarian restaurant, then enjoy a leisurely browse through the local op shops. With Paige still unsure of her plans, whether she will return to Australia or spend Christmas in England, the farewell is tinged with melancholy.

Another day finds us back in Dalston, London, where we finally share a meal with Emma and her family. Despite staying in their house for a week earlier in the trip, this is our first chance to see them face to face, and lunch becomes a long, easy afternoon of conversation. Emma's sister, my cousin Danielle, joins us with her own family, and together we strengthen family bonds before our departure.

Caversham Court Gardens, site of the lively fete we enjoyed earlier in the year, has been hosting outdoor cinema nights all summer, with the final screening set for Harry Potter and the Deathly Hallows. Returning in the early evening from our lunch with Emma, we find the night cold and miserable, rain teeming down in sheets. Passing the gardens, Darryl and I can only shake our heads in bemusement at the sight of families huddled under umbrellas, stoically watching the film. It feels like one last reminder of just how stalwart the British really are.

Two days before our departure, Charlotte, Derek and Fudge return to reclaim their house, which proves fortuitous for us, as it means another chance to enjoy Charlotte's excellent cooking. Our final day in England is spent discarding items that no longer fit into our cases, packing up the barbecue—likely destined never to see the light of day again—and taking short walks between showers of rain. On one such walk, a final memory of England takes shape when we notice the gardens and footpaths of nearby houses crawling with slugs.

'Look at the size of them!' Darryl exclaims.

'They're half the size of your foot,' I reply, wrinkling my nose.

'I've never seen slugs so big, nor so many!'

Monday, 11 September arrives, and it's with a sombre mood that we bid farewell to Charlotte, Derek and Fudge. Their generosity has made this trip possible, and we will always be grateful. While Derek readies his pushbike for his regular Monday morning ride, Charlotte drives us to Reading Station, from where it's a quick and easy train journey to Heathrow—one of the world's busiest airports.

Our Qantas flight, code-sharing with Emirates, is scheduled to depart from Terminal 3, and in line with all the advice we had read, we allowed ourselves a healthy three hours to clear customs. To our surprise, there's no outbound passport control to clear; everything is taken care of at check-in, where our bags are collected, boarding passes issued, and passports briefly sighted.

'Well, that was quick,' I say to Darryl, barely 20 minutes later. 'Now what are we going to do for the next two and three-quarter hours?'

Using up the last of our English pounds in a nearby coffee shop helps pass the time, as does wandering through the plentiful duty-free shops, and before long, we are being herded onto our plane. It's our first time flying Qantas long haul, and we have been looking forward to the experience.

Six hours later, we touch down at Dubai International Airport and agree that the flight has been one of the more disappointing of our travels. The crew, far from the professional stewards we had expected, proved the most laid-back and blasé we have ever encountered. By the time we land, the cabin is a mess—pillows, blankets, earphones and plastic wrapping strewn about, with no attempt at garbage collection.

'It'll be interesting to compare this with our Emirates flight next,' I comment.

'I don't think it will be hard to beat this one,' Darryl replies.

Unsure how Darryl would cope with sitting cramped in a plane for hours on end, we have chosen to stop in Dubai rather than fly any further today. It's a good decision as after sitting for so long, Darryl is tired, stiff and sore. We have also elected to stay at the Dubai International Terminal Hotel, which means that not only do we not have to leave the airport, but we also do not have to pass through customs. Our bags should be waiting for us in Hong Kong, and our hotel bed here is mere metres from our arrival gate.

Despite it being 11:30 pm, the airport throngs with people, and the sight of a hotel employee clutching a sign with my name is gratefully welcomed. He leads us on a strange, almost surreal adventure that takes us by airport train to the next terminal, hustles us through a security check, and finally delivers us to our hotel, tucked conveniently among the duty-free. With a quick explanation of how to find our onward flight, he disappears, and half an hour after arrival, showered and refreshed, we fall into our king-size bed.

With the hotel fully enclosed within the world's third-busiest airport, no sunlight penetrates, and our sleep in the pitch-black, cavernous room is deep and satisfying. We wake restored, and 15 hours after touchdown, board our Emirates plane. It's been a fun, easy stopover—one we would happily repeat.

The following flight, which has us disembarking seven hours later at Hong Kong airport, is as far removed from our earlier one as we could have hoped. Professionalism replaces the blasé attitude. Orderliness replaces chaos.

'There was even a better movie selection,' Darryl comments wryly.

'Funny. I thought Qantas would be much better. Unfortunately, our next flight is also with Qantas,' I reply.

'Hopefully, they redeem themselves.'

Having had my interest sparked years ago by James Clavell's epic novel *Tai-Pan*—and later consolidated when a girlfriend moved here—Hong Kong has long been on my list of places to visit. With roots stretching back over a thousand years, the thriving cosmopolitan city we know today was shaped 180 years ago, when Britain defeated China's Qing Dynasty in the First Opium War and forced the cession of Hong Kong

Island. It soon grew into a major centre for international trade. Fast forward to 1997, when Hong Kong was handed back to China, and the story only becomes more intriguing. Under the principle of 'One Country, Two Systems', it remains a Special Administrative Region of communist China while retaining its capitalist economy, independent judiciary, free trade, and freedom of speech. Little wonder we're eager to finally experience it for ourselves.

Like our arrival in Dubai, we land in Hong Kong in the dead of night. Anticipating this, we've pre-booked a hotel pick-up, and the sight of yet another sign bearing my name feels both welcoming and rather fun—though Darryl is less amused.

'How come the signs are always in your name?'

'Because I'm the one who booked them.'

'You could have booked it in my name at least once,' he grumbles.

'Well, next time I will,' I promise.

It's well after midnight when we finally reach the Royal Pacific Hotel and Towers, though judging by the crowds milling in the lobby, you would never guess the hour. Our spacious, air-conditioned room greets us with a sweeping view of illuminated skyscrapers rising over a broad stretch of water. After a quick shower, we both fall gratefully into bed.

Day one of our four-day stopover finds me mid-morning looking out over Hong Kong's Victoria Harbour as I perform my yoga routine and meditate on the view. Before me, steep hills tumble into a vast harbour dotted with countless boats, while high-rise buildings cling precariously to the slopes before clustering thickly at the base. Hong Kong is home to more skyscrapers than any other city in the world—over 2,000—and the proof is right here in front of me.

Our hotel sits directly above the China Ferry Terminal, and after yoga, I linger by the window, watching heavily laden ferries come and go. Breakfast is included, and once again we are treated to the joy of a multinational buffet where dim sims, dumplings and noodles sit comfortably beside croissants, hash browns and sausages.

With an eight-hour time difference from London, we expect some signs of jet lag, so today is set aside for relaxation and light exploration close to our hotel. Hong Kong is divided into 18 political districts, and we are staying in Tsim Sha Tsui (TST), on the Kowloon Peninsula. We chose this location for its proximity to Kowloon Park, Temple Street Night Market, and Harbour City—Hong Kong's largest shopping centre—and are eager to step outside and experience the bustle of the city streets.

With such a slow start, it is close to lunchtime before we finally leave the comfort of our hotel and, stepping from the cool air-conditioned foyer, we are greeted instantly and forcefully by Hong Kong in all its hot, humid splendour. The temperature hovers around 35 degrees with humidity soaring skyward, an abrupt reminder that we are once again back in Asia.

Having arrived in the pitch dark, this is the first chance we have had to properly take in our surroundings, and the sight is memorable. Wide, pedestrian-clogged footpaths spill past shops offering every imaginable kind of wares, while the sky above is barely visible through the forest of high-rise buildings. Many of these towers, to our surprise, are in a dilapidated state, draped in bamboo scaffolding, their exteriors sprouting aged, wheezing air-conditioning units.

With the footpaths so crowded and the temperature so unappealing, it's an easy decision to duck into the Harbour City Shopping Centre, where we have plenty of time to cool off while exploring some of its 800-plus shops. Stretching for more than three kilometres, the complex eventually delivers us to the harbour front and, stepping out of the air-conditioned comfort, we find ourselves among large groups of browsing tourists.

'It's Hong Kong's equivalent of Hollywood's Walk of Fame,' I read from a sign announcing that we've reached the

Avenue of Stars.

'Anyone we recognise?' Darryl asks.

'Absolutely no one,' I reply.

'Let's head back to the hotel via Kowloon Park,' Darryl suggests. 'Hopefully, the park will be a bit cooler.'

Connected to our hotel by a solid concrete walkway, which, rather alarmingly, sways as we cross, Kowloon Park proves to be a welcome oasis in the midst of the busy concrete jungle. Beneath a canopy of shady trees, we pause at turtle-choked ponds and marvel at the surprising flocks of flamingos basking in the sun.

'Never thought I'd see flamingos in the middle of a city,' I say to Darryl.

'Especially not this city,' he agrees.

The heat of the city and the travel have caught up with Darryl, so while he rests, I continue exploring. Beneath our hotel, I discover a small but bustling shopping mall filled with locals, and in one of its grocery stores, I stock up on a few necessities. A couple of pots of easy noodles—just add water—take care of dinner, while a block of chocolate provides dessert. With such a simple meal, preparation is minimal and cleanup almost non-existent, leaving us with plenty of time to secure a good spot for tonight's much-anticipated light show.

First staged in 2004, the Symphony of Lights is a nightly orchestration of music, lasers and beams that illuminate Victoria Harbour each evening at 8 pm for up to ten minutes. Though we could easily watch from our hotel room, we decide for our first night to join the crowd on the jetty rooftop below. With the temperature finally easing after dark, the show is nothing short of spectacular.

'Look where we are,' I grin. 'Standing over Hong Kong Harbour with this incredible light show blazing above us. How crazy is that?'

The next morning dawns bright, if a little smoggy. With a long day ahead, I skip my yoga and simply stand at the window, taking in the view. Far in the distance rises Victoria Peak, and today we will be making our way to its summit as part of the full-day tour we've booked. Recommended by a friend, the tour promises to give us a true taste of Hong Kong.

BUCKET LISTS AND WALKING STICKS

The tour begins shortly after breakfast with the arrival of a minivan, where we meet our guide and the six fellow travellers joining us for the day. Our first destination is Hong Kong's central business district, located across the harbour. To reach it, we take the Cross-Harbour Tunnel—an underwater passage that feels both impressive and a little nerve-wracking.

'This tunnel was built in 1972,' our guide explains. 'Today, it is one of the busiest roads in the world, carrying up to 117,000 vehicles a day.'

As expected, Hong Kong's central business district is a hive of activity, its streets filled with suited workers hurrying between meetings. What strikes us most is the contrast between the gleaming glass skyscrapers and the stately remnants of British colonial architecture still holding their place among them.

From here, our journey turns upward. The van winds its way along Peak Road before depositing us at the entrance to the Peak Tram. In operation since 1888, this steep tramway remains the most thrilling way to tackle the 550-metre climb to the city's highest hill—and the most direct.

At the summit, we are rewarded with a breathtaking 360-degree panorama. We count ourselves lucky: the smog that had hung over the city earlier has lifted, revealing a clear view of the skyline and harbour. With Hong Kong often shrouded in haze from neighbouring China's pollution, we could easily have arrived to find our outlook totally obscured.

Leaving the sweeping views of Victoria Peak behind, we rejoin our van and soon arrive at the Aberdeen Fishing Village. Once a bustling hub, this 19th-century port supported some 600 traditional junks and around 6,000 residents. But with the fishing industry gradually relocated to mainland China over the past two decades, the community has dwindled.

Today, as we climb aboard our own junk and weave past a scattering of traditional boats, the contrast is striking: their weathered hulls bobbing alongside sleek, million-dollar yachts belonging to Hong Kong's elite. The village feels less like a working harbour now and more like a living exhibit for tourists.

'Do fishermen still live and work here?' someone in our group asks.

'Yes, they still fish from here,' our guide replies. 'But no one lives on the boats anymore. These days, it's more famous as a movie location.'

Part of our tour includes a stop at a diamond factory, where the intrigue of watching glittering new pieces being crafted is quickly overshadowed by the relentless spruiking of the sales staff.

'You like this ring? For you, only 20,000 Australian dollars!' one insists.

We escape with our wallets intact and, not long after, find ourselves gliding upward on the world's longest covered outdoor escalator. Stretching for more than 800 metres, it is kitsch but entertaining—and an easy way to navigate the city's teeming streets.

As the day draws to a close and the sun sinks low on the horizon, our tour concludes with a dinner cruise around the harbour. Against the backdrop of the Symphony of Lights, we enjoy a feast of international dishes, accompanied by a few glasses of wine. It feels like the perfect finale to a thoroughly enjoyable day.

Darryl, who has been without a watch for the entire trip, wakes determined to finally remedy the situation. Our hunt for a suitable timepiece dictates our final day in Hong Kong, giving us the perfect excuse to explore the city further. Navigating ferries and the MTR (Mass Transit Railway), we travel deeper afield until we finally locate the elusive watch in the bustling Causeway Bay district.

'After all this searching, you're happy with a Seiko?' I exclaim.

'I like Seikos,' Darryl replies. 'My first watch was a Seiko.'

As evening draws in, we take another wander through Kowloon Park before winding the night down with a stroll through the nearby

BUCKET LISTS AND WALKING STICKS

Temple Street Night Market. Also known as the Men's Market, it overflows with everything from menswear to mobile phones to antiques. It's crowded and hot, and it is with some relief that we escape to a little restaurant overlooking Victoria Harbour. Here we feast on more Asian delicacies while gazing one last time at Hong Kong's captivating light show.

As if mourning the close of our adventure, we wake to the thickest smog yet. A heavy cloud of pollution, so often associated with China's vast cities, has swallowed Hong Kong, and we feel quietly relieved that our flight leaves in just a few hours. Driving back towards the airport and away from the densest parts of the city, the haze begins to lift, revealing an incredible scale of development.

'Look at the size of that bridge!' Darryl exclaims. 'And there's another one.'

Having arrived under cover of darkness, we had missed the sprawling highways and massive bridges now under construction, stretching across deep gorges. The sheer scale of it all is a striking testament to China's immense wealth and relentless growth.

Hong Kong security and customs are navigated quickly and without fuss, and after pausing only long enough to pick up a few last-minute duty-free gifts, we soon find ourselves aboard our Brisbane-bound Qantas flight. This time the crew prove far more professional than on our earlier leg, and as the hours stretch slowly ahead, we are given ample space for thought and reflection.

It has been almost seven months to the day since we set off on this amazing adventure. We have done things we will never forget: sailed halfway around the world, wandered through ancient Petra, followed an aqueduct in Tuscany, and even tracked down Doc Martin. We have seen sights that will stay with us for a lifetime: the Suez Canal, Malta's limestone walls, the empty platforms of Brussels' train station, Bedouins in the desert, and the endless oil silos of Khor Al Fakkan.

Spending time with our children in a foreign country has been a special gift. We have always wanted to show them that there is more to the world than the Byron Shire, and today, with Paige happily settled in London and Pierce off enjoying himself at Germany's Oktoberfest, it feels as though we have succeeded.

And while we are carrying a few extra kilos—the 6-1 diet well and truly forgotten for now—the enjoyment we have had and the variety of food sampled, from Prague's trdelniks to countless other treats, make every bite worth it.

They say travel is good for you, and looking at Darryl beside me, I can only agree. Though he still needs his heavy medications and daily rest, he is stronger and healthier than he was seven months ago, and he has even managed to wean himself off the anti-depressants—something that once seemed impossible. I hope that it stays this way once we return to our everyday lives.

As the plane begins its descent and the city of Brisbane starts to appear below, I turn to Darryl.

'It's over. But what a journey! By my count, we've checked off 13 bucket list items and travelled through 19 countries. And that walking stick tip you bought in Florence—is still perfect.'

'It is.' Darryl grins. 'It's been an amazing experience, but I'm ready to be home. Seven months is a long time to be away.'

'I can't believe it's gone so quickly,' I say. 'Would you do it again?'

'I would.'

'That's good,' I smile. 'Because I'm thinking about the Panama Canal next.'

AUTHOR'S NOTE

More From Emma Scattergood

I write my adventure books with two purposes in mind. The first is to share my experiences with you—whether it be an awe-inspiring glimpse of an ancient civilisation at Petra, a thrilling train ride across Mongolia, standing beside the sacred Ganges at Varanasi, the feeling of loneliness while crossing the Atlantic Ocean, or what it's like to have your breasts amputated.

I also write to inform. If you learn something from my books, then I have succeeded. Of course, I hope you learn many things.

If you would like to know more about me, please visit:
 ⚲ https://linktr.ee/emmascattergood
or browse my website:
 🌐 http://darmatravels.com

Emma Scattergood
October 2025

Previous Books by Emma Scattergood

Next Chapter Travel: More Bucket List Adventures
Australia to Europe by Sea, Greece, Türkiye & India by Rail

'Because life is short and we've still got places to see.'

Four years after their last global journey, and with cancer, recovery, and lockdowns finally behind them, Emma and Darryl board a cruise ship bound for Europe. The route?

From Australia to Greece via South Africa, Mauritius, Morocco, and more.

From there, it is trains and buses across ancient Greek landscapes, through Bulgaria and Türkiye, and deep into the heart of India. But this is no packaged tour.

There are bucket list sights, yes—but also sleepless nights, questionable coach drivers, lost passengers at borders, and the humbling realisation that Indian hawkers can outsmart you with QR codes. There are rooftop breakfasts, muesli under the stars, and generous strangers who appear just when needed.

Told with honesty and humour, *Next Chapter Travel* is a story of resilience, curiosity, and connection—a reminder that life is short, and journeys are what shape us.

Next Chapter Travel

Itchy Feet and Bucket Lists: A Global Adventure

I've pulled the bucket list back out. Amongst what's left are the Trans-Siberian Express, the Terracotta Army, the Swiss Alps and the Panama Canal.

Easy words spoken over an avocado on toast breakfast—catalyst for a global adventure. A 24 country, 57,000-kilometre unforgettable journey across the steppes of Mongolia, the wilderness of Siberia, Putin's Russia. Through strike-torn France, Europe during winter and over the lonely Atlantic and Pacific Oceans.

Commencing in October 2019 and undertaken by author Emma and injured husband Darryl, the trip will cement their belief that travel is the epitome of learning and the antidote for depression. And while providing an education on the incredible places visited, there will also be lessons on staying one step ahead of a developing pandemic, Google translate, food poisoning and train accidents. Throw in some weighty goals like having a rum in Barbados, a coffee in Guatemala and guacamole in Mexico; it might even be the cure for their itchy feet.

<u>Itchy Feet & Bucket Lists</u>

My Breast Cancer Adventure: Or What Can Happen Following a Breast Cancer Diagnosis

A journey does not always involve travel.
So discovered adventurer Emma Scattergood.

In 2022, Emma was diagnosed with stage 3 invasive lobular breast cancer. Unsure what it really meant, she channelled her energy into understanding and fighting this increasingly common disease—and soon realised it was another journey worth sharing.

This insightful and often entertaining book is the result: an 18-month roller-coaster through diagnosis, double mastectomy, chemotherapy, radiation and hormone therapy. A deeply personal experience that also explores integrative approaches, infections, supplements, diet, exercise and more.

Told with honesty, humour and compassion, Emma aims to:

- Shine a light on how breast cancer is detected—and what can happen next.
- Offer guidance and reassurance to the newly diagnosed.
- Provide insight for those who have never faced it.

To broaden the picture, Emma includes stories from eleven other women—each with their own unique path and perspective on survival.

My Breast Cancer Adventure

ABOUT THE AUTHOR

Emma Scattergood is the author of *Next Chapter Travel*, *Itchy Feet & Bucket Lists*, and *My Breast Cancer Adventure*, as well as the creator of the darmatravels.com blog. Transported overland from England to Australia via Afghanistan and India before her first birthday, travel has always played an important role in her life. With qualifications in accounting and tourism, and a degree in business, Emma retired early to care for her injured husband. For the past twenty years, a laminated bucket list has lived in her wallet.

www.ingramcontent.com/pod-product-compliance
Lightning Source LLC
Chambersburg PA
CBHW031238290426
44109CB00012B/343